# Classic Cycling Race Routes

**CHRIS SIDWELLS**

Published by AA Publishing (a trading name of AA Media Limited,
whose registered office is Fanum House, Basing View, Basingstoke
RG21 4EA; registered number 06112600).

Editor
Donna Wood

Design and layout
Liz Baldin

Picture Editor
James Tims

Image retouching and internal repro
Ian Little

Cartography by Lovell Johns Limited
OpenStreetMap.org data © OpenStreetMap contributors, CC-BY-SA
NASA terrain courtesy of Esri

Produced by AA Publishing
© Copyright AA Media Limited 2013

ISBN: 978-0-7495-7410-9

A05009

The contents of this book are believed correct at the time of printing.
Nevertheless, the publishers cannot be held responsible for any errors
or omissions or for changes in the details given in this book or for
the consequences of any reliance on the information provided by the
same. This does not affect your statutory rights.

Although a small number of images in this book show people riding
without safety helmets, the publishers strongly advise that helmets
should be worn when attempting any of the race routes.

Printed in Dubai by Oriental Press

**theAA.com/shop**

GARMIN

# Classic Cycling Race Routes

Download the race routes in this book at
theaa.com/cycling-race-routes

# Preface

This book contains the 52 classic cycling routes of Europe, one for every week of the year. In the main, the routes were inspired by professional races, or by mass-participation cyclosportive events. In some cases they contain additional elements from a race's history to give you a better feel for it.

Reading about these routes, some younger readers might be inspired to become professional cyclists one day, and perhaps compete in great European classics such as Paris–Roubaix, the Tour of Flanders or Milan–San Remo, or they may take on one of cycling's Grand Tours: the Tour de France, Giro d'Italia or Vuelta a España.

For the rest of us, most of these famous races also have all-comers events that anyone can enter, called cyclosportives. They aren't races in the strict, legal terms of what a race is (at least in the UK they aren't), but the participants are timed on the route and most of them try to achieve the best time they can.

There are stand-alone cyclosportive events that have great routes too, and some of these are included in the book. In fact, the UK and Ireland section is filled exclusively with cyclosportive routes, as our two countries don't have any historic professional races yet.

Some of the European events are also part of the UCI (cycling's governing body) World Cycling Tour, which is essentially an age-group race series. Take part in one of these events and you stand a chance of qualifying for a final, in which riders compete within their age-group bands to become world cycling champions. A few of these routes are included in the book, too.

You can use the route information in two ways. The first is to take part in the official event for each route where there is one, and I urge you to do that as a first choice because the atmosphere and camaraderie of these events, where thousands of like-minded souls take part, all enjoying doing something they love, is incredible. And you could even end up being a world champion. Secondly, though, there is enough information in these pages to ride each route, or a version of it, independently of the official event at any time you like, as long as the roads are open.

There's a description of each route with background information and little titbits of history. Plus there are maps and directions for each route, as well as profiles that show where all the hills are located. Where the hills are significant, there's information on how long and steep they are, and how much height is gained when you climb them. Height gain is more useful than their overall altitude, which you can get from maps anyway.

Enjoy the book, use it for planning and setting objectives, but above all get out and ride these routes. They represent some of the finest cycling experiences you could ever have.

*Chris Sidwells*

# Contents

# Introduction

**Basic equipment: your bike**

This book is about attempting the best cycling challenges available on the roads of Europe. True, there's one ride in England and one in Italy that have a lot of off-road stretches, and some of the roads in the others are really rough, but the best type of bike to take on these challenges is still a road bike.

As with any piece of sports kit, road bikes come at a wide range of prices; and they are prices that rise exponentially in comparison to the advantage they give. Put simply, once you go over a certain price, you pay a lot more for a bike that is only a tiny bit better. It's the materials, the way they are used and the engineering involved that determine price, although fashion and the manufacturer's pedigree have a bearing too.

The heart of a bike is its frame, and the most common frame materials are aluminium, carbon fibre and titanium. Steel bikes have made a bit of a comeback recently, having been out of fashion for a while. The frame is what everything else works around. It holds the bike together and affects its performance more than any other single component. A good-quality bike frame should be light, stiff so it transfers your pedalling forces efficiently to the road, and it should be able to absorb or at least deaden minor bumps in the road. Frames come in a range of sizes, and the frame size denotes the size of a bike.

Broadly speaking, the size of bike you need is determined by the length of your inside leg measured from your crotch to the floor without your shoes on. There are other considerations, and in a good bike shop these should be discussed when you buy. However, if the size of bike the shop recommends is outside the ranges shown in the table, right, you should consider whether it is a good bike shop.

Most of the cheaper road bikes have aluminium frames, but that doesn't mean that aluminium is a poor frame material, because it's not. It's a reflection of the fact that aluminium is plentiful and fairly easy to work with. Aluminium works well at the heart of a road bike so long as it's combined with carbon-fibre forks, and most aluminium frames are. Aluminium is relatively light, quite stiff, and it absorbs shocks well, which are the properties you are looking for in a frame. A quality aluminium-framed bike that would be perfect for taking on the challenges in this book can be bought for around £1,000, maybe a bit less.

Carbon fibre is generally a step up from aluminium. It's lighter, it can be stiffer, and it's better at absorbing shocks than aluminium. Quality carbon-fibre bikes can be bought in the £1,000 to £1,500 price range, and from there they go right up to £10,000 and more. What you are paying for in a more expensive bike is lighter equipment and a lighter frame that's still very stiff, and probably a frame that will keep its properties for a long time. This is because there are many ways to use carbon fibre, some of which are more

## Choosing the correct size bike

| Inside leg measurement | Frame size | Bike size |
|---|---|---|
| 75–78cm | 46–51cm | Small |
| 79–82cm | 50–54cm | Medium |
| 83–86cm | 53–57cm | Large |
| 87–90cm | 56–60cm | Extra large |

refined but come with increased research, development and labour costs. On more expensive bikes, the matrix that the raw carbon fibre is set in will be more expensive and work better, too.

Titanium bikes have the highest starting price. That's because titanium is rare and difficult to work with. Titanium makes a good bike frame for challenges like the ones in this book, though. Titanium is light and quite stiff, but its real benefit for riding long distances – and distance features in most cycling challenges – is how well it absorbs shocks. Not big shocks, no frame material will do that, but the irregularities in road surfaces that produce something cyclists call road noise. Absorbing road noise means a more comfortable ride, and more comfort means less fatigue.

## Gearing

If you are buying a new bike, the quality of the equipment on it tends to increase with the quality of the frame. But within that broad trend there are things to consider if you are buying it to take on some of the challenges in this book, and the most important of those is gearing.

Hills are part of the challenge of cycling. They are a test of strength and stamina, and they are what multiple gears were invented for. Until recently, almost all bikes had roughly the same gears, but now it's possible to buy bikes with lower gears because they are fitted with a compact chainset. If you are attempting challenges with mountains or very steep hills in them (and most in this book do have mountains and/or steep hills), then a bike with a compact chainset is the best tool for the job.

Just like in a car, you have to change down the gears when cycling uphill to avoid straining your engine, which in the case of cycling is you. Compact chainsets allow you to use lower gears, but because most modern road bikes have 20 ratios to choose from, you still have high gears to use downhill and on the flat. Compact chainsets work so well that some of the best racers in the tours of France, Italy and Spain use them for some of the mountain stages.

## Adjusting your rear gear changer for smooth shifts

From time to time you may find that your chain doesn't shift smoothly from one gear ratio to the next. It might jump over a sprocket, missing it out, or the gear shift is slow or the chain jumps or makes excessive noise. The best way to cure all these faults is to set up your gear shifts from scratch by following these steps. You'll need some Allen keys and a screwdriver.

**Step 1.** Shift to the largest chainring and smallest sprocket.
**Step 2.** Loosen the cable clamp bolt on the rear gear changer, or rear mech as it's known in cycling, and turn the barrel adjuster until it's at half its range.

**Step 3.** Turn the pedals backwards. If the chain doesn't run smoothly through the mech's little jockey wheels, use the screwdriver in the high adjuster (a screw on the mech usually marked 'H'), turning one way then another while back-pedalling until it does run smoothly.
**Step 4.** Reconnect the cable, keeping it under tension while you tighten the cable clamp bolt.
**Step 5.** Use the shifter to shift the chain, one sprocket at a time, over the cassette. One click of the shifter should make one gear shift. If the shifter clicks and the chain doesn't go to the next sprocket, turn the barrel adjuster outwards until it does.

If the chain shifts past the sprocket, turn the barrel adjuster inwards until it sits on the correct sprocket.
**Step 6.** Shift through to the largest sprocket, but if the chain goes beyond that, or the jockey wheels touch the rear wheel spokes, you need to screw the low (marked 'L') gear adjuster inwards until the chain runs smoothly on the largest sprocket.
**Step 7.** Occasionally the rear mech won't shift to the largest sprocket because the upper jockey wheel is rubbing against the sprocket. There's a screw on the rear mech where it joins the gear hanger on the bike's frame. Screw this in until the jockey wheel clears the largest sprocket.

# Using a GPS device

You've poured untold hours, miles and sweat into your training, so it's worth considering buying a purpose-built device to capture, share and relive every detail. A touchscreen GPS bike computer can give you live tracking, wireless data transfers, and social media sharing. But the major advantage of such a device is in helping you plan, download and follow new routes while at the same time improving your performance during training and racing by giving you accurate real-time feedback.

Garmin was the first to bring GPS to the cycling computer market – the first to let cyclists put their ride on the map and record detailed metrics with accurate GPS data. Its Edge products have continued to evolve and can now give you all the details of your ride, including:

- Distance: GPS-based for accuracy and works anywhere in the world
- Route planning: simply plan routes on Garmin Connect and send to your device, then select the desired route and follow the turn-by-turn instructions
- Speed: current, average, last lap and more
- Elevation: ascent/descent, grade and more
- Speed/cadence
- Heart rate
- Maps: a built-in map compatible with optional detailed street or topographic maps for navigation and guidance on- and off-road
- Weather conditions: forecasts and alerts
- Personal records: your Edge device can display personal bests such as farthest distance, most ascent gained, fastest 40km and best 20-minute power

The Garmin touchscreen devices are robust, waterproof and glove-friendly. They allow you to customise data fields and device settings for different types of cycling activity, such as road, mountain or touring, and to switch profiles with a tap of the screen.

One of Garmin's newest innovations is the ability to pair your Edge device with your smartphone, so that even when home may be miles away, you can stay connected and share all the details of your ride with your friends, family – and rivals. With the Garmin Connect mobile app, Edge tracks the data and sends it to your phone using a Bluetooth® connection. These wireless uploads of your rides mean that you can instantly store, share and analyse every detail of your ride from the road. You can search for other users' routes – ideal for exploring new areas – and share your favourite routes with other Garmin Connect users.

The LiveTrack feature allows your friends and family to follow your races and training activities in real time. You can invite followers using email or social media, and they can view your stats and location on the map through a Garmin Connect tracking page. The social media sharing feature also allows you to post an update on Facebook, Twitter and other social media networks immediately after your ride, with a link to all the data about your completed activity.

All routes in this book can be downloaded to your Garmin at **theaa.com/cycling-race-routes**

GARMIN®

## Accessories

A bag that fits under your saddle is a key requirement. Put a set of tyre levers and at least one spare inner tube inside it. Keep the valve cap on the inner tube and wrap the tube in cling film to prevent other things in the bag from chafing it.

Multi-tools are like Swiss army knives for bikes. Basically, they consist of various-sized Allen keys and a screwdriver that fit inside a penknife-type handle. Some multi-tools have a chain-link extractor as well. If your multi-tool doesn't, then it's wise to carry one of these and learn how

### Tip

You need to carry some things to support your effort on any ride, but it's best if these are attached to your bike, not you, so that you are able to ride as light as possible. Drinks go in bottles held on the frame in special cages. You also need an under-the-saddle bag to carry spares such as an inner tube and a multi-tool device in case you need to do any running repairs.

to use it. There are some great bike maintenance books on sale to help with that. Other things you should carry in the bag are a couple of zip ties, because you'd be amazed what emergency repairs you can do with them. You could keep some emergency money in the saddlebag too, but again, wrap it in cling film otherwise it rattles about and can wear a hole in the inner tube.

A GPS device is essential when doing these challenge rides outside an event. They also provide great feedback during an event, so that you know you are on the correct route, and in training, when you can see improvements in average speed, power or heart rate as you get fitter.

### How to repair a puncture

Remove the wheel, then insert the blunt end of a tyre lever between the tyre and wheel rim. Lever the edge of the tyre over the rim. With the lever still under the tyre, hook its other end around a spoke. Insert the second lever and push this around the tyre to lift it off, then remove the inner tube. If the tyre is tight, you might need to hook the second tyre lever to a spoke and use the third one to remove the tyre.

Lift the tyre completely off the wheel and inspect it inside and out for cuts and anything sticking through it. A deeply cut tyre needs replacing. Remove any objects lodged in the tyre by pulling them out from the outside. Tweezers are useful for this.

Inflate the inner tube and locate the puncture by listening for escaping air. Mark where it is, then work around the whole tube, listening in case there are more holes. Deflate the tube and roughen its surface around the hole with abrasive. Select a repair patch and spread a thin layer of glue that is slightly larger than the repair patch over the roughened area of the tube.

Allow the glue to go tacky then peel the backing from the patch and firmly press the patch, back-side down, onto the glue. Ensure that the patch's edges are flat and keep pressure on it for about a minute. Use the abrasive to dust some French chalk onto the repair and allow the glue to dry fully.

Put one side of the tyre on the rim. Inflate the tube slightly and push its valve down through the rim hole. Work the whole of the tube onto the rim and under the tyre. Push the valve upwards slightly and lift the other side of the tyre over the rim. Work the rest of the tyre back onto the rim. If it proves difficult, use a tyre lever to help fit the last part.

If you have a puncture out on the road, it's best to simply replace the punctured inner tube with a spare one you should always carry, then repair the punctured one when you return home. That can then be your spare tube on future rides.

## Clothing

The final piece in your equipment jigsaw is clothing, and what you wear is just as crucial as having a good and well-maintained bike. Modern cycling clothing is, on the whole, well thought out and absolutely the only kit to wear for the challenges in this book.

Let's start with your feet and work up. Cycling-specific shoes are a must, and ideally they should be married to clipless pedals. Clipless pedals work rather like ski boots fit on skis. You step into the pedal and engage a cleat on the sole of your shoes with the retention device on the pedal. To release your foot you just flick your heel out sideways. Clipless pedals ensure that you harness as much power as possible from your body into going forwards.

There are two types of shoe and pedal combination: one designed specifically for road riding and the other for off-road, although off-road pedals can be used for both. In fact, off-road shoes are great for more leisurely cycling, because you can walk around in them quite easily too. And they would definitely come in useful when riding some of the challenges in this book that use off-road trails and rough roads.

Cycling-specific clothing includes socks. Summer cycling socks are thin and help move sweat away from your feet, while winter ones are thicker and a lot warmer.

Shorts are next. Bib shorts are best because they have integral loops that go over your shoulders and they are cut high at the back, so that your lower back is always covered. Back pain can be caused by lower back muscles getting cold, and bib shorts help prevent this. Shorts should have a lining in the crotch area that prevents chafing. There are women-specific shorts with a different cut and different-shaped lining to men's. Shorts are not an area for saving money. Buy the best quality you can afford, and if a particular brand suits you, then stick with it.

Cycling tops are short- or long-sleeved and have pockets at the rear for carrying food to eat while you ride. You can pop your mobile phone in a jersey pocket too; some even have custom-made pockets for mobiles. Tops should fit closely but not too tightly. Tops with full zips are perfect for summer because you can pull the zip down to let the air circulate around your upper body when it's hot. A base layer to go under a top is also advisable. Again, these should be cycling-specific and made from material that transports sweat away from your skin. Thin base layers are for summer and thicker ones with long sleeves are for winter.

You should always wear gloves when cycling: full ones in winter or when it's cold, and fingerless gloves called track mitts when it's warm. Gloves stop sweat from your hands affecting your grip on the handlebars, and they protect your hands from getting sore or grazed if you fall.

Always wear a cycling helmet whenever you ride. Just consider it an essential. It's not the law to wear one in Britain, but it is in some countries in Europe. A helmet makes sense. There are arguments that it won't save a life in a really bad crash with maximum head impact, but helmets definitely reduce the effects of other impacts, and they have saved many lives and have prevented or reduced countless injuries.

The suggestions above are cycling basics for warm weather. It's good to have several pairs of socks and at least two tops and two sets of shorts so that you can rotate them, but you also need extra clothing so that you can keep riding in cooler or even cold weather.

Again, starting with the feet, get some cycling-specific winter socks. Overshoes are a necessity too. They are usually

waterproof, they stretch over your cycling shoes, and they are essential for winter riding.

Protect your legs with leg warmers, which fit under your shorts and cover your legs down to your ankles, or bib tights, which are like bib shorts except that they have long legs and are made from a thicker material.

Long-sleeved tops range from thin, simple ones for autumn days to thicker, quite technical tops for wearing in really cold weather. Wear a thicker long-sleeved base layer underneath the top. You'll learn by trial and error which thickness of top suits which weather condition. Sometimes it might even be necessary to wear a thin mid-layer, but heavy-duty tops are so good nowadays that this doesn't happen very often. Anyway, if the weather is that bad you may be better off training indoors (see 'Turbo trainers').

You also need a thin rain- and windproof top if you are doing these challenges. There are some amazing ones on the market that roll up and fit into a pocket, but they can be lifesavers if the weather closes in on top of a big hill or a mountain.

The gilet is another great invention for cyclists. It's a thin sleeveless top that is usually windproof and sometimes waterproof. Gilets are perfect to wear over your thinner long-sleeved tops on days that are cold but not quite cold enough for a thick winter top. They also work if you set off riding in the chill of a spring morning, because you can take the gilet off and carry it in your pocket when the day warms up. Gilets are adaptable pieces of clothing because they fill in the gaps between your other clothing.

Full-finger gloves are a must on cold days, while other things to consider buying to combat cold or wet weather are a skull cap to wear under your helmet, and a buff that can act as a scarf or face mask. The final must-have for wet-weather riding is mudguards for your bike. They don't have to be fitted permanently – you can buy mudguards that clip on and off in seconds – but they can make the difference between comfort and misery in the rain.

## Turbo trainers

Turbo trainers are devices that let you train indoors when the weather is too bad to go outside. They are also perfect for covering some of the very short-duration training that can have a positive effect on your fitness, but needs to be done with precision and total focus.

Turbos come in two types: those that support the back end of your bike while the front wheel is mounted on a block to keep the bike level, and those where you remove the front wheel and the front and back of your bike are supported by the turbo trainer. You can also buy some trainers called rollers, but while these work well, they require skill and practice before you extract the full benefit from them. Turbo trainers are a simpler option.

They work by the rear wheel running against a roller, on which there is a device designed to increase the resistance you have to pedal against. The simplest-designed turbos have a fan attached to the roller, and as the roller spins, so does the fan. The fan's blades don't slice through the air; they are set at an angle to pick air up. The faster the rear wheel goes, the faster the fan spins and the more

air the blades pick up. This is similar to what happens when you ride outside: the faster you go. the more air resistance you meet.

Air resistance is increasingly being replaced on modern turbo trainers by fluid resistance, where the fan spins in oil. This works in the same way as air resistance; the harder you ride the more resistance there is, but fluid trainers feel smoother and they are quieter.

Resistance on a turbo's roller can also be provided magnetically, but relying totally on magnets gives a less 'real-life' feel to riding on a turbo. Having said that, you can dial in the resistance you want to ride against, and so replicate riding uphill. The best turbo trainers combine a fan, either air or fluid, and magnetic braking to give a real outdoor-riding feel.

When you ride on a turbo trainer you produce a lot of heat, so you need some sort of electric fan to keep you cool. It's also a good idea to protect the floor under the trainer and have a towel over your handlebars and front part of your bike to soak up sweat drops. Sweat is salty and quite corrosive.

Turbo trainers are used for pre-race warm-ups as well as for training

A professional bike-fit is a good investment in your cycling performance

## Bike set-up

Setting up your bike so that it fits you perfectly is crucial. You'd be surprised at how much power can be gained from establishing the correct position on your bike, and because we are all different, the riding position that best suits us is individual. This is not just because two people of the same size can have different-length limbs, but also because we each have different histories and what we have done in the past can affect how we sit on a bike and ride it.

The best thing to do is get a professional bike-fit from a qualified technician. Many bike shops have qualified bike-fitters on staff, and a number of physiotherapists have added bike-fitting to their professional skills. There are even bike-fitting specialists whose sole business is helping people get the most from their riding position.

There are some basic principles to follow when setting up your riding position, and it's best to go through these before having a professional bike-fit. The first thing to do is to set your seat height. The simplest way to do this is to sit on your bike without shoes on and place your heel on the pedals. Turn the cranks backwards and when the pedal is at the bottom of each revolution your leg should be straight but not stretched. Move the saddle up or down to achieve this.

Set the fore and aft position of your saddle so that you get the maximum power from your leg muscles during each pedal revolution. Your front knee must be over the centre of the front pedal when the cranks are parallel to the floor. Get someone to help you with this using a spirit level or a plumb line. Place the level or line just behind your kneecap on the outside of your leg and ask your helper to see where it is, relative to the centre of the pedal spindle. Move the saddle back or forwards so that your knee is directly over the pedal spindle. When you get the saddle in the right place, ensure that its surface is absolutely flat and parallel to the floor.

Now check the position of your handlebars. Hold the bottom of the handlebars and look down at your front. The top of the handlebars should obscure your front wheel hub. If you can see the hub in front of your handlebars, the handlebar stem is too short. If you can see the hub behind the handlebars, the stem is too long. You must buy the correct length stem and fit it, or have it fitted.

These are the basics regarding setting up your riding position. Once you have carried them out you can start training for any challenge. But as training proceeds and your fitness develops, it's a good idea to get a professional bike-fit, too.

# Creating a training plan

## Building stamina

All of the challenges in this book are long-distance ones, so stamina is crucial and your training should focus on building it. But what is stamina? It's the ability to keep doing something for a long time. In a cyclist's case it means conditioning the body's muscles to work for extended periods by strengthening them and increasing the rate and efficiency with which the heart and lungs can supply oxygen and nutrients to fuel their work.

So, riding your bike for extended periods must feature in your training for a long-distance cycling challenge, but perhaps not as much as you might think. If you can train your body to work harder than necessary to meet the demands that long-distance challenges place on it, albeit for shorter periods, then it copes better with working at a lesser intensity for longer.

This training principle is like approaching the objective of lifting a 10-kilogram weight 10 times by training to lift a 100-kilogram weight once. Once you can lift the 100 kilograms once, lifting 10 kilograms 10 times becomes a whole lot easier.

This analogy simplifies things a lot, because although there's more to cycling 100-plus miles over all kinds of terrain than there is to lifting weights, it demonstrates the principle of overload. Your body responds well to overload, as long as you don't overload it too much in one go and you make sure that you provide the building blocks and the time to rebuild it.

To get fitter and stronger you need to push your body just a little harder than it's used to, overloading it slightly but not too much. Then you rest and eat the right foods to give your body the time and the materials it needs to repair. The repair process gears up to cope with the overload, so

you end up a bit fitter and stronger than before. The basic training equation is therefore:

**Overload + Rest + Correct nutrition = Increased strength and fitness**

You create overload by increasing the intensity you ride at, the duration you ride for, or both at the same time. But be careful with both at the same time because too much overload may cause breakdown in the form of injury or illness, both of which will set you back.

The best way to control overload is to control how hard you work in training. Controlling duration is easy – you just add more time to a session – but to control intensity you need to measure some kind of parameter. You can do that by recording perceived exertion, heart rate or power output; perceived exertion is the least accurate representation of intensity and power output is the most accurate. In fact, perceived exertion only really works if you've been cycling and training successfully for a long time, and it isn't an effective measure if you haven't.

Before you start, though, you need a baseline from which individual doses of training can be prescribed. The intensity you can ride at for a period of one hour is the best baseline, and you can determine this by doing a test.

Pick a day when you have recovered completely from your last training session. You can do the test on the road, but you need to repeat it as training progresses to maintain some accuracy, so you would need to pick days with exactly the same weather conditions. It's much better therefore to do the test with your bike on a turbo trainer. You also need a heart-rate monitor that records average heart rate or a power-measuring device that has an average power facility.

## The test protocol

Warm up by riding at a steadily increasing intensity for 10 minutes, then spin in a lower gear for another five. After that you ride as hard as you can for three minutes, then spin in a low gear for two minutes. For the next five minutes, sprint flat out for 10 seconds every minute, recovering for the remaining 50 seconds by spinning the pedals in a low gear. Now ride easy for five minutes and get ready for the test. You need to zero your heart-rate monitor or power device ready to start recording when you start the test, then just focus on making a solid 20-minute effort where you ride as hard as you can for 20 minutes.

That's the key: you have to go as hard as you can for 20 minutes but spread the effort over that period. When you've finished, measure your average heart rate or power output and subtract 5 per cent if you are an experienced, fit, racing cyclist, or 10 per cent if you are less fit or less experienced. This should give you the heart rate or power output that you could maintain for one hour, but only for one hour. That's your baseline figure. Training doses can be worked out as percentages of that figure. Each percentage range is called a training intensity level.

Cyclist doing a 20-minute heart-rate test

| Level | Stage | Percentage of one-hour heart rate | Percentage of one-hour power |
|---|---|---|---|
| 1 | Recovery | < 65% | < 55% |
| 2 | Stamina | 66–80% | 56–75% |
| 3 | Tempo | 81–95% | 76–90% |
| 4 | Performance | 96–105% | 91–100% |
| 5 | Super | 106%+ | 101–115% |
| 6 | Anaerobic | N/A | 116%+ |

Training sessions are based on the above intensity levels and range from one hour at level 1 for recovery through two to four hours of level 2, to 20-minute repeats of level 3, especially the upper end of level 3, and finally to much shorter bouts of levels 4, 5 and 6. The bouts of specific effort are called intervals and training with them is interval training.

Training at each level develops a particular physical capacity. Level 2 does exactly what it says on the tin and boosts your stamina by training your body to use fats for fuel instead of sugar. Our bodies carry limited amounts of sugar, but even the skinniest person has enough fat to survive for days and ride for hours. Training at level 2 increases the intensity at which you can ride while burning fats and saving sugar stores for more intense efforts, such as the ones you need to make when riding up hills.

Training at level 3 increases pedalling efficiency and the overall efficiency with which your body burns fuel. It helps to increase cruising speed and makes sustaining it easier. Training at the top end of this level, which some coaches call the 'sweet spot', increases the exercise intensity level at which our bodies start producing chemicals that tend to slow us down. In short, it helps you to ride with more intensity for longer.

Level 4 training also does this, but at more cost to your body. You can't do as much level 4 training as you can upper level 3, so the total training effect and potential from level 4 is less than from upper level 3. It's a subtle difference but worth knowing. Level 4 is effective but should be used sparingly in a training programme.

Before you start training you should have a plan. Your plan is like a map that takes you where you want to be. With regard to this book, your destination is being able to take on the challenges within it, but a plan is also like a recipe: you mix in training sessions in order to get fitter, and they have to be mixed in the right proportions.

The sessions that will form the 'key ingredients' when training for long-distance cycling challenges are as follows:

## Key ingredients

**1.** Riding for extended periods at level 2

**2.** Riding for one hour at the lower end of level 3 (tempo)

**3.** Riding intervals of 10 to 20 minutes at upper level 3 (the 'sweet spot'), with five minutes of easy riding between each

**4.** Riding intervals of five to six minutes at level 4 with the same length of easy riding between each

**5.** Riding intervals of two to three minutes at level 5 with double the length of each interval of easy riding between each

**6.** Riding intervals of one minute at level 6 with two minutes of easy riding between each

**7.** Riding intervals of 15 to 30 seconds at maximum effort, with three times the interval length of easy riding between each

## Making a plan

You know how much time you've got to train, and how long you've got to get ready for a challenge, so you can take the above ingredients and create a training plan that runs over a number of weeks or months. The overall thing to bear in mind is the mix of training you need, which should be something like this.

Around 80 or 90 per cent of your training should be done by riding in the level 2 to level 4 range, broken down further into 60 per cent at level 2, 30 per cent at level 3 and 10 per cent at level 4.

Of the 30 per cent at level 3, at least half should be in the upper level 3 or 'sweet spot' range. The remaining 10 to 20 per cent of your training time should be at level 5 and above, or level 1 to recover.

It's a good idea to write down ina  diary what training you did, how it felt and what outcomes you had. After a while, the diary becomes your training manual because you can look at it and see what mix of training works for you.

Coaches used to believe that training should progress, starting with a large volume of lower intensity work to build a base, then moving on to shorter amounts of higher intensity training to build form near to the event or challenge an athlete is training for. This approach is called periodisation.

Nowadays, though, more and more coaches think that training should be mixed, with all levels of training practised throughout a training plan, but each one should be focused on for two to three weeks so its effects can take hold. Coaches who use this method believe that training like this helps athletes to focus on building all the abilities they need to perform. This approach can help an athlete eradicate any weaknesses as well as building on strengths.

It's the way Bradley Wiggins trained to win the 2012 Tour de France. He started in November 2011 by focusing on a weakness he had, which was climbing steep hills, and he addressed it by doing some very short but intense interval training right at the start of his plan.

Still, the mainstay of training for long-distance cycling challenges is riding at level 2 to build your stamina. Every week you ride, every session apart from very slow recovery ones should have some level 2 riding in it, either in a long-duration session dedicated to level 2, or as a warm-up and cool-down before and after more intense training. For the rest of your training, it's a good idea to do what Wiggins did and focus on your weaknesses first.

If you don't ride well up short, steep climbs (Scenario 1), try riding intervals at level 5 or 6 on short hills. If you get left behind when a group ride gets fast, or are always dropping back after corners, then do some of the same kind of training but on the flat or on your turbo trainer.

If you aren't good at maintaining a fast pace for a long time or you don't feel strong on longer climbs (Scenario 2), start with sessions 3 and 4 from the key ingredients box and focus on them, mixing them in with level 2 riding. Here are the typical week's training sessions that would address these two scenarios.

Be wholehearted in your training and commit to every session

## Scenario 1

Do session 5 and session 6 from the key ingredients box with at least one day of easy riding at level 1 for one hour, or total rest, between each session. Ride at level 2 before and after the intervals, and have one day when you ride for at least two hours at level 2. If there's time in the week and you have recovered from all the other sessions, repeat session 5 or 6 on another day.

## Scenario 2

Do session 3 and session 4 with at least one day of easy riding at level 1 for one hour, or total rest, between each one. Ride at level 2 before and after each session, and have one day when you ride for at least two hours at level 2. If there is

time in the week and you have recovered from all the other sessions, repeat session 3 or 4 on another day.

Do the specified training in either of the scenarios for two to three weeks, so the adaptations to it can really take hold on your body. Then do three weeks where you train based on sessions 2 and 3 of the key ingredients box. After that, if you started with sessions designed to address Scenario 1, use the sessions for Scenario 2 for two to three weeks, and vice versa.

These training combinations are great for improving weakness and for boosting specific areas of your fitness. They should be repeated through a training cycle in the build-up to a challenge, if there's time. However, most of

your training for the challenges in this book should be made up of weeks where you combine sessions 2 and 3 from the key ingredients box. That's because the adaptations these sessions stimulate are the ones you need most in order to attempt long-distance cycling challenges. You should do twice as many weeks of this sort of training as any you do in the scenarios. Regard it as your bread-and-butter training.

Session 7 in the key ingredients box should be treated as you would a strong flavouring in cooking. It's very effective training because it creates a big overload stimulus to every facet of your fitness, but like a strong flavouring it needs adding to your training with care. From time to time during each year do two sessions per week of this training for three weeks with some easy riding, and riding at level 2, for two or three days between them.

Not all your training should be done on your bike. One key to riding hard is to have a strong core, and that's achieved by conditioning the muscles in the mid-section of your body. A strong core gives your legs a solid platform to push against, whereas a weak core means your upper body gets lifted slightly when your legs push down, which soaks up some of their power. Consider the analogy of sitting on a skateboard and pushing against a barrel with your legs. The barrel will move one way but you will move the other on the skateboard. Now, if you push the barrel while sitting on floor with your back against a solid wall, only the barrel moves.

Having a strong core is like pushing with your back up against a wall. None of your leg energy is wasted; it all goes into turning the pedals. A strong core locks your pelvis onto the bike saddle, and it provides a solid platform for your legs to push against when you are out of the saddle.

Core muscles are those at the front and sides of your abdomen and in your lower back. There are lots of exercises that target core muscles, and many of them are more effective if you do them on a Swiss ball.

Your breathing muscles also play a part in stabilising your core, and along with it they have a direct effect on your cycling performance. Breathing muscles can be trained in isolation by using a POWERbreathe or similar device. Both the ball and breathing devices are relatively cheap bits of kit, but using them boosts cycling performance in a way that no amount of on-the-bike training can.

## Extra training

Resistance training is worth doing to build extra power in your legs, especially during the winter and/or if you are over 40. Over-40s tend to lose muscle fibres if they don't load them up by lifting weights or pushing against some sort of heavy resistance.

Lifting and other kinds of resistance training are also very good for maintaining bone health. Load-bearing exercise stimulates bone tissue renewal, but cycling isn't load bearing because your bike bears the load. It's the only downside of cycling as a form of exercise, but a bit of weight or resistance training rectifies this.

Running is a load-bearing exercise and a great substitute for cycling if the weather is bad, or if you are away without your bike, or even if you haven't got time for a bike ride. You need minimal equipment for running, it takes very little time to get changed into running kit, and there are no tyres to pump up or anything to check – like there is before you go for a bike ride. Running uses many of the same muscles that cycling does, only in a different way, and it's a great cardiovascular workout, just like cycling.

However, if you want to use running as part of your training you must keep it up and run at least once a week throughout the year so that your muscles stay used to it. And if you start running from scratch, you must start with short distances and build up slowly. Ten or 15 minutes will do for a first session, then build up the duration you run by no more than 10 per cent per outing.

# Challenge-ride nutrition

There are two sides to cycling nutrition: what you eat and drink to support your training, and what you eat and drink to support your effort when riding a challenge.

In training you need to eat and drink to get the most from each session, both during the session and while recovering after it. The objective of training nutrition is to help your body become lean and efficient. That means reducing your body fat percentage while preserving or even building lean muscle, and getting your body to work like a lean burn engine so that it gets a greater proportion of its energy by burning fats rather than by burning sugar.

There are books on how to do this, and specialists who dedicate their lives to helping athletes optimise their diets so that their bodies make the desired changes. However, the first principle of what to eat and drink to support your training is that you must fuel your workouts. That means eating before training sessions, but at least two hours before so that you don't start training on a full stomach.

It also means eating during a workout if it's longer than an hour. There are many things you can eat while cycling, but the broad choice is between real food and sports nutrition products. It is entirely up to you which you use; they both do the job, providing the real foods you eat have lots of easily available energy, so we are talking cakes and fruit, especially bananas. Sports nutrition products are more refined in the way they work and also more precise.

It is crucial to stay well hydrated. This means drinking lots of water throughout the day and while you train. The test of whether you are well hydrated is simple. You should be peeing fairly regularly and your urine should be clear or light yellow. If it's not then you must drink more until it is.

Drinks taken during exercise can contain nutrients too, such as sugars for energy and electrolytes to keep your muscles working optimally, but on long rides it's advisable to drink plain water from time to time as well. A good idea is to have two bottles on your bike, one with an energy electrolyte drink and the other with plain water in it.

After completing a tough training ride you should immediately eat something containing carbohydrates and protein. Some energy bars have the right mix of the two, but a tuna sandwich works well too.

The trick with eating to support your training but at the same time cutting body fat is to match your food intake to the amount of work you do. Try to eat less on non-training days or easy days. The reason you should try to cut body fat is that it doesn't contribute anything to your cycling performance. Quite the opposite, in fact – it detracts from it, particularly when riding up hills. Imagine cycling uphill with two or three 1-kilogram bags of sugar strapped to your back; you would definitely feel them there.

Protein can help boost cycling performance. Protein breaks down into the building blocks of muscle, the building blocks your body uses to make repairs in direct response to the training stimulus you place on it. If you don't eat enough good-quality protein you won't adapt to training fully, so you won't improveas much.

Animal proteins are the best source, but you can build muscle with vegetable proteins too, although you might need specialist advice on how to do it. This is because many vegetable proteins aren't complete proteins and they must be eaten in certain combinations to provide all the building blocks your body needs.

On hard training days eat 1.5 to 2 grams of protein per kilogram of body weight. Spread protein consumption throughout the day, because if you take too much at once your body cannot process it and it will get converted to fat.

Fats are an important part of your diet. You need to eat a certain amount of fat each day for optimum health but you should eat much more unsaturated than saturated fat and avoid processed fats completely. Fats help your body work to its full potential. Some, like the omega fats, can help you recover, maintain a good environment inside your body and even help you to build lean muscle. Again, there's a lot of good advice around that's beyond the remit of this book, but it's well worth keeping up with the latest ideas on performance nutrition that come from top professional cycling teams such as Team Sky.

## Fuelling up for a challenge ride

Challenge-ride nutrition starts the day before the ride, when you should eat extra carbohydrates to ensure that your stores of this fuel are full. Drink plenty of water but avoid alcohol as it has a dehydrating effect and puts a strain on your metabolism. One or two small beers or glasses of wine are OK though, provided you are used to them.

A carbohydrate-rich breakfast will set you up for a challenge ride. It's OK to eat protein at breakfast too; eggs are good. A favourite Tour de France riders' breakfast starts with cereal and yoghurt then takes in an omelette, maybe with cheese in it, and pasta with some bread as well.

Drink plenty of water before the ride. Coffee and tea are allowed – a strong black coffee may even help your performance, but don't drink too much coffee as the caffeine in it can cause you to pee more. Avoid fruit juices as they can cause gastric stress. You can start drinking as soon as you start riding. In fact, it's a good idea to set your watch to beep every 20 minutes to remind you to drink. You can drink in between these 20-minute intervals too.

Start eating after the first hour. You need lots of carbohydrates in the form of sugars to fuel your effort. Aim to consume 60 grams an hour, but don't think more is better, because 60 grams of glucose is all the body can process in an hour. However, recent research has revealed that your body can process 90 grams per hour of a 2:1 glucose–fructose mix.

Well ahead of the challenge, practise this eating pattern from time to time by doing a long hard ride where you eat the amounts prescribed above. You must get your body used to processing this amount of carbohydrate in training otherwise it won't do it during the challenge.

Fuelling a race or a challenge ride effort is where sports nutrition products come into their own. It's very hard to eat 60 grams of glucose an hour using normal foods, whereas there are energy gels on the market that deliver almost that amount in one shot.

Experiment with gels, energy bars and drinks when you are training, noting how many grams of sugar (which can be glucose, fructose or a substance called maltodextrin) they deliver per hit. Once you are happy with a product, stick with it. However, be aware that challenge events are often sponsored by sports nutrition companies that provide samples of their products at the feed stations. Find out which company is sponsoring the event and use their products in training so that you get used to them, or carry you own, or do both.

Finally, carrying water in one of your bottles has the extra benefit of being useful to cool you off on hot days. You must keep drinking to replace fluid lost through sweat, but pouring cool water over your head and legs cuts sweat rates down and reduces the amount of blood your body uses to shift heat to your skin, where it's lost through radiation. Doing that means your blood gets on with its primary task of transporting oxygen and fuel to working muscles. It also makes you feel better, and preserving good morale is crucial when taking on the challenges in this book.

UK & Ireland

Perthshire, Scotland

**Distance** 130 kilometres | 81 miles
**Total climbing** 1,949 metres | 6,390 feet
**Route key** A mountain climb and a timed 1-kilometre sprint

# 1 Etape Caledonia

The Etape Caledonia hit the headlines a few years ago because it was the first closed-road cyclosportive to take place in the UK, which was great for the participants but hard to swallow for some local residents. That's all water under the bridge now, and the event is a success today because of its stunning scenery, and it's a challenge because of the ever-changing nature of its route.

The mountains, lochs and glens of Perth and Kinross make the Etape Caledonia event memorable, but the simplicity of its route makes it a very accessible ride on any day of the year when the weather works for you. You must be certain that conditions will be safe and suitable throughout the ride, because this is the Scottish Highlands and it can get very wild very quickly.

The event starts and finishes in Pitlochry, but Aberfeldy is also on the route and would make a perfect base. The closed roads are a selling point of the Etape Caledonia, but, as with many parts of Scotland, there is very little traffic on them for the rest of the year, and for the most part the route stays clear of main roads.

The feeling of tranquillity and freedom of mind evoked by this challenge kicks in as soon as you leave Pitlochry and head west along the north side of Loch Tummel. You ride a beautiful twisting forested road that leads to a hydroelectric power station at the loch's western end, and to the start of the first test of the Etape Caledonia.

The closed roads in the event already provide the illusion of being in one of the great professional races, but at this point you can go for the green jersey competition with a timed 1-kilometre sprint. It starts after the sharp right and left bends following the hydroelectric power station and runs alongside the River Tummel aqueduct. Have a go: ride as fast as you can for 1 kilometre on this section. Two minutes 20

seconds was a good time in the 2012 event. It's not flat and there is often a headwind here.

Continuing west, you reach Loch Rannoch to begin a full circuit of the loch. It's 9 miles long and has the Tay Forest Park on its southern shore, but the crowning glory of Loch Rannoch is seeing the conical Schiehallion, the mountain this route climbs, reflected in its deep, mysterious waters.

It's worth pausing at the end of the loch to peer into the distance, because in the far west, the legendary mountains of Glencoe are visible. Turn left to cross the River Gaur here to follow the smaller and rougher south loch road, keeping right past Kinloch Rannoch to the start of Schiehallion.

The timed mountain section starts after the road leaves the loch, and just after it starts to climb. The exact point is 42.5 miles into the ride. Push hard from here until the top. The road rises in a series of steep steps with flatter sections in between. The fastest time in 2012 was just over six minutes, but sub-nine for men and sub-12 for women is good.

The descent is long and needs treating with respect because the road is narrow with lots of bends and the perennial mountain threat of wandering sheep. You turn right onto a wider road but still continue downhill.

A sharp right after the descent takes you behind Drummond Hill towards the shores of Loch Tay, where you keep left to ride through the Appin of Dull and follow the scenic road on the left bank of the River Tay back to Pitlochry.

The final section is a joy. There is just one stretch of main road, which crosses a flood plain formed where the River Tummel meets the Tay. Also, when you turn left off it just after Ballinloan, there's a short but very steep climb, and another a little further along the road. They are the final stings in the tail of the Etape Caledonia. It's a great circuit in stunning scenery, but one that is very achievable too.

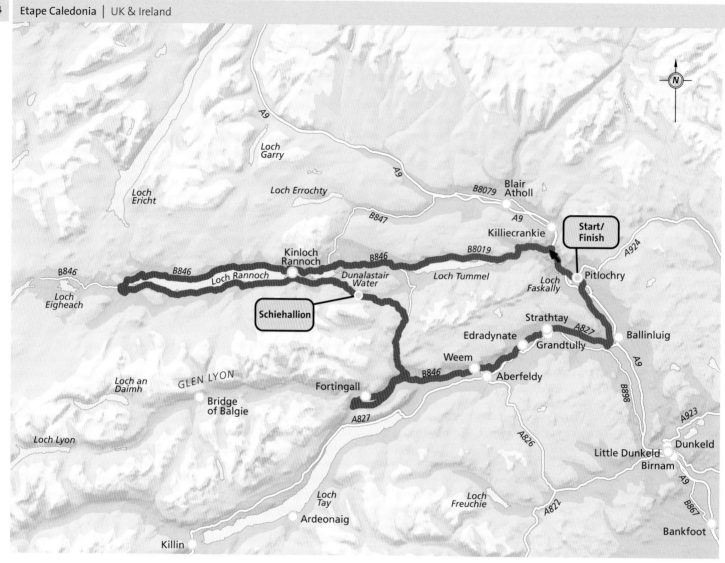

# Directions

▲ From Pitlochry town centre follow the main street northwest to the roundabout and take the second exit, the B8019. Follow this road all along the north side of Loch Tummel then Loch Rannoch. Turn left at the end of Loch Rannoch and follow its south side eastwards.

▲ Keep right at the end of the loch to climb Schiehallion. Turn right on the descent, continue down to take the first right and follow a minor road on the north bank of the River Lyon. Go left after the bridge and follow the south bank of the Lyon east. Take the first left, then turn right on the B846. Continue straight on where the B846 goes sharp right and follow this minor road to join the A827, still going east. Take the first left and follow this road back to Pitlochry town centre.

3.31km
169m
5% a.v.
10% max

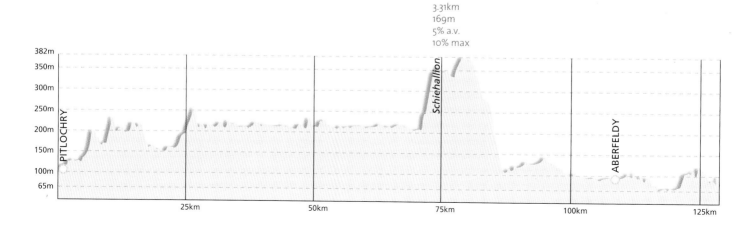

Scotland provides a dramatic and challenging landscape for racing

Wide valleys and steep hills characterise the final part of the Etape Caledonia

**Website**
www.etapecaledonia.co.uk

**Date**
Usually the second Sunday in May.

**Why the name?**
Caledonia was the name the Romans gave to Scotland. Schiehallion is known as the fairy mountain of the Caledonians.

**Anything else?**
This route is just south of the Cairngorm Mountains, where there are some fantastic cycling challenges including the climb of The Lecht, Britain's highest main road, and the Tour de France-style climb to the ski station on the Cairngorms. The Lecht is on the A939 between Cock Bridge and Tomintoul and the Cairngorm Mountains are accessed through Aviemore.

**Don't forget**
If you do this challenge outside of the Etape event you need to take all your food and drink with you, as there are very few shops. Tell somebody your route if you are going solo.

Northumberland

**Distance** 166.4 kilometres | 104 miles
**Total climbing** 2,374 metres | 7,789 feet
**Route key** Eight tough climbs

# 2 The Cyclone

Northumberland is the secret jewel in Britain's crown. Wide-open views, quiet roads and mysterious forests lie under a big, big sky. The Cyclone route is an all-encompassing loop running north of Newcastle to the Cheviots (the chain of high, wild hills that Northumberland shares with Scotland), past the great Kielder and Wark Forests then shadowing Hadrian's Wall on the way back towards Newcastle.

The Cyclone event starts at the Newcastle Falcons Rugby Club in Kingston Park, in the north of the city, but if you are riding this challenge at other times it's probably better to start in Ponteland, about 12 kilometres (7 miles) northwest of there. Parking facilities are better and you lose the only uninteresting section of the route.

The route heads northwest through a network of lanes that become increasingly undulating, with the undulations trending upwards all the way to Rothbury, a town with a frontier feel. It stands on a little cliff above the River Coquet and on the southern edge of the Cheviot Hills, Northumberland's mountains.

The route continues northwest then runs below the rounded mass of Cushat Law before turning south past Harbottle Castle. From there it follows the River Coquet downstream then swings left to climb over Billsmoor. You descend into Redesdale then climb out of it to begin the hardest part of the Cyclone. You'll have noticed by now that the countryside has grown wilder. You are riding through Reiver country.

Border Reivers were legendary cattle rustlers who lived on both sides of the English and Scottish border and ran their territories as if they were independent of either country.

They lived in fortress-like dwellings called bastle houses; you occasionally see their ruins and the imposing peel towers built by the Reiver clan leaders. Reivers were such a problem that Elizabeth I considered fortifying Hadrian's Wall, south of here, against them, and forgoing part of her kingdom. However, when James I succeeded her, he waged an effective war against the Reivers and brought their reign to an end.

As you ride through this sparse, northern scenery, the Reiver legends help bring the landscape to life. Reiver law said that anyone who had been raided had the right to track and make counter-raids. This was called the 'hot trod'. Visualising the dashing raids and the grim, vengeful pursuits across this trackless land helps add steel to your resolve as you pedal through it.

The highest point of the ride comes after a long climb up Troughend Common, where the Pennine Way footpath crosses the road at right angles. Another climb over Hareshaw Common, then Hareshaw Head, follows. Then there's a long descent to Bellingham, where you cross the North Tyne river.

Most of the Cyclone's climbs are long and steady, but in the next phase they become short and sharp. Ealingham Rigg and Wark Common are both very steep, then a lumpy passage takes you away from the North Tyne to the A68 and the last sting of the Cyclone, the Ryal, where Bradley Wiggins attacked to win the Beaumont Trophy road race in 2009, weeks before finishing third in the Tour de France. This dead-straight road climbs in two giant steps. Afterwards, all that's left is mostly downhill to run through some pretty villages back to Ponteland and the start.

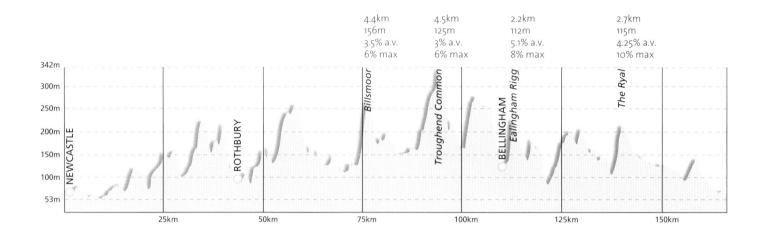

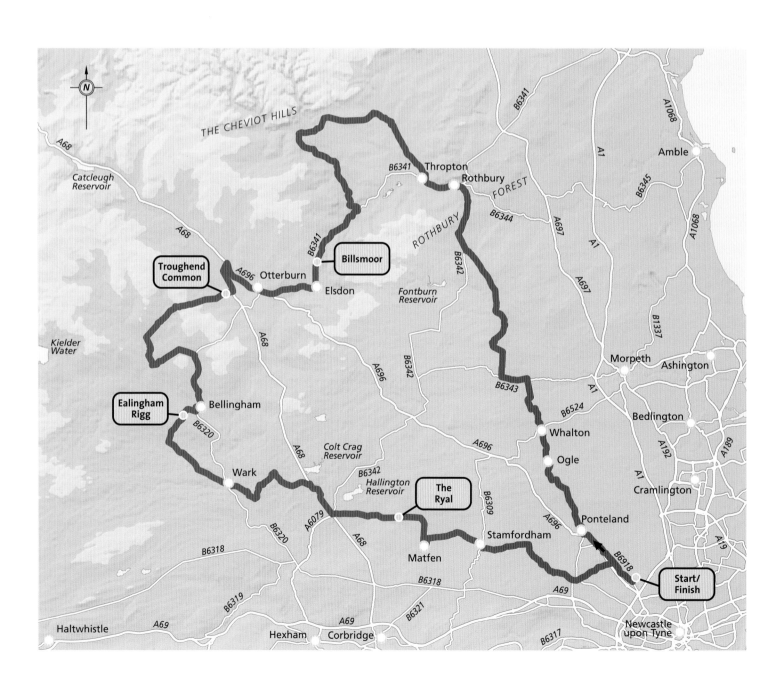

# ▌Directions

▲ Go north on the B6918 then A696 to Ponteland, where you turn right on North Road and follow this through Ogle and Whalton then Meldon to the B6343, where you turn left. Take the first right after Meldon Park to Rothbury.

▲ Turn left on the B6341 then go right at Thropton and follow this road northwest then west to Alwinton. Turn left and follow the river southeast through Harbottle to the B6341. Turn right and continue to the A696 where you turn right again. Turn left in Elishaw on the A68 then turn right just before Troughend village. Turn left to Greenhaugh then go left to the B6320 where you turn right to Bellingham.

▲ Turn right after crossing the river, then go left to Wark and continue over the river, following the road to the A68. Turn right then go left on the B6342 and take the first right off it. Continue through Matfen and Stamfordham then back to the B6918 where you turn left for Ponteland or right for Kingston Park.

**Website**
www.virginmoneycyclone.co.uk

**Date**
The end of June.

**Why the name?**
Organiser Peter Harrison named it after all the battles he's had with the weather across this wild terrain.

**Anything else?**
There is a road from Alwinton, which is on the most northerly section of the Cyclone route, that runs for almost 20 kilometres (12.5 miles) up a wonderful secret valley, steadily uphill for most of the way, to the remains of a Roman camp. Riding it should be on every British cyclist's bucket list.

**Don't forget**
This ride is high and wild and in the north of England. It can get cold, it can rain, and there isn't much shelter. Plan to ride it on a good-

**Riding the Ryal**

weather day and take all the high-ride gear with you that you normally would. There are a number of villages and cafes on the route, but mostly in the first and fourth quarter. You must carry sufficient food and drink with you to get through the middle section.

Two pro racers who both studied in Newcastle and trained on the Cyclone's roads: James Moss in black and Ross Creber in blue

Cumbria

| | |
|---|---|
| **Distance** | 179.2 kilometres \| 112 miles |
| **Total climbing** | 3,800 metres \| 12,464 feet |
| **Route key** | 10 killer climbs |

# **3** The Fred Whitton Challenge

A circuit of Britain's Lake District crossing every major pass in one voluptuous loop, the Fred Whitton Challenge is as hard as it is beautiful. A test without compromise – there are no alternative routes, no choices but a chain of steep hills that challenge your legs, your spirit and even your patience. This is not a casual undertaking; you will be out there for a long time in a very tough environment.

The reward is immense as you rip almost 4,000 vertical metres from the route. This is the hardest British sportive, and anyone who does it wears the Fred Whitton Challenge medal with pride. Getting round is an achievement, but some take the challenge even further. They try to beat their best time, and the elite even try to get close to Cumbrian cycling legend Rob Jebb's sub-six-hour record ride.

Sub six hours is amazing for a challenge that's easily the equivalent of a hard Tour de France stage, except that France hasn't got climbs this steep – at least not concentrated in one small area. Their names are a litany of pain: Kirkstone, Honister, Newlands and the formidable twin passes of Hardknott and Wrynose.

The official Fred Whitton Challenge starts and finishes in Coniston, although you could choose any of the towns that the challenge passes through for an unofficial attempt. The thing about starting and finishing at Coniston, though, is that the two hardest climbs, Hardknott and Wrynose, come last, but it's downhill almost all the way from the top.

The Coniston start begins with the climb of Hawkshead Hill. It's tough, but nothing like what's in store. Kirkstone Pass starts at the left turn from the A591 called Holbeck Lane and it's steep. This joins the main road at Townhead, where the climbing relents slightly.

The descent of Kirkstone is fast, so take care. It flattens as you reach Patterdale, where England's third-highest mountain, Helvellyn, towers above you on your left. You ride along the peaceful shore of Ullswater lake, then climb up to Matterdale End and descend to reach the A66. This is the only really busy road on the whole route and it leads to Keswick and Borrowdale, where the next big climb, Honister Pass, begins.

Honister Pass leads to Buttermere and the bottom of Newlands Pass, which in turn leads to the start of Whinlatter. This is a hard section but one of jaw-dropping beauty. Buttermere is majestic – one of the quietest Lakeland valleys nestling between two high walls of solid mountain. The entry from Honister reveals Buttermere's splendour.

Whinlatter takes you back into Buttermere lower down the valley where there's a short hill before Loweswater, then the climb of Fangs Brow. You are now on the western edges of the Lakes in a land of low fells, and there's a long, undulating ride to Eskdale and the final act of the Fred Whitton: the Hardknott and Wrynose passes.

Treat them with respect. They would be a challenge without all the hard miles and brutal climbing you've done so far. In fact, one of the secrets of this ride is to spread your effort and don't get carried away on the first few climbs. The other is to use the flatter sections in which to eat and drink, so you don't have to do it near the six key climbs.

Climb with good technique. Engage bottom gear, ride the outside of the corners because the insides are steeper, and pedal smoothly to prevent wheelspin, especially in the wet. Finally, take care when descending; these climbs go down as steeply as they go up and the corners are treacherous.

Coniston is about 9 miles from the Wrynose summit, and it's downhill all the way with just two tiny but cruel climbs. And finally you've finished; you've met the challenge, all 112 miles and 3,800 metres uphill of it.

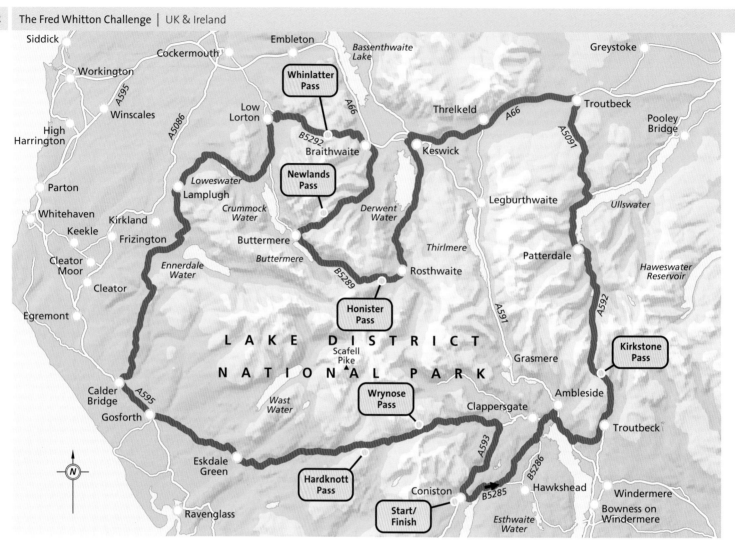

# Directions

▲ From Coniston, follow the B5285 and turn left at High Cross to climb Hawkshead Hill. Descend to join the B5286 and turn left to Clappersgate. Turn right and right again to join the A5095 south. After a mile turn left at Holbeck Lane and climb to the top of Kirkstone Pass. Descend and carry on to Ullswater and to the junction with the A5091, and turn left. Turn left on the A66 at Troutbeck and ride to Keswick.

▲ From Keswick, follow the B5289 south to Seatoller and take the right fork over Honister to Buttermere village. Turn right and climb Newlands. Keep left to Braithwaite and turn left onto the B5292 to climb Whinlatter. Turn left in Low Lorton and right to Loweswater, then left after Fangs Brow to Lamplugh.

▲ Keep left at Lamplugh and turn left onto the minor road to Croasdale then go right to Ennerdale Bridge, where you turn left and head south to Calder Bridge. Turn left onto the A595. Turn left at Gosforth to Eskdale Green. Turn first left after the village to pass Dalegarth station. Climb over Hardknott and Wrynose passes. Continue until the A593 junction. Turn right to Coniston.

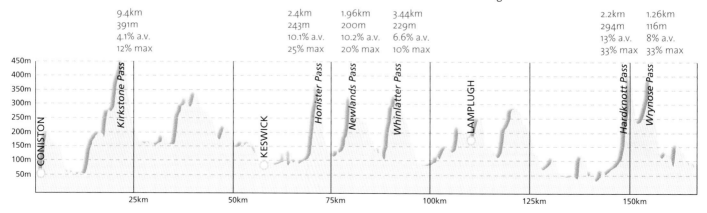

One tough climb follows another in the Fred Whitton Challenge

If traffic allows, it's best to ride wide on steep corners like this to avoid the steeper inside line

### Website
www.fredwhittonchallenge.org.uk

### Date
The first Sunday after May Day.

### Why the name?
Fred Whitton was the driving force behind a local cycling club, the Lakes Road Club, and a highly regarded and popular race organiser who died in 1998 aged 50.

### Anything else?
Full details of the Four Seasons Fred Whitton Challenge are on their website, but basically you get a card from SPORTident and post a time for the challenge whenever you want. Simply get the card stamped at the start and finish in Coniston and at several checkpoints along the route. All submitted times appear on the Fred Whitton website, so you can see how you compare with other riders.

### Don't forget
Take ample spares and plenty of food and drink, but there's no need to overload because there are lots of shops and cafes along the way. You will be going high, so dress for temperature changes. The Lake District is famous for rain, so a folding waterproof top is a must.

County Durham

**Distance**  124.2 kilometres | 77.6 miles
**Total climbing**  2,313 metres | 7,587 feet
**Route key**  Six major climbs and plenty of undulations in between

# **4** Etape Pennines

The north Pennines are high, lonely and beautiful, with fantastic views and some of the longest, hardest hills in Britain. That's what makes the Etape Pennines a real challenge, especially when you add in the open nature of the terrain. It's wild and windswept here, but this ride is one every cyclist should try, if only for the fact that you ride over the highest surfaced road in England.

The 2013 event started in Barnard Castle, the gateway town to northern Britain. From here, you don't get long to settle into your stride before the first hill kicks in, although Langleydale Common is nothing like what's to come.

The descent of Langleydale leads to the 20-kilometre point, and the next big climb is 40 kilometres away, but the section leading to it is very heavy going with several short but very steep climbs in an intricate route. Watch out for the steep rise up the valley side just after crossing the River Wear. Wilk's Hill near Esh Winning is tough too.

The really serious climbing starts just southwest of Consett with a long pull over Muggleswick Common to 466 metres (1,528 feet). A long descent follows that has several steep sections and leads to Blanchland, where another major climb starts. This is Cuthbert's Hill and it breaks the 500-metre barrier. It also has a very difficult descent where the road is unfenced and gusting wind can cause scary moments. It's wickedly steep near the bottom. Focus on keeping your centre of gravity low, hold the handlebars low, and keep your speed down to a point where you feel in control of your bike.

One descent leading to the start of the next climb is a feature of this ride. Scarsike Head and Race Head come in quick succession, both their summits well over 500 metres, but they are just the prelude to the star hill of this ride. First, though, because the Etape Pennines is a closed-road event, there's a lumpy detour of back roads around Wearhead to negotiate. If you did this ride at any other time, you could cross straight over the A689 to Ireshopeburn.

Whatever, you will now be at the foot of Langdon Fell and facing a long, exposed, steep in places and almost dead-straight slog to 627 metres (2,057 feet). You don't often get to ride this high on a road in Britain. Only one surfaced climb is higher – The Lecht in Scotland. There are higher roads, some close to the top of Weardale, where you are now, but they aren't surfaced all the way and some are just bridleways, or tracks that were roads many years ago.

The descent of Langdon Fell is long, straight and exposed. It takes you into Teesdale, which is gentler looking than Weardale. You follow the youthful, splashing River Tees downhill to Middleton. The worst is over now: there's a short climb called High Dyke just after Middleton-in-Teesdale, and another a few miles later. Then it's downhill all the way back to Barnard Castle.

The Etape Pennines is one of the best challenges in this book. The high, gaunt hills here give nothing away, and getting around this route is a real achievement. It's not as long as some other challenges, but it's a real test, and you definitely have to enjoy climbing hills to do it.

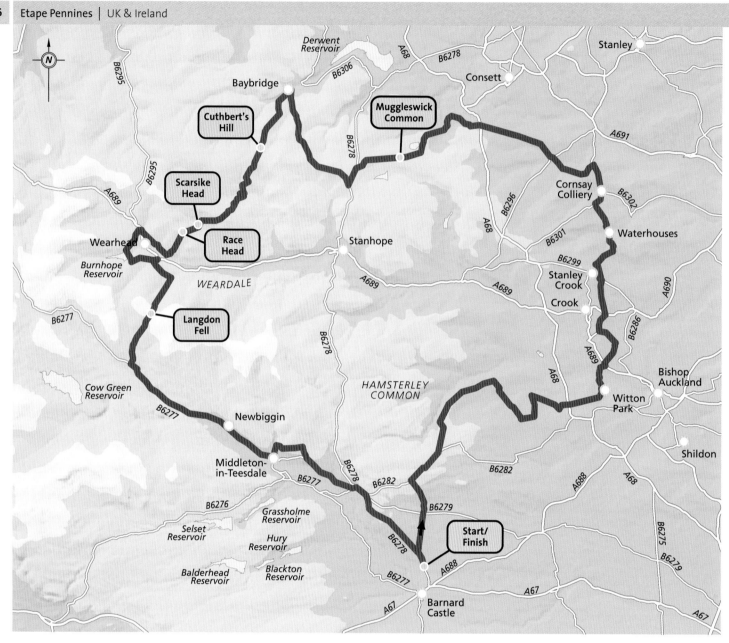

# ▌Directions

▲ From the start in Barnard Castle head north on the B6278 and fork right at Rose Cottage. Continue north over the B6279 and turn right on the B6282. Take the left fork before Woodland then turn left and follow this road to continue straight where the Hamsterley Road turns left. Take the first left, then the first left again, then go right. Take the second left to cross the A68 then turn left through Witton Park and go over the weir, crossing the A689 then the A690 just east of Crook.

▲ Continue northeast through Stanley Crook then turn left and follow this road north to go right on the B6301. Turn left at the top of Wilk's Hill, then take the first right to cross the B6296. Continue through Rowley to cross the A68 and follow this road uphill over Muggleswick Common. Turn left at the summit then first right and descend to Baybridge, where you turn left to climb Cuthbert's Hill. Take care on the descent and turn right then left over Rookhope Burn to climb Scarsike Head then Race Head.

▲ During the Etape Pennines event follow direction signs around Wearhead, but outside the event descend to the A689 then turn right then first left. Keep left then turn right to climb Langdon Fell. Turn left on the B6277 after the descent and follow this road to Middleton-in-Teesdale. Turn left at the sharp right bend then take the first right, then go right again to turn left on the B6282 to Eggleston. Turn right on the B6278 and follow this road back to Barnard Castle.

## Website
www.etapepennines.co.uk

## Date
Early October.

## Why the name?
Etape means stage in French, and the most famous all-comers cycling event is the Etape du Tour, which means a stage of the Tour de France. The Etape Pennines is modelled on that event.

## Anything else?
Langdon Fell isn't the only high hill here. Swinhope Head runs parallel to it, about 5 miles east, and its summit is 607 metres (1,991 feet). But if you are feeling brave and have a cyclo-cross or mountain bike, there's Grasshills Causeway about 3 miles west. It runs parallel to the Langdon Fell climb, but it's partly unsurfaced, and its summit is 674 metres (2,211 feet). Going further afield to Alston there's a track over Skirwith Fell, a former mine road, that touches 758 metres (2,486 feet). If you like hills, this part of Britain is the ideal adventure playground.

## Don't forget
Pay close attention to the weather forecast and dress accordingly. Take a rainproof top with you even if it's not raining, gloves and a thin hat that you could put under your helmet if it gets cold.

**The Etape Pennines uses some of the highest, wildest roads in Britain**

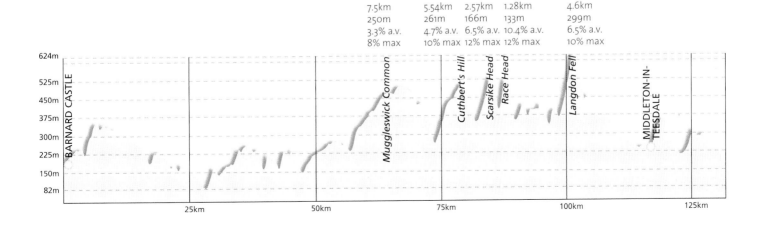

| | 7.5km | 5.54km | 2.57km | 1.28km | 4.6km |
|---|---|---|---|---|---|
| | 250m | 261m | 166m | 133m | 299m |
| | 3.3% a.v. | 4.7% a.v. | 6.5% a.v. | 10.4% a.v. | 6.5% a.v. |
| | 8% max | 10% max | 12% max | 12% max | 10% max |

North Yorkshire

**Distance** 133 kilometres | 83 miles
**Total climbing** 2,340 metres | 7,675 feet
**Route key** Three very hard, very steep climbs with some tough undulations between them

# 5 The Ryedale Rumble

This new cyclosportive event had a stuttering start when it was cancelled in 2012, but at the time of writing it is set to run again in 2013. However, it has its place in this book not because of its history, but because it's located in the North Yorkshire Moors, an area that is the perfect setting for a cycling challenge. Because the Rumble doesn't have the history of other events in this book, we've used an adapted version for you to follow.

The moors are high and wild with wide-open views; an undulating plateau that's deeply dissected in places. Some fearsome climbs have been created by the steep sides coupled with the deep dissections, including one of the hardest in the country – and the Ryedale Rumble goes up it.

The event starts at Gilling Castle, but Ampleforth is just around the corner on the route and is a great place to start if you want to try this challenge at any other time. The first leg plays in the foothills of the moors, going east then south near Coxwold, then it heads northwest along a lovely undulating lane where the famous white horse carved into this part of the North Yorkshire Moors is visible. This area is known as the Hambleton Hills.

Look out too for the gliders circling above one of the most famous climbs in this area, Sutton Bank. But that is a main-road climb; the Rumble's route heads into the moors by another climb a few miles further north, Sneck Yate Bank, sometimes called Boltby Bank. Pace yourself up this; it's steep but there's steeper to come.

The next section is one of the best of the ride. You turn sharp right at the summit of Sneck Yate and ride along the ridge of the Hambleton Hills along a dead-straight road. Then the route heads east past Rievaulx Abbey to Helmsley on the north side of Ryedale, the wide, flat-bottomed valley that gives this ride its name.

The next climb is Helmsley Moor, and the scenery now is typical of the inner moor. It's a long climb going north with some steep ups and downs that takes you to Cockayne, under Bransdale Moor. The climbs come thick and fast now. You go up Shaw Ridge, which has a very steep start, then descend to Gillamoor. After that there's a long climb north over Harland Moor, a short, steep descent and the brutal Blakey Bank, just after Church Houses.

The steep climbs in this area demand respect. It's no good trying to hammer up them like you might do in the Surrey Hills, for example. They are too long for that. Treat them like long climbs; gear down, stay seated if possible and don't give any one climb too much effort, except for one. After continuing to Rosedale Head you descend to Rosedale Abbey, where the Ryedale Rumble confronts you with Rosedale Chimney. You are 60 miles into the ride, you will be tired, but you will have to give everything you've got just to ride up the Chimney. The difficulty of any climb is the sum of its length and its gradient. Rosedale Chimney is one of the hardest in the country. But as you catch your breath while riding over the dome of Spaunton Moor, console yourself that the worst is behind you now.

A descent into Hutton-le-Hole leads to a stretch along the lovely River Dove, which you follow into Ryedale. The final leg of the ride meanders, a bit like the rivers here, but it does so with a purpose. There are little outcrops of hills in this flat valley, and you go over them. Caukleys Bank is steep but short, then there's a section from Hovingham going west that undulates through some woodland before taking you north to the event finish, or a little bit further to Ampleforth. Several of the roads on this route have been used for the national men's and women's elite road race championships and in stages of the Tour of Britain.

On a ride of constant hills, it's best to spin your legs quickly and ride in the saddle for as long as possible on each one

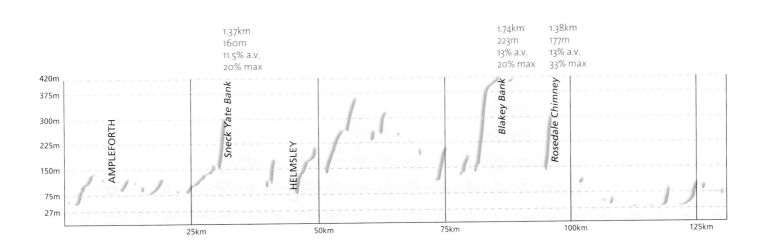

1.37km
160m
11.5% a.v.
20% max

1.74km
223m
13% a.v.
20% max

1.38km
177m
13% a.v.
33% max

# Directions

▲ From Gilling Castle turn left on the B1363, then left at Oswaldkirk. Ride through Ampleforth then turn left to Byland Abbey. Turn right then take the first left after Elm Hag Lake. Turn right on Whinny Bank and follow the road through Kilburn and Osgoodby, where you turn right then turn left on the A170 to Sutton-under-Whitestonecliffe. Turn right and follow this road north to turn right at the Boltby Trekking Centre and climb Sneck Yate Bank.

▲ Turn right at the top of the hill then go left on Wethercote Lane through Old Byland and past Rievaulx Abbey to turn right on the B1257. Join the A170 east in Helmsley and turn left on Carlton Road. Follow this road through Cockayne then head south on Bransdale Road then Fadmoor Bank to Gillamoor, where you turn left. Go through the village, follow the main street up Gillamoor Bank and turn left on High Lane. Continue north, following Daleside Road to Thorn Wath Lane, go right through Church Houses and up Blakey Bank.

▲ Turn left at the top of the hill, then turn right and carry on to Rosedale Abbey. Turn right to climb Rosedale Chimney and descend to Hutton-le-Hole to continue south over the A170. Take the first right to Great Edstone; take the third right, cross the river and go right again. Turn left on Ings Lane, go right on Muscoates Lane, left through Nunnington to join the B1257 south, then turn right in Hovingham and follow this road to Coulton, where you turn right. Turn right on the B1363 then turn left to Gilling Castle.

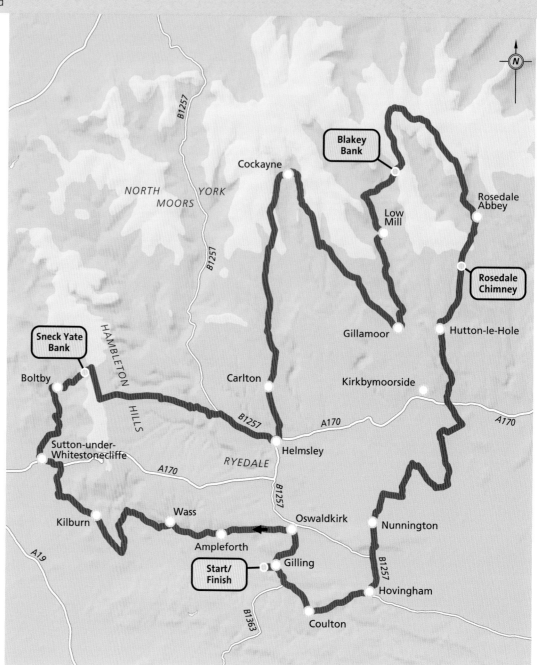

## Website
www.bcyorkshire.co.uk

## Date
September.

## Why the name?
Ryedale is where the event starts and finishes.

## Anything else?
There's plenty. This ride explores only the western moors; there is wonderful cycling country to be found further east, and to the north, in an area known as the Cleveland Hills. Then there's the Yorkshire Wolds, just south of Ryedale. The Wolds are not as high as the moors, nor do they have such spectacular valleys or hills, but they are quiet, beautiful, and not visited as much as the Yorkshire Moors.

## Don't forget
You are going high, so take the usual rainproof/windproof top in case you need it, and perhaps some light gloves if you do this challenge in spring or autumn, especially if rain is forecast. The villages are fairly spread out, so take a good supply of food and drink with you.

**Distance** 180 kilometres | 112 miles
**Total climbing** 3,500 metres | 11,480 feet
**Route key** Four major climbs with a lot of steep undulations in between

# **6** Etape du Dales

The Yorkshire Dales have been a playground for cyclists ever since the bike was invented. Their southern edge is on Leeds, and Bradford's doorstep, and the Dales stretch north as far as the imagination. Or so it must have seemed to the 19th-century mill, factory and office workers who explored them by bike back then.

Green valleys, gaunt hills and vivid slashes of limestone crags, that's the Dales, and the Etape is a celebration of their scenery. It drives right up and down the backbone of the Dales, visiting the valleys one after the other against the grain, so the route generally drops into and has to climb out of them. This is the Etape du Dales' unique challenge.

It starts and finishes in the south, in Grassington, and the route begins by climbing steadily up Wharfedale, almost to the river's head, to the base of the first big hill of the day. At 589 metres (1,932 feet), Fleet Moss is the highest road climb in the Dales, and one of the highest in England. But it's made harder because it climbs in steps, and that makes getting into a rhythm difficult.

Constant gradients help cyclists focus on their pedal rhythm and their breathing, which together make half of the key to good climbing. The other facets are fitness and power-to-weight ratio. But Fleet Moss imposes its own rhythm; you can't set yours. You will be in and out of the saddle, shifting gears, but it helps to know where the steep sections are. The climb is 4.4 kilometres (2.75 miles) long, and the steepest bits are at 250 metres (820 feet), 1.7 kilometres (1 mile) and then 3.3 kilometres (2 miles), just before the summit. Watch your bike computer and count them down – it helps.

The descent to Hawes is fast, then you have the south side of Buttertubs Pass to climb. This is high again, 526 metres (1,726 feet), but it's in two parts with a steep first half and steadier second. Like many Dales climbs, Buttertubs is wild and exposed, a hedgeless track with no shelter.

The descent of Buttertubs leads to Swaledale, then there's a short but steep climb over into Arkengarthdale. Named after Arkle Beck, this is the northernmost dale, and the climb to Tan Hill is the northernmost part of this route. The Dales grow wilder as you ride north, and this dale, scarred by old lead mines, is quite desolate. You despair of seeing any sign of human habitation, and then a pub appears.

It's not a mirage: it's the Tan Hill Inn, the highest pub in Britain at 528 metres (1,732 feet) and the start of the run south. Keld is the first place you reach after the bumpy descent of West Stones Dale, then the southerly progress is halted by a long slog up Birkdale Common and over Nateby Common to Nateby. The section from Nateby to the Moorcock Inn up the valley road is uphill but relatively easy. Use it to eat and drink and prepare for the Etape du Dales' final stage.

You clamber over Garsdale Head then turn left to climb Galloway Gate, more commonly known by cyclists as the Coal Road. It starts with a very steep section and has a tricky descent into Dent, where one of the founding fathers of geology, Adam Sedgwick (1785–1873), was born.

The ride gets even harder, with lots of spirit-sapping short, steep hills. The roads are heavy too; what cyclists describe as 'grippy'. Through Ribblehead to Horton in Ribblesdale it gets harder. Five miles further on in Stainforth you start the final climb, Halton Gill. It wouldn't feel so tough at the start of the ride, but at this stage it's really punishing. Focus on the fact that at the top there's just 15 miles left, almost all downhill.

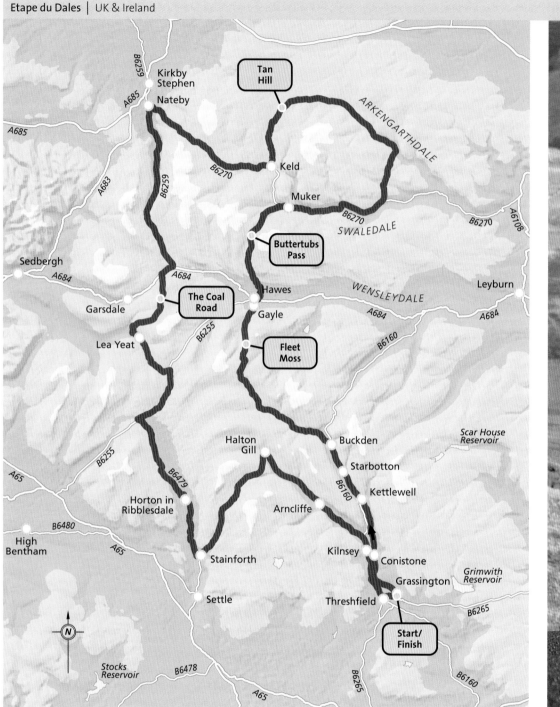

# ❙ Directions

▲ In Grassington, turn right off the B6265 to ride northwest to Conistone. Continue to Kettlewell, then turn right and stay on the B6160(NW) to Buckden. At Buckden fork left and go through Hubberholme then over Fleet Moss to Hawes. Turn right onto the A684, ride through Hawes, then follow signs to Simonstone. After Buttertubs Pass, turn right at the end of the descent to Muker. Stay on the B6270(E) through Gunnerside to Low Row,

then take a sharp left up a steep climb in the direction of Langthwaite. At the bottom of the descent into Arkengarthdale turn left to Tan Hill, then left to Keld. In Keld, turn right on the B6270 to Nateby, then left onto the B6259 to the Moorcock Inn.

▲ From there, turn right in the direction of Garsdale for one mile, then left towards Garsdale station up the steep Coal Road.

Proceed into Dent and descend to Lea Yeat and then turn left to Newby Head, where you turn right on the B6255 and continue to Ribblehead viaduct. Turn left to Horton in Ribblesdale, then stay on the B6479 to Stainforth. Take a left to Halton Gill, then a right to Litton, and continue on to Arncliffe. At Kilnsey stay on the B6160(S) to Threshfield, then turn left back to Grassington.

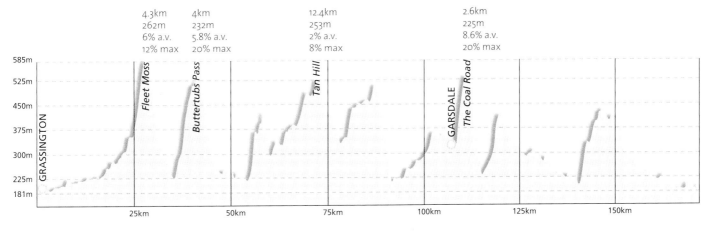

| | 4.3km | 4km | | 12.4km | | | 2.6km |
| | 262m | 232m | | 253m | | | 225m |
| | 6% a.v. | 5.8% a.v. | | 2% a.v. | | | 8.6% a.v. |
| | 12% max | 20% max | | 8% max | | | 20% max |

585m
525m — *Fleet Moss* — *Buttertubs Pass* — *Tan Hill* — GARSDALE — *The Coal Road*
450m
375m — GRASSINGTON
300m
225m
181m

25km · 50km · 75km · 100km · 125km · 150km

Dales scenery varies from green sheltered valleys to wild, exposed rocky tops

Previous page: On steeper sections of long climbs like this, there's no alternative but to get out of the saddle and push for all you are worth

### Website
www.daveraynerfund.co.uk then click on 'Etape du Dales'.

### Date
Usually the middle of May.

### Why the name?
It was a spoof on the French Etape du Tour, a stage of the Tour de France for all-comers, but now the Tour is coming to Yorkshire the Etape tag is perfect.

### Anything else?
There's loads more to explore here. The ride doesn't touch the west or east fringes of the Dales. Then there's the other big Yorkshire Dales cycling event: the Three Peaks Cyclo-Cross. That is definitely a challenge, but one you can only do on the day of the official event, as it crosses private property.

### Don't forget
Catch bad weather on this ride and it doubles the difficulty. You need good clothing so that you can remain as comfortable as possible. Even if the weather is good, take everything you normally would for a mountain challenge. This ride goes pretty high and temperatures can drop without warning. The weather can change suddenly too.

The Peak District

**Distance** 160 kilometres | 100 miles
**Total climbing** 1,400 metres | 4,590 feet
**Route key** One super-steep climb and a passage through the edge of the Peak District. The roads are rough in places

# 7 The Cheshire Cat

The Cheshire Cat explores everything that Cheshire has to offer. The pastoral beauty of its quiet lanes (where the cows that produce Cheshire cheese munch contentedly on lush green grass), its industrial heritage and its hills combine in a testing but accessible challenge named after the grinning cat-like creature in Lewis Carroll's *Alice in Wonderland*.

This is a good ride if you are new to cycling. The event starts in Crewe, a location that rolls out the real difficulties, including the infamous Mow Cop hill, early on. That's why it suits someone who is new to challenging bike rides. The ride is long, but the hardest parts come early, while you are still strong, although there is also a tough hill at around three-quarters distance that grabs your attention. The Cheshire Cat is a good stepping stone towards some of the more demanding challenges in this book.

From Crewe, the route heads straight for the Cheshire–Staffordshire border. It's very distinct here because it runs along the top of a ridge, and the top is where you're going. The climb of Mow Cop is not subtle. It rises fast enough for you to get the bends; at least it feels like the bends when you are gasping for breath at the top.

The road begins to undulate as you approach Mow Cop, then there's a flat stretch alongside the Cheshire Ring Canal. Then you turn right. You don't get the full impact at first. The road rises, but there's a right-angled right bend so you can't see what's ahead.

After the next left you can. The road kicks up, flattens a bit, then kicks up again in front of a pub called the Cheshire View. There used to be a sign here saying that the gradient was 30 per cent. It's gone now, but some locals reckon that the council surveyors came here one day and found that the gradient was nearer 40 per cent. They didn't have a sign for that so they took the old one away.

True or village myth, this bit of Mow Cop is a brutal experience. The Cheshire Cat organisers film riders here and award medals to anyone who doesn't get off and walk, but plenty still do. It's steep before the pub and the same for at least 100 metres afterwards as well, then you go sharp left where it's flatter, but after a right turn there is still a long pull to the top.

Conquering Mow Cop is a real achievement; one you can savour as you ride along the ridge and gaze down on the Cheshire Plain, where in one sweep you can see the mountains of North Wales, Liverpool and the Wirral, Manchester, and the Pennine hills behind it. Not for long though; there's a sharp descent then a short slog across to Congleton, where the route tiptoes right around the edges of the town. You then thread your way across the Cheshire Plain, enjoying its leafy lanes, to Delamere Forest, where the Cheshire Cat grins again. Bad things happen in forests, and the Yeld is quite bad. There must be something about Cheshire and laser-straight hills because that's just what this is: a mile of dead-straight and narrow road crossing a lovely round hill.

The route goes around Kelsall then turns for home and follows the Shropshire Union Canal before dropping south to cross the Peckforton Hills at Harthill. You'll see Cholmondeley Castle on the descent, or at least its gardens and deer park. They make the perfect prelude for the last idyllic look around the lanes as you head through Nantwich back to Crewe.

# Directions

▲ From Crewe, head south to Shavington. Turn left over the A500 and follow this road through Haslington, Hassall, Rode Heath and Scholar Green, where you follow the canal and take the second turning on the right. Climb Mow Cop and turn left after the summit, then go around the east side of Congleton and head northwest through Twemlow Green to Goostrey, where you turn left to Holmes Chapel.

▲ Turn right then left just before the M6 and follow this road west to cross the A533 just south of Middlewich. Turn left. Take the first right, then first left, then go left again, right, and right again through Church Minshull to turn right in Cholmondeston. Turn left to Eaton then turn right to the Delamere Forest Park.

▲ Turn left in Hatchmere, then left in Woodside, then first left and right to climb the Yeld. Descend through Kelsall and turn right at Westwood Common. Take the first left, go across the A51 and turn second right to Brown Heath. Cross the canal and take the first left, then follow signs to Tattenhall. Turn left in Tattenhall to Burwardsley, where you turn right and climb through Harthill. Take the second left to Cholmondeley and cross the A49, then follow signs to Nantwich. Go straight through Nantwich and take the second exit at the roundabout before the A500 dual carriageway and follow this road back to Crewe.

**The 2009 British road race champion Kristian House climbing Mow Cop**

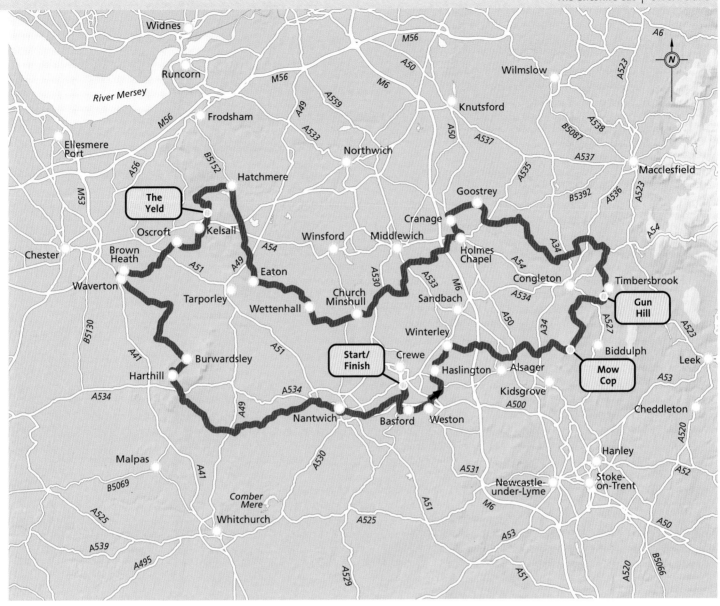

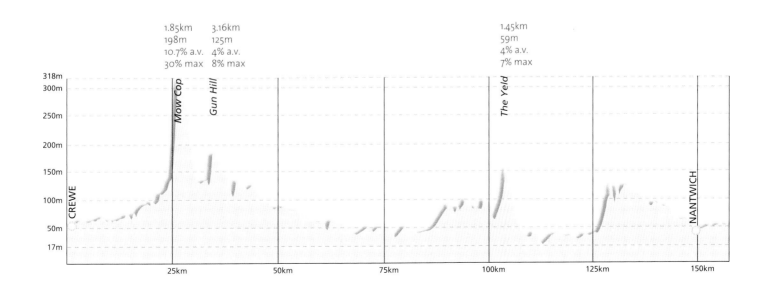

The Cheshire Cat traverses varied scenery and attracts a wide range of cyclists, many of them riding for good causes

**Website**
www.kilotogo.com and click on 'Events' to find the Cheshire Cat

**Date**
March.

**Why the name?**
It's thought that the connection between a grinning cat and Cheshire comes from the area's centuries-old milk production industry. A cat would grin in a dairy, wouldn't it?

**Anything else?**
Manchester is nearby, the base for British cycling's international racers, and the Cheshire lanes are one of their favourite training areas. You might find yourself in good company.

**Don't forget**
The event is held in March, so take enough clothing to meet every eventuality. Once you have assessed the weather, though, most of the route is at lower levels, so the only additional clothing you need with you is a gilet or light rain top.

The Peak District

**Distance** 157 kilometres | 98 miles
**Total climbing** 1,500 metres | 4,730 feet
**Route key** Three major hill climbs and one rollercoaster series of shorter but steeper ones

# 8 Tour of the Peak

The Peak District is an upland area providing breathing space for the people in the surrounding towns and cities. It's separated by geology into two halves, the High Peak and the White Peak, and while this challenge covers both areas, most of it is set in the lofty and leaner landscape of the High Peak.

The event starts close to the border between the two in Chapel-en-le-Frith, on the west side, but you could start in any of the many towns and villages on the route. The limestone White Peak is green, pleasant and full of little rivers and knotty woods. The craggy edges and much darker landscape of the High Peak surround it like an enclosing fist.

The first leg of the ride from Chapel-en-le-Frith explores one of the Dark Peak's grasping fingers. You go southwest to Macclesfield, where the Cat and Fiddle Pass starts in the town centre. It's a lot of climbing, well over 10 kilometres, but the gradient isn't too severe and prevailing winds push you up to the pub at the top that gave the pass its name.

The descent is straight and fast at first, but it ends with a series of bends that you must respect. You skirt the south side of Buxton for a short passage through the White Peak, where you'll see and feel the change. The hills are smaller now but steep in places, and you ride through the pretty stone villages of Miller's Dale and Tideswell Dale to reach Castleton by a very steep descent. This is where one of the hardest challenges of the ride begins.

Winnats Pass is a collapsed cavern: its roof caved in to create a deep slash in the cliff edge. The whole of this area is undermined by caves that were created when underground streams dissolved the rock. You can't see the climb at first. You seem to be riding towards a solid wall, then the cliff parts and you see the road wriggling up ahead at a breathtaking pitch. Treat Winnats with respect and ride within your means; there's still a long way to go.

There's another short climb after the summit before you drop into Edale, and into the High Peak. There's a lull in the severity now, so use it to refuel. A short stretch alongside Ladybower Reservoir and a dragging main road climb takes you to the head of a wild roller-coaster ride called the Strines. You go down three times – down three steep descents with sharp hairpin bends over streams at the bottom – then you go up three times, just as steeply, and the last one, Ewden, is a killer. It's longer and steeper than the others, which are both about 800 metres (2,624 feet) long.

The countryside after the Strines is rugged. A bleak slog over Thurlstone Moor leads to Holmfirth, *Last of the Summer Wine* country, and the start of another iconic climb at Holmbridge. Holme Moss is on the route of stage two of the 2014 Tour de France. It has featured in the Tour of Britain and the Leeds Classic, so many of the world's best cyclists will have passed this way. It's a long, hard climb with a tough mid-section made tougher because if you started at Chapel-en-le-Frith you will have ridden 60 miles by now.

You can see why High Peak is sometimes called the Dark Peak on Holme Moss's descent. Over on the other side of the valley the gaunt, trackless plateau of Bleaklow Hill rears up like a black fortress. There are no trees here; the slopes are covered with sharp, wiry grass which tough-looking sheep chew on while they look at you with disdain. Be wary of them.

The bottom of the valley is even darker. It's the start of the Woodhead Pass, so there is a lot of heavy traffic coming out of Manchester here, another reason to take care. A quick flick left between Torside and Woodhead reservoirs and you are climbing again, and things begin to feel better. The valley doesn't look so threatening from this side and, once through Glossop, there are two relatively easy climbs, Chunel and Chinley Head, before a short descent into Chapel-en-le-Frith.

# Directions

▲ Leave Chapel-en-le-Frith by the B5470 heading southwest to Macclesfield. Go left at the first roundabout to climb over the Cat and Fiddle Pass but cross the A53 near Buxton then follow the A5270 and go right on the A6.

▲ Take the first left and follow this road, forking left after the A623, and ride through Little Hucklow to Castleton. Turn left at the main road in Castleton to climb Winnats Pass then follow signs from the top to Edale. Turn left in Hope then left to Bamford and right on the A57 towards Sheffield.

▲ Take the first left and keep left for the Strines series of climbs to Langsett then follow the signposts to Holmfirth. Turn left at the bottom of the hill and keep straight on the A6024 over Holme Moss. Go right after the descent then first left to climb across the side of the Woodhead Valley to Glossop, where you continue south on the A624 to Chapel-en-le-Frith.

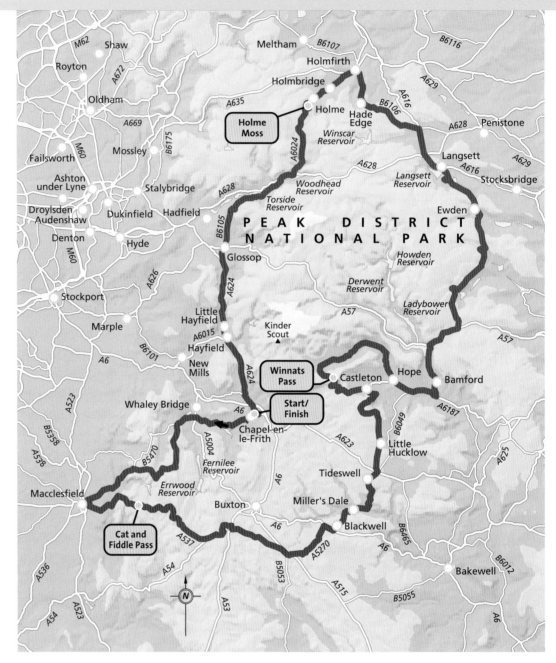

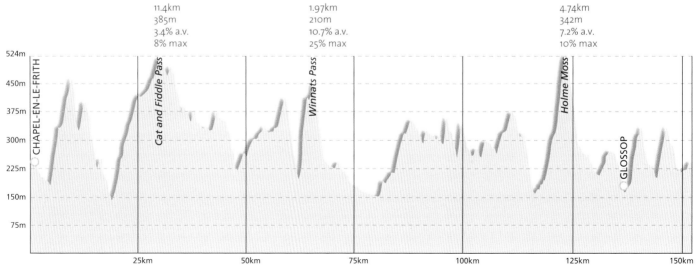

Riding out of Winnats Pass, which you can just see in the background

**Website**
www.kilotogo.com and click on 'Events'.

**Date**
Early June.

**Why the name?**
It's a tour of the Peak District but it also remembers a race that was a British classic but is no longer with us.

**Anything else?**
The ride focuses on the High Peak. The Derbyshire Dales, which this route passes through only briefly, are beautiful and well worth exploring.

**Don't forget**
The usual bodywarmer/light rain jacket that you should always take with you even on summer rides in the British hills. There are lots of towns and cafes on the route, so you don't need to take everything you will eat and drink with you. Take great care when descending on the Strines section. It's mostly surrounded by thick woodland, so it takes a longish spell of dry weather for the roads to really dry out. The great Belgian racer Tom Boonen once crashed here when he hit a wet patch during a Tour of Britain stage. It's even worse in winter, when ice lingers here for ages.

Shropshire

**Distance** 160 kilometres | 100 miles
**Total climbing** 1,600 metres | 5,250 feet
**Route key** Three medium-sized mountains

# 9 The Shropshire Mynd

This ride is a perfect introduction to the extended effort involved in climbing mountains on a bike. It crosses three: one that's shortish but steep and two that are much longer but have easier gradients. The ride also explores the surrounding hills, and straddles the Wales–England border.

Confusingly, two of the mountains on this ride have almost the same name. The first is the Long Mynd – 'mynd' being a derivation of the Welsh word for mountain – so its name is Long Mountain. And that's exactly what it is: a long, thin, undulating steep-sided ridge that stands just east of Bishop's Castle.

The 2012 event, then called Wild Edric, started at Bishop's Castle, but the organiser has changed its name and it is likely to stay the Shropshire Mynd from now on. Bishop's Castle is the best place to start the ride if you do it outside of the event anyway, as it's only 13 kilometres (8 miles) away from the first slopes, which is just right for warming up your legs.

The Long Mynd has several roads scrambling over it, all of varying severity, but the Shropshire Mynd uses one of the easier ones. The southern ascent is harder and the way you are going is much steeper in the opposite direction – worth remembering when you are descending the other side.

The road tops out at 485 metres (1,590 feet), quite close to the Long Mynd's summit, Pole Hill, which is 516 metres (1,692 feet). Have a look around on reaching the top; the views east and west are spectacular, with the Welsh mountains one way and the West Midlands the other. The descent is pretty scary in places and quite exposed, with long drops towards the end, so take care and brake early. There's the temptation to look down into the valley below. Don't do it – just focus on the road in front of you.

Church Stretton, a lovely little Victorian holiday town, lies on the other side of the mountain. Leave it to head north,

making a detour to climb a small but nasty hill at Comley. Continue north then west towards Wales for the next big challenge. It's a good idea to eat and drink early on in this section so you have plenty of power for the next climb.

You cross into Wales while climbing Long Mountain, quite close to its 342-metre (1,122-foot) summit. It's not clear why this mountain has the English name and Long Mynd has the Welsh version; perhaps it's because a much older border, Offa's Dyke, is still a little further west. It's a straightforward climb with a long, straight descent, but be careful towards the end because it becomes very steep as you skirt the edge of a small pine forest. Scrub off extra speed here by braking until you are descending at a speed that's within your comfort zone.

A change of direction in Montgomery takes you along a winding and severely strength-sapping road that goes further into Wales. Then there's a short, easy section alongside the River Severn, which is your next big refuelling opportunity because the majority of the next 10 miles is uphill, so much so that all the climbing can be lumped in together and called one mountain.

You start climbing in Abermule then follow the Mule Valley towards its source. There's a short descent near Dolfor, then you climb the twisting road up the final mountain, Banc Gorddwr. This climb, called Kerry Hill, is one of the longest in the UK and has a tricky descent, but this time the tricky bit comes just after the summit through some steep and very sharp bends. After that, the route follows the River Teme all the way down to Knighton and into England again.

There are two hard climbs left now, both on the main road and both crossing well over the 1,000-foot contour. Then you descend to Clun and follow the River Clun downhill before the final, gently undulating stretch back to Bishop's Castle.

Climbing the Long Mynd

Shropshire is an overlooked gem for cycling, full of rolling hills and empty roads

# I Directions

▲ Ride east out of Bishop's Castle to the A488 then turn right on the B4383. Join the A489 for 100 metres then carry straight on towards Norbury, but turn right just before you enter the village and follow the River Onny north to Ratlinghope. Turn right and climb over the Long Mynd. Turn left in Church Stretton on the B5477 then right on the A49 and first left off it to climb through Comley, where you bear left. Then turn right, and go left through Longnor to Condover.

▲ Turn left, then first right, then first left to Longden. Turn right then left, then right and over the A488 to Cruckton. Turn left on the B4386 and go through Westbury to Vennington, where the Long Mountain climb starts. In Kingswood turn left on the A490 then continue straight on the B4388 to Montgomery.

▲ Turn right on the B4385 and continue riding straight on, on the B4386, at the point where the B4385 goes right, under the railway. Turn left in Abermule on the B4368. Turn right on the A489 and then first left after Kerry (Ceri). Follow this road through Dolfor and join the B4355 to climb over Banc Gorddwr. Descend to Knighton, where you turn left on the A488 to Clun. Turn right on the B4368 then turn left on the B4385 and follow this road back to Bishop's Castle.

**Website**
www.kilotogo.com and click on 'Events'.

**Date**
Mid-September.

**Why the name?**
It celebrates the Long Mynd, which is a beautiful little mountain, and the fact that Shropshire is a great but often overlooked place to ride.

**Anything else?**
Linking all six ascents of the Long Mynd in one ride is a great challenge. Shropshire's dales between Church Stretton and Much Wenlock are worth exploring.

**Don't forget**
Hone your cornering skills and always brake in a straight line. The descents on this ride demand respect. Take your normal changeable weather gear: you'll be going over 1,000 feet three times, so the temperature could drop.

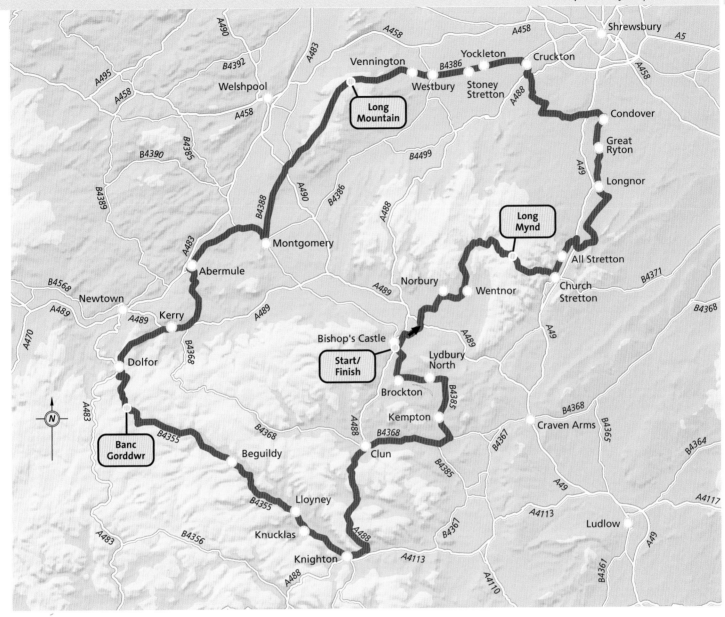

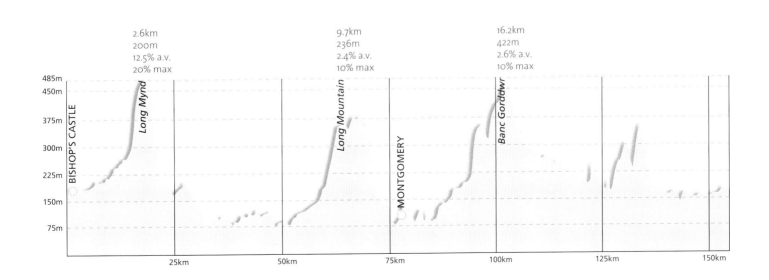

**Distance**  243.2 kilometres | 152 miles
**Route key**  There are no hills bigger than a bridge. Coping with the distance is the key here

# **10** Flat Out in the Fens

Flat Out in the Fens is the longest cyclosportive event in Britain by far. It's flat, but 152 miles is an epic distance, over 50 per cent longer than most challenges in this book. Long-distance cycling brings its own problems, and you'll need to do some special preparation for this ride or else bits of you will hurt in a way they have never hurt before.

Then there's Public Enemy Number One for Fenland cyclists: the wind. This ride takes place right behind the Wash, the wide-open indentation in the east coast where four major rivers empty into the North Sea. The Fens are flat, and parts of them were marsh and frequently under the North Sea before they were drained and turned into fertile crop-growing land.

Flat Out in the Fens starts in Peterborough, and that's probably the best starting place if you do this ride at any other time too. The route goes through Cambridgeshire, Norfolk and Lincolnshire and roughly traces the outline of the Fens. The ride's beauty comes from the Fenland sky; it's big here. And the patchwork of fields under it, dissected by dead-straight ditches, dykes and canals, seem to roll on forever.

The Fenland road network is fascinating. The straight roads you see running across the flat polders of Holland are mostly in the inner core of the Fens, called the Peat Fen, much of which is reclaimed marshland. The Flat Out route sticks to the Outer Fens, the sandy fen, an older area of land where the roads tend to wriggle around field and parish boundaries or alongside winding rivers.

The first leg of the ride goes out across the Bedford Level, past the Hundred Foot Drain, one of the earliest of many similar large drainage ditches that helped create the Fens. Then it follows the meanders of the River Great Ouse, where the magnificent Ely Cathedral dominates the scenery for

most of the way. Through Downham Market you get the first tangy whiff of the sea, as the route enters a fascinating part of the Fens. The network of lanes here is so dense and so varied that if you are doing this ride outside the Flat Out in the Fens event you must take some form of navigational aid for this section, even if it's just a copy of the ride map.

The route tracks around the northern edge of the lanes, about four to seven miles from the Wash, tiptoeing around Holbeach then filtering through the edges of Spalding. You break through the 100-mile barrier during this section, and the distance will start to have an effect.

There are some more tips on long-distance riding in the 'Don't forget' section, but the most important component in riding long distances is you, and it's the bits of you that don't usually get stressed by cycling that will be affected. Hands, arms, shoulders, back and neck can all develop game-breaking pain that can prevent you from continuing.

One way to condition them is to ride long distances in training, but that is inefficient and time consuming. It's much better to do what round-the-world cyclist Mark Beaumont did and use weight training to strengthen and condition the upper parts of your body. A good fitness instructor or a trainer will be able to advise you on suitable exercises if you tell them what you are training for.

If you are suffering at the 100-mile point, the final leg is bound to be a struggle. Where the route has followed mostly winding roads so far, it now spears dead straight across Deeping Fen. A headwind here can make things messy, and you are heading southwest, making headwinds more likely, for another 18 miles. Finally, turn east and ride around Peterborough before finishing where you started 152 miles ago. Outside the event it's advisable to ride with a group of friends of similar ability. It's a very long way on your own.

Top: Spalding Cycling Club enjoying the Fenland roads. Bottom: Not only are there no hills in the Fens, parts of this ride lie below sea level

**Website**
www.kilotogo.com. Click on 'Events' and look for Flat Out in the Fens.

**Date**
June.

**Why the name?**
The Fens are flat.

**Anything else?**
Getting lost in the web of lanes between Wisbech, Holbeach and Spalding makes a great bike ride. It's like cycling must have felt during the 1940s and '50s.

**Don't forget**
Wear your tried-and-tested kit, in particular the most comfortable shorts you have. It's also worth investing in some help for your hands. If you are not doing the ride in winter (and that's inadvisable because you'll be riding for hours and could end up riding in darkness), then you could try some anatomically designed track mitts. Take plenty of food and drink and don't set off too fast. One hundred miles is really only halfway on this one.

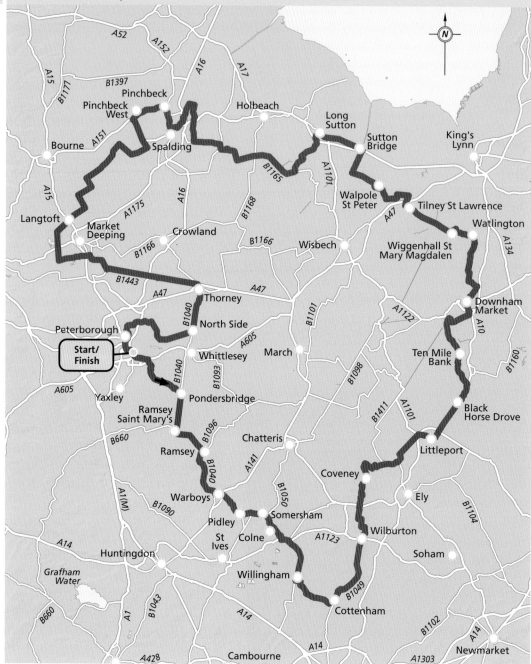

# ▌Directions

▲ In Peterborough go east on the A605 then right on the B1095 to Ramsey. Continue on the B1040 and B1050 through Warboys and Willingham, left to Cottenham, then north to Littleport. Follow the Great Ouse left bank north to Downham Market. Go through Downham Market to Watlington, turn left to Tilney St Lawrence, then go right over the A47 and follow signs to Walpole St Peter, Sutton Bridge and Long Sutton.

▲ Turn left on the B1390 then right on the B1165. Take the first right after Weston Hills. Go north to Wykeham, turn left, left again, go through the north side of Spalding, turn right to Pinchbeck.

▲ Take the B1180 to Pinchbeck West, turn left on the A151 and continue straight where the A151 turns left to Spalding. Take the first right then second left. Follow this road through Langtoft. Go south at the lakes through West Deeping. Take the first left to go through Northborough, then turn left at Waterfowl World and continue to Thorney. Follow the B1040 to North Side, turn right and head back into Peterborough.

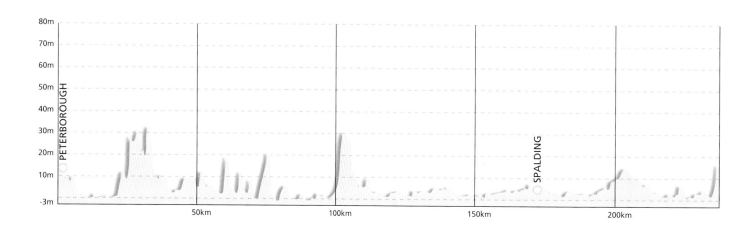

The Midlands

**Distance** 100 kilometres | 62 miles
**Total climbing** 1,700 metres | 5,576 feet
**Route key** Mastering the many off-road sections of bridleway on the route

# **11** Hell of the North Cotswolds

The North Cotswolds is the perfect place for a cycling challenge. Testing hills and wide-open views make cycling here a great experience, but the Hell of the North Cotswolds, or Honc as it's affectionately known, has another dimension. Its fascinating and quite intricate route includes a number of off-road sections, forgotten roads and tracks that are mostly designated as bridleways today.

Note the word 'mostly'. Some small off-road sections are footpaths where permission to ride has been obtained by the event organisers. That permission is only valid on event day. You cannot ride these sections at any other time. There aren't many, and some you could walk, otherwise a spot of map reading will give you a road option around the section.

The event starts in Winchcombe, close to the Cotswold Edge, where this upland chalk area rises steeply out of the lower Severn Valley. You ride along the top of the Edge near the end, but turn away from it at first, with an opening five miles of tiny lanes before the first off-road stretch.

Overall, these sections are a mix of narrow single tracks composed of mud, grass or stones. The key to riding off-road sections is not to make sudden changes of direction and to stay in the saddle using low gears, so that you make smooth progress by having good traction with the rear wheel.

Braking should always be done while you are going in a straight line, although that's true for road riding too. The big difference with braking off-road is that it should be smoother, which means pulling the brake levers slowly but steadily, and you must start to slow down earlier.

Descending over loose or slippery surfaces requires a very delicate and controlled touch. Control your speed by braking regularly and well in advance of any turns. It's important to place your centre of gravity even further back on your bike.

On gentle descents it's enough to sit a little further back in the saddle, but on steep ones you should support your weight with your legs, get out of the saddle and hang your backside as far back as possible. Keep your arms straight, but flex your elbows and knees to absorb shocks.

The River Eye and the Windrush valleys are particularly beautiful, and you ride through Upper Slaughter, one of the most attractive and least touristy Cotswold villages. The ride gets very hilly now though, and a steep track down to Barton is exciting. Take care: it's very steep near the end.

The route twists and turns after Turkdean, using sections of the Diamond Way and the Gloucestershire Way. Then there's a hard off-road climb after Salperton. The same general principles apply to climbing off-road as they do to riding on the flat. Try not to get out of the saddle, sit down and use lower gears, and keep your weight over your rear wheel to increase its traction. If you have to get out of the saddle, pull on your handlebars with straight arms and continue to keep your weight as far back as possible. And remember, it's often just as quick to get off and walk up.

A couple of exciting off-road descents take you to the Cotswold Edge, directly above Cheltenham. This is almost the final section of the ride but it's visually the best. It's mostly off-road along a track that is right on the edge. The feeling of exposure at times is breathtaking, as are the views across the Severn Valley to the greying bulk of the Black Mountains in Wales.

After riding under Cleeve Cloud and around the peak of Cleeve Hill there is a footpath section, so if you aren't participating in the event you must drop down to the B4632 and turn right back to Winchcombe. Otherwise, a long, sweeping off-road descent leads to the B4632, and a quick sprint to the finish.

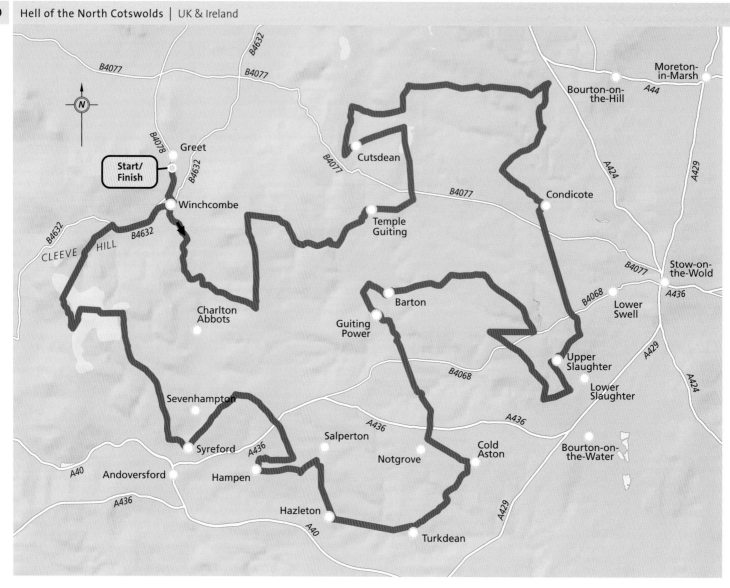

# Directions

▲ Go south through Winchcombe on the B4078. Turn left and second right on Vineyard Street. Follow this road south, keep left at the next two junctions, then turn left at the top of the hill. Continue north to the T-junction, turn right and keep right, then take the left fork then turn left. Go left after the next hill then first right to Temple Guiting and turn right on the bridleway in the village. Turn left at the end. Cross the B4077 then turn left at the second crossroads to Cutsdean. Turn right after the village, then right after the architectural heritage site, then left at the next crossroads. Turn right on the bridleway and head east on a mix of roads and bridleways to a junction just west of the A424, where you turn right.

▲ Take the second left to Condicote, where you turn right at the church and follow the dead-straight road (Condicote Lane) over the B4077 and B4068. Take the first right to Upper Slaughter. Follow the road sharp left then go right on the next bridleway, following it across the road. Turn right on another bridleway joining the road you crossed and turn left. Continue over the B4068, and take the first bridleway on the right. Where that joins the B4068 turn left on another bridleway heading northwest. Turn left when this joins the road and take the first right after the crossroads to Barton. Turn left after the stream, go left on the bridleway to Guiting Power, turn left then first right, and keep right to cross the B4068 and the A436.

▲ Take the first left to Cold Aston. Turn right. Follow Macmillan Way to Turkdean. Continue on a bridleway to Hazleton. Turn right then go straight on at the church on the bridleway to Salperton Park, then turn left on the road. Go left, right and left, then right through Hampen, right then first left. Continue northwest over the A436, taking the first bridleway on the left. Turn right on the road, through Syreford, fork left then take the first right. Follow this road northwest. Go left shortly after it becomes a bridleway. The next section, on footpaths, is only open on ride day. At other times, dismount and walk 500 metres on the footpath to some radio masts. Turn left on the road, right on a bridleway that joins the road, and descend to Prestbury. Turn right on the B4632 to climb Cleeve Hill and descend into Winchcombe.

### Website
www.honc.org.uk

### Date
Mid-April.

### Why the name?
The Hell of the North is the name given to the cobblestone and rough tracks section of the great French road race classic, Paris–Roubaix (see page 113). The first Cotswolds event was held in 1984 and it was the idea of Pat and Tim Gordon, who had both ridden the cyclosportive version of Paris–Roubaix.

### Anything else?
There are many more bridleways you could explore throughout the Cotswolds.

### Don't forget
Bring your off-road riding skills. Be aware all the time of keeping weight over your rear wheel to give it traction, and do everything as you would on the road but do it a lot smoother and take longer over doing it. Don't grip your handlebars too tightly; try to guide your bike where you want it to go rather than steer it.

If you ride this outside of the event you must obey the no footpath riding rule. Footpaths are indicated on OS maps with a short-dashed red line, bridleways with long-dashed red lines.

**A mountain bike works well on the off-road sections of this ride**

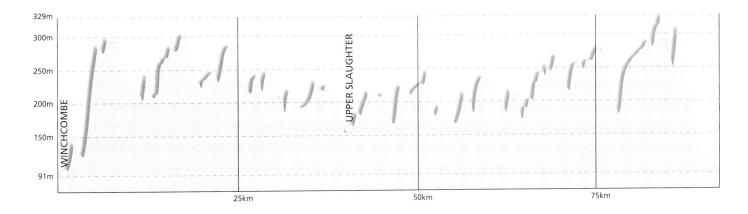

Surrey and Sussex

**Distance** 160 kilometres | 100 miles
**Total climbing** 1,666 metres | 5,465 feet
**Route key** Six significant hills in two blocks of three, one just after the start and the other close to the finish

# **12** The Ups and Downs

The Ups and Downs sportive route flits between the North Downs and the Low Weald, almost reaching the South Downs, and runs from Surrey into Sussex and back again. It is hilly but the hills come in distinct blocks, both of which are in the Surrey Hills area of the North Downs.

The Surrey Hills became part of the international cycling landscape after hosting the 2012 Olympic road races. The Olympiads went up Box Hill and used the roads on the east side of the Dorking Gap, but although this ride starts in Dorking, it heads west. If anything, though, that makes the ride better. Box Hill was picked because it was good for spectators. There are much more challenging hills in the North Downs, and they are all west of the Dorking Gap.

The first hill comes right after the start. You climb past Denbies Vineyard, up one of the Downs' edges and onto Ranmore Common. The next climb, in Effingham Forest, is long but not too steep, then there's a much harder pull up through Hurtwood, and that's the first hill block done. You descend to Cranleigh and into the Low Weald.

Weald is a Saxon word meaning wood. The modern German word for wood is *wald,* so you can see the connection. Roads in the South Downs and the Weald run through some really lovely old woodland, the typically English broadleaved woods that are an absolute glory to behold at bluebell time. The Ups and Downs event is held towards the end of April, when the North Downs and the Low Weald are at their most beautiful.

The route is much flatter now – flat enough to accommodate an airfield at Dunsfold. This is where the motoring show *Top Gear* do a lot of their filming, and where their 'Star in a Reasonably Priced Car' feature is shot. The route passes within metres of the airfield, so if you hear the sound of tortured tyres and engines, that's why.

There's a short detour into the Downs after the route turns north towards Godalming, but it soon turns back and meanders over the wide Weald towards the South Downs. The Weald section of the Ups and Downs is quite long and it trends downwards right to the southern tip of this ride. Enjoy the wonderful scenery on this section and eat and drink plenty, because you need to gather your strength for the turn north near Billingshurst.

Now the road rises steadily to Ewhurst, and the ridge of the Surrey Hills looms larger all of the way. Ewhurst lies at their feet. Take a deep breath because you've now got to climb the steep side of Hurtwood. Descend that, go through Peaslake and change direction again to climb up a valley road, after which there's another about turn to climb the *pièce de résistance* of this ride, Leith Hill, the highest hill in the North Downs.

There are several ways to get there, but the Ups and Downs chose the best. You climb towards Coldharbour, keeping to the right of Leith Hill, then suddenly switch left to make a summit bid. The road is narrow, steep and lined with trees that tower over you. It's worth stopping at the top to look back at the view over the way you've just come, with the Weald stretching off into the distance.

You continue north after Leith Hill with just one big hill to go, but it's a killer. White Down comes after a tricky descent over Abinger Common, right after crossing the A25 Guildford road. It's not steep until you cross a railway bridge, then it pitches up before a sharp left and right bend that are even steeper. Ride the inside of the left and outside of the right-hander because it eases the gradient slightly. That's useful to know because White Down is steep for another 500 metres after the bends, but once at the top it's mostly downhill for the final push to the finish line.

The Ups and Downs is one of the best spring rides in the country

# Directions

▲ The official ride opens with a short loop through Westhumble to Ranmore Common, but it starts with a stretch of busy dual carriageway, so outside the event it's best to go straight to Ranmore Common. Head west from Dorking over Ranmore Common and continue downhill to the T-junction, where you turn left. Follow this road over the A25 through Shere, then continue south through Hurtwood to Cranleigh.

▲ Turn right in Cranleigh and head south then west to Alfold Crossways on the A281. Cross the A281 and ride through Dunsfold then go north to join the B2130 and head for Godalming. Turn left on the outskirts of Godalming and continue south through Hambledon and Chiddingfold, where you turn left. Take the first left then keep right, then go left and left again to Plaistow. Turn first right after Plaistow and go south through Kirdford then north to Loxwood.

▲ Turn right, go northeast over the A281, then right and first left to Ewhurst. Turn right just before Ewhurst, cross the B2127 and follow the Ewhurst road to Peaslake. Keep right, join the B2126 Holmbury road, and continue south. Skirt the southern edge of Gatton Manor Hotel golf course, then head north. Turn right on Ockley Road, go left, then take the first left on Broomhall Road. Go left again on Abinger Road. Go right, cross the A25, climb White Down and turn right on Ranmore Road back to Dorking.

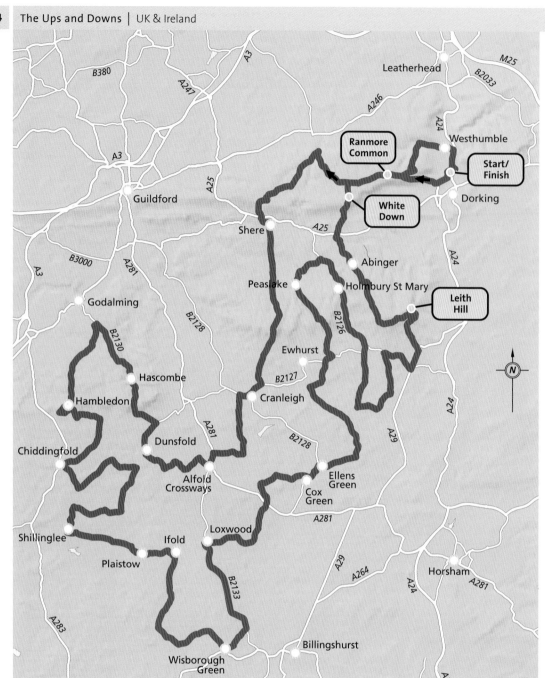

**Website**
www.ukcyclingevents.co.uk

**Date**
The end of April.

**Why the name?**
You are going up and down the North Downs.

**Anything else?**
There's a lot more of the Downs and Low Weald to explore either side of this ride.

**Don't forget**
Take a light wind- and/or rainproof top. This is a complicated route on a lot of little lanes, so a navigation device would be helpful.

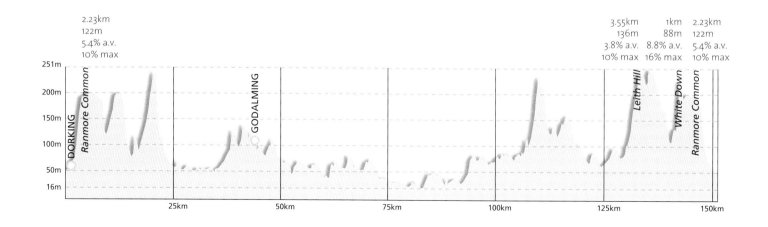

**Distance** 160 kilometres | 100 miles
**Total climbing** 1,585 metres | 5,200 feet
**Route key** Lots of hills with Wylye Down, Fovant Down, Middle Down, King Alfred's Tower and Gare Hill being the standouts

# **13** The Lionheart

This is a great ride through the Wiltshire Downs that lie west of Salisbury, and up and down the hills that encircle the north end of Blackmore Vale. It takes its name from the Lions of Longleat, because the event starts outside Longleat House and the first part of the route runs through Longleat Estate and past the big cats enclosure. There are plenty of other exotic animals around, so it's a really unusual send-off.

The first climb comes while you are still inside the park, and serves as a great warm-up. Then there's a longish and much flatter section through the pretty Wylye Valley. Chalk rivers like the Wylye are a feature of the first part of this ride, and so are the chalk downs. You climb over them for the first time from Wylye village, then you descend through Fovant Wood to the village of Fovant, which is the first feed stop in the sportive event.

Don't eat too much though, as the climb of Fovant Down comes next and it's hard. A steep, straight descent with a sharp left at the bottom takes you into the Ebble Valley, where you go right in Mount Sorrel, near a watercress farm, to climb again. This is the start of a loop back into the Ebble Valley, where you face another climb over the Downs. This one has a steep, twisting descent that can catch you out if you go into the bends too fast, so take care.

Just short of Tisbury you turn left and head west along the River Sem Valley to Semley, from where you cross the Blackmore Vale to Mere. The ride changes character after this section. There are still hills but they become even steeper and they go through woodland rather than across open country.

Pen Hill, just after passing the lakes of Stourhead, a popular National Trust property, is typical of them. The surrounding pine trees smell as sharp as a cough sweet and help clear your lungs ready for even harder hills to come.

One of those is King Alfred's Tower, a folly built on a hill, which you can see for miles around. Legend has it that this is where King Alfred unfurled his standard to mark the Saxon conquest of England, and the tower was built in the 18th century to mark that historic event. It's a long, straight climb that gets very steep towards the top, and it goes through the same pine forest as Pen Hill, which means that even on dry days there could be moisture on the descent. Take care again because pine needles mixed with water make a very slippery surface. The King Alfred's Tower climb is a timed section of the Lionheart sportive.

The next section is easier until Bruton. Use it to eat and drink so that you are stoked up and ready for the last roar of the Lionheart. Creech Hill is not as bad as King Alfred's but it's still quite hard, especially since by now you have around 80 miles in your legs. The views from the top are amazing though, and the descent is another fast one that requires care. Then, from Evercreech, the leg through Stoney Stratton and Westcome is very hard work because it undulates unmercifully.

There is one big climb left now, and it's Gare Hill, which is longer than the recent hills you've climbed but the gradient is easier. You're back in the pinewoods, which feels refreshing at this stage, and that's a boon because the succession of steep hills exact a real toll. As on all rides, the wooded sections require extra attention because fallen leaves can make the road slippery, and the roads don't dry and ice doesn't melt as quickly as on uncovered roads.

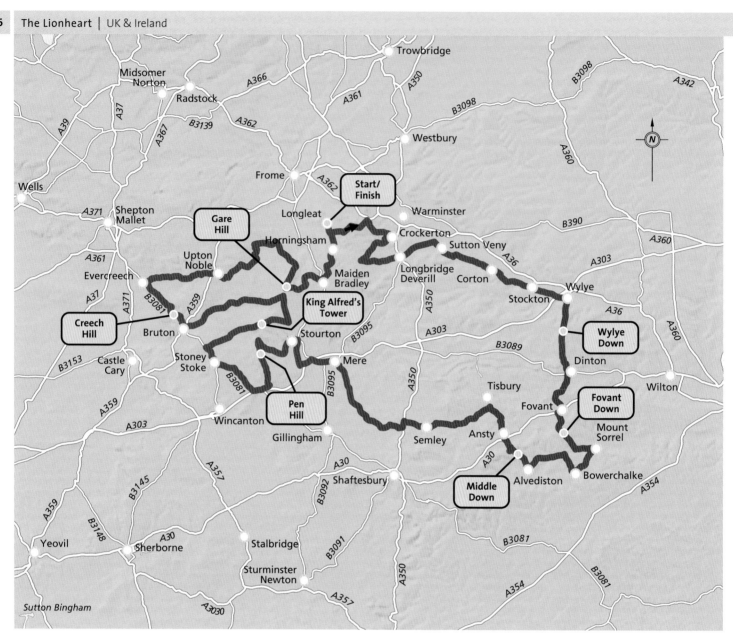

# Directions

▲ After a loop north around the safari park in Longleat head to Crockerton where you go left twice and right at the third junction to Longbridge Deverill, where you continue over the A350 and follow the River Wylye through Corton and Stockton. Turn right at Wylye and climb Wylye Down. Descend to Dinton and continue through Fovant to turn right then left across the A30 and climb Fovant Down. Turn left after the descent, then right in Mount Sorrel and right again in Bowerchalke.

▲ Turn left after the descent, then right in Alvediston to climb Middle Down. Continue over the A30 to just south of Tisbury and turn left before the River Sem to follow it west to Semley. Follow directions to Mere, where you turn left on the B3095 and go under the A303 to turn left to Zeals then right to Stourton, where you go left to climb Pen Hill. Turn sharp left at the summit and descend through Penselwood to join the B3081 west. Go through Stoney Stoke, go right at Redlynch crossroads and follow this road over King Alfred's Tower.

▲ Turn left at Kilmington Common, left again to descend Druly Hill, and continue to Bruton. In the village, turn right and follow the B3081 over Creech Hill. Turn right at the church in Evercreech; follow this road through Batcombe. Continue through Upton Noble, turn left to Witham Friary, then left again, then go straight on just before the pylons, where the road bends sharp right. Go right to climb through Gare Hill village, continue then turn left to Maiden Bradley. Cross the B3092 then go left to Horningsham to enter Longleat Park.

**Chalk Downs scenery is a feature of the first part of the Lionheart**

### Website
www.thelionheart.co.uk

### Date
March.

### Why the name?
Well, it's the lions at Longleat, isn't it?

### Anything else?
The drovers roads running the length of the Downs are worth exploring. They run right along the apexes of the hills and there are amazing views to either side. The one that runs from Salisbury racecourse almost all the way to Shaftesbury is a delight. A mountain bike or cyclo-cross bike is best for this but a road bike with thick tyres is OK.

### Don't forget
There's nothing too high to climb on this route, so just a light wind- and waterproof top that fits in your back pocket is all you need for extra weather protection. The Downs roads are exposed, so strong winds will make this ride a good deal harder. Take care when crossing the main roads on the route.

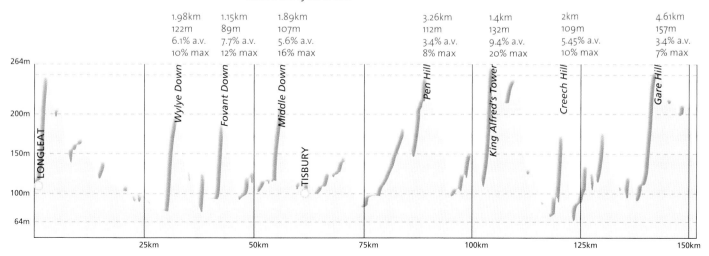

**Distance** 160 kilometres | 100 miles
**Total climbing** 670 metres | 2,200 feet
**Route key** The constant rolling nature of the route

# **14** The New Forest Epic

The New Forest is a great place for cycling, and the Epic route is the best way to experience the area. The route goes right through the heart of the forest, uses the most bike-friendly roads and lets you experience both faces of this unique area: the larger forest south of the A31 and the more broken mix of woods and open heath to the north.

The ride starts in Brockenhurst, from where you head over Beaulieu Moor then go down towards the south coast before following Beaulieu River inland. The river is tidal and Southampton Water is only a few miles further east, so the New Forest Epic has a seaside feel to its start. But that ends as you approach the busy town of Lyndhurst and enter the forest proper.

The ride has been relatively flat so far, but soon after passing under the M27 at just over 30 miles it starts to get hilly. Not too hilly though; the climb over Longcross Plain is quite mild and fairly typical of this ride. The challenge of the New Forest Epic is its distance, which of course cannot be underestimated, and neither can the constantly rolling nature of the route. It's an ideal introduction to cycling challenges. If you are new to them, starting with this event would be a good plan.

You're on the heathland side of the New Forest now, breaking clear of the woods to cross the River Blackwater, then you follow the River Dun upstream to West Dean, which is roughly the halfway mark. Dean Hill is quite spectacular. It's an escarpment that you climb by its easy dip slope, then ride along the top of the ridge formed by its other side, which is very steep.

In many respects this is a ride of rivers as well as forests. The route joins the Avon just south of Salisbury, following it south to Woodgreen, where a long climb starts and continues through Hale to Bramshaw Telegraph on the top of Deadman Hill. Bramshaw Telegraph earned its strange name during the Napoleonic Wars, when it was part of a hilltop shutter light communication system that ran between the Admiralty in London and where their ships were in Plymouth. In good weather it took about 20 minutes for a message to travel the distance.

A long descent leads back to the River Avon for a short stretch to South Gorley, where the climb of Rockford Common starts. You are on the final leg now, and it's the best of the whole ride. You go under the A31 and into the heart of the forest again to ride along the Bolderwood Arboretum Ornamental Drive.

This is lined with a variety of majestic old trees, including many ancient oaks. The oldest is the Knightwood Oak, also known as the Queen of the Forest. It's been here for over 500 years, has a girth of 7.4 metres (24 feet) and is still growing. It's on your left, just before the route crosses the A35.

The next section is the Rhinefield Ornamental Drive, where there are two giant redwood trees and two giant sequoias. One of the sequoias is 51 metres (167 feet) high, and the others aren't far short of that. The drive leads into Brockenhurst but the race route shies away from it at this point to loop south along Long Slade Bottom and finally approach the village from the same direction as the famous Lymington Flyer railway line.

**Top: Riding through the more open northern half of the New Forest. Bottom left: Some of the specimen fir trees along the Ornamental Drive.
Bottom right: The Beaulieu River**

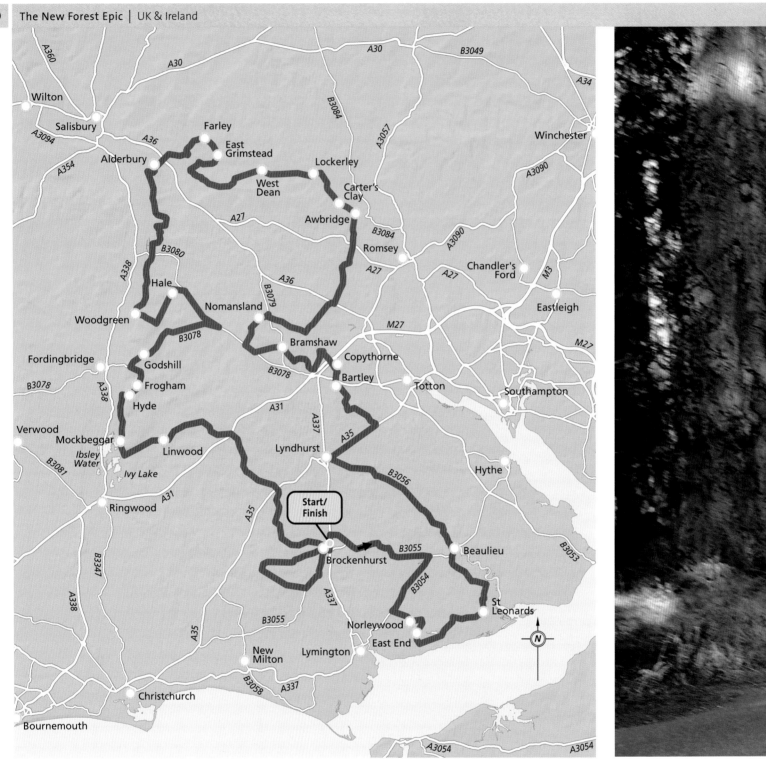

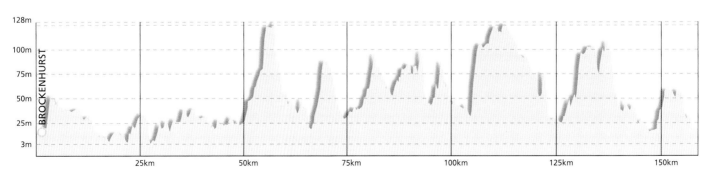

Riding in a woodland's dappled light is sheer joy

# Directions

▲ From the centre of Brockenhurst head north and turn right on the B3055 east then southeast. Turn right on the B3054 then go left through Norleywood and East End, then turn left at the No Through Road sign and follow this road through Beaulieu to join the B3056 going northwest to Lyndhurst. Turn right on the A35, then left on Woodlands Road and head north across the A336 and under the M27. Turn left then go north along the east side of Bramshaw Golf Course, but on entering Bramshaw turn left to Nomansland, where you turn right then left to cross the A36 at Crawley Hill. Continue north to Kent's Oak.

▲ Turn left and ride through Carter's Clay, Lockerley and East Dean. Fork left in West Dean to climb over to West Grimstead then East Grimstead. Turn right and follow this road to Farley, where you head southwest over the A36 and continue south to Woodgreen, where you turn left. Then go left to Hale and right onto the B3080 to climb Deadman Hill.

▲ Turn sharp right at the summit (Bramshaw Telegraph) and follow the B3078 to Godshill, where you turn left and right through Blissford, Hyde, North Gorley and South Gorley then through Mockbeggar. Take the first left after Mockbeggar through Linwood then go right and under the A31 to enter the forest. Turn right on the Bolderwood Arboretum Ornamental Drive and continue south over the A35 into Brockenhurst, but turn right after entering the village on Burley Road. Take the first left outside the village then turn left on the B3055 to re-enter it.

**Website**
www.ukcyclingevents.co.uk

**Date**
June.

**Why the name?**
It's not because the New Forest is new. It was planted at the time of William the Conqueror as a hunting ground for him and his family.

**Anything else?**
The New Forest is an ideal family cycling location with lots of quiet roads and easy trails.

**Don't forget**
This is a low-altitude ride in the south of England, so if you are going to get great cycling weather anywhere in the UK it should be here. Just take the normal clothing you would take in case of rain.

Sussex

**Distance** 167.5 kilometres | 104.7 miles
**Total climbing** 1,435 metres | 4,700 feet
**Route key** Five big climbs with constant undulations between

# **15** The South Downs Epic

The South Downs is an impressive upland area that runs west to east and parallel to the south coast of England between Winchester and Eastbourne. The South Downs Epic explores the Downs' higher and wider mid-section, where the countryside is at its best, and where the terrain presents a tough but accessible cycling challenge.

The ride kicks off in the beautiful cathedral town of Chichester, and starts climbing right from the word go. The Downs look really impressive from the towns and villages, such as Chichester, that lie to the north or south. You get an immediate impression of their size and steepness. In a certain light they look solid and impregnable, but then the light changes slightly and you notice the folds and dry valleys in their sides.

The first climb is Kennel Hill, then you continue along a steady rise that runs parallel with the undulating Downs summit ridge. This takes you to one of the main roads running north to south through the Downs, and to an exciting descent of Duncton Hill, where there are fantastic views over the River Rother to Petworth and beyond.

You dodge east of Petworth then head into the Low Weald for a while, but this is one of the most engaging things about this route – it keeps taking you away from the Downs, letting you get a good look at them, then it takes you back in, which it does now at Lickfold.

Bexley Hill is one of the hardest on this ride. It clambers up the steep side of the Downs at a slant to make the gradient tolerable, but it's still very steep. You are getting on for 40 miles into the ride now and the temptation is to hammer these hills, but don't do it. Keep things under control, spreading your effort wisely, because like a lot of rides in hilly areas, it's not just the named climbs of the South Downs that test your strength – it's all the smaller hills in between them as well.

Two of these taxing little climbs come in the next leg; one as you go north over Woolbeding Common and the other when you head south just before Rogate, which climbs steeply right next to Combe Hill. There's a slight lull after Rogate, from where you cross the flat bottom of the Rother Valley. Use this section to prepare for the next climb; it's a tough one.

Harting Hill starts just outside East Harting at the attractively named Turkey Island. It's an easy climb at first, but the middle section is very steep, and then it drags on to the summit. The reward is a long, sweeping downhill ride to East Marden, followed by a very difficult lumpy road that leads to the southern ascent of Tower Hill. The ride will be beginning to bite now, with over 60 miles done, a lot of them on these unforgiving Downs lanes.

There's some respite from the suffering while you circle Butser Hill, which at 270 metres (886 feet) is the highest point of the Downs, then you climb over Old Winchester Hill and the southern shoulder of Weather Down and clamber over the southern side of Butser Hill to reach 235 metres (771 feet), the highest point of the South Downs Epic.

That's 85 miles completed, and thankfully there's very little pain to come. Just one short climb leading up to a dead-straight road called the Broad Walk, which goes through Stansted Forest, before a generally pleasant downhill run back to Chichester.

# Directions

▲ Start in Chichester and go north on the A286. Turn right in Lavant and left up Kennel Hill, then bear right to the A285, where you turn left. Turn right just before Petworth and go left on the A283, then turn right on Kingspitt Lane to go under the A272 and follow this road via Rickmans Lane to Plaistow. Go north on Dunsfold Road then turn left on Shillinglee Road.

▲ Cross the A283 and take the first left to Lickfold. Fork right and climb Bexley Hill. Turn right at Cowdray Park on the A272 and go straight ahead at the T-junction, then follow signs to Redford. Go through Redford and turn left at the next T-junction. Go straight at the next two crossroads then fork left and take the next left to cross the A272 in Rogate. Continue south to South Harting, where you turn left. Turn right in East Harting to climb Harting Hill then go left on the B2141. Turn right to East Marden then go right on the B2146 to climb over Tower Hill. Follow this road to Petersfield Golf Course, where you turn left.

▲ Ride through Buriton, Weston, Ramsdean and East Meon to West Meon. Turn left on the A32 then left again in Warnford. Turn left opposite Hyden Farm Lane then take the first right and go right again over Butser Hill, then turn right and go over the A3 to Finchdean. Head for Forestside but turn right then left to go through Aldsworth and Funtington and back to Chichester.

Pro racers James Moss (left) and Peter Hawkins (right) training in the South Downs

## Website
www.ukcyclingevents.co.uk

## Date
Late September or October.

## Why the name?
The South Downs are geologically the same as the North Downs, but they are different because they are separated by the Weald. The Downs are the northern and southern edges of what was a huge dome of chalk that covered the Weald. The top part of the dome eroded to reveal the clay Weald and effectively separate the two Downs areas.

## Anything else?
If you are an off-road cyclist you have to ride at least some of the South Downs Way. It's a brilliant experience as it goes the whole length of the Downs, 100 miles, along its summit ridge line.

## Don't forget
Take normal wet-weather precautions and don't go too fast too early on this one; it's deceptive and you think it's easy when it's not.

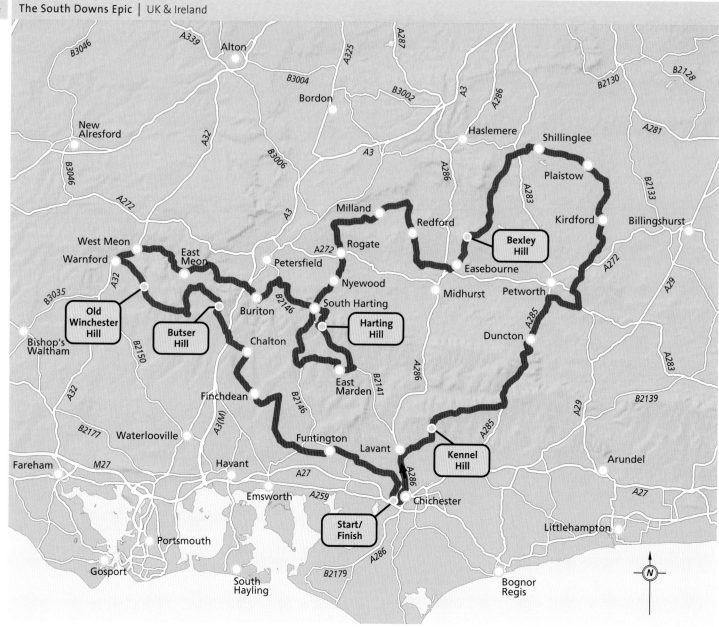

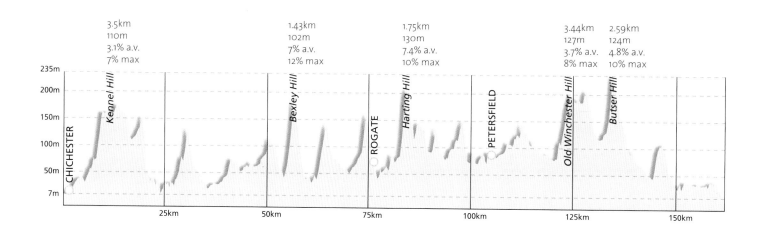

The West Country

**Distance**  536 kilometres | 335 miles
**Total climbing**  7,672 metres | 25,164 feet
**Route key**  This is a three-day challenge, so the day-to-day build-up of fatigue is something extra to cope with.
It also has five major hills or ranges of hills spread over its three stages

# **16** The Tour of Wessex

Multi-stage events are a big feature of professional cycling. The biggest race of all, the Tour de France, is a multi-stage race. However, it's quite rare to find promoters offering a multi-stage challenge that's open to the rest of us. The Tour of Wessex is one of very few in the world, and it's the biggest, but it has a lot more going for it than its duration. The three stages go through some gorgeous countryside, reaching out in different directions to explore the scenic gems of an ancient kingdom.

## Day One

All the stages start and finish in the Somerset town of Somerton. Stage one is 107 miles long and goes north then east, exploring the Mendips and the hills around the Blackmore Vale. It begins with a lovely 25-mile flat ride over the Somerset Levels, which is a joy and tempts you to ride hard, but don't do it. Not only are there lots of hills to come today, but there are two more days after this, with the third day probably the hardest of all.

Cheddar Gorge is a hard climb to open with, especially the first part of it, but it's spectacular. So are the views you get from the undulating top of the Mendips before descending into the historic city of Wells. There's another undulating section before the climb of King Alfred's Tower, which you'll be familiar with if you've ridden the Lionheart. There's some duplication of the Lionheart route here, but only for short sections, and it ends at the Redlynch crossroads, where the Wessex stage heads west and back to Somerton.

So that's Day One done, but every day in a stage race has a night stage, and the night stage is when you recover. If you ate and drank as you normally would in a single-day challenge, you'll end the stage in reasonable shape. What you need now is a light meal that mixes carbohydrates with protein. Recovery drinks will do this, or something like a tuna sandwich, but recovery drinks are easier to consume when you are tired. Keep sipping a drink while you travel to your accommodation, and continue drinking throughout the evening. Eat a proper meal including a dessert as soon as possible, to build up energy for tomorrow. Your evening meal should contain plenty of carbohydrates, plus a normal serving of protein, and you need time to digest it before you sleep.

**Mastering the hills of inland Dorset is a key part of the event**

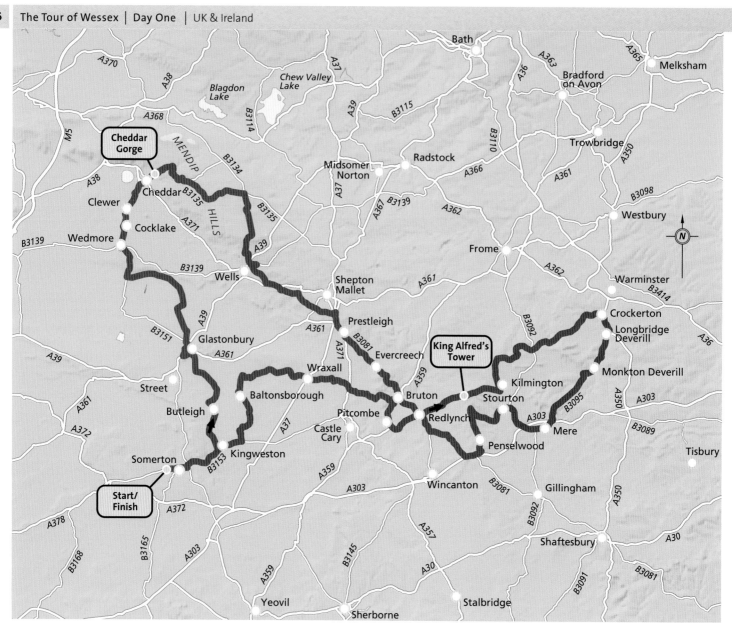

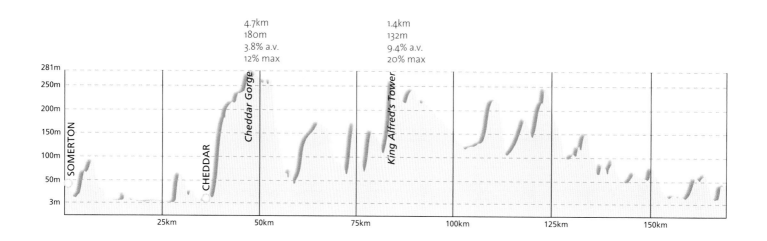

# ▌ Directions

### Day One

▲ Head east on the B3153 and turn left to Butleigh. Go right around Street, then to the west of Glastonbury on the A39. Turn left off the third roundabout, take the first right and follow this road and turn right. Continue to meet the A371 and turn right to Cheddar. Climb Cheddar Gorge and continue over the summit on the B3135, then turn right to Wells.

▲ Go south through Wells to join the A371. Turn right on the Old Wells Road then right again to join the A37. Follow that south, then continue south on the A371. Turn left to Evercreech then go through Bruton and turn left at Redlynch to climb over King Alfred's Tower.

▲ Turn left at Kilmington Common and do a loop northeast to Crockerton then south to Longbridge Deverill and Monkton Deverill, then southwest to Mere. Follow the B3092 to the left turn to Stourton, then turn right just past New Lake, then left at the top of the hill to descend through Penselwood. Turn right and follow the B3081 to Redlynch crossroads, where you turn left. Then go right on the A359 to Bruton where you turn left on Wyke Road and head west through Ditcheat, Wraxall and Hembridge to Coxbridge. Turn left and head south through Baltonsborough and Barton St David to the B3153 where you turn right and head back to Somerton.

**Cheddar Gorge is one hill where you do have to ride out of the saddle, especially up the first part of it**

**Whiteway Hill is exposed and the wind can add to its difficulty**

## Day Two

The second day heads to the south coast. It's an easy start again, but the hills come soon after Yeovil, with the climb of High Stoy just before Cerne Abbas providing a serious test. There's another hard climb out of Cerne Abbas through Piddle Wood, then the route relents so you can bowl downhill and enjoy the scenery across the Frome Valley before the hills start again at Winfrith Newburgh.

These hills go around the back of Lulworth and into an area called Purbeck, where the English Channel is very close. You get a tantalising glimpse of the sea at the top of the hardest climb, which is called Whiteway Hill. The descent ends in Corfe Castle and there's a long, flat section next, to Wareham. It's important to use sections like this to eat and drink in single-day challenges, but even more important when taking on something like the Tour of Wessex.

After Wareham the road begins to undulate, then it gets hilly after the A35, culminating in the climb of Bulbarrow Hill, just after Milton Abbas. You've done 82 out of 116 miles today, and at 264 metres (866 feet), this is the highest place on the stage. It's mostly downhill from here to Somerton, although there is a hard climb through Charlton Horethorne. When you get to the top it's 17 miles to the finish, mostly downhill.

Get organised at the finish. Drink your recovery drink or eat a sandwich, start sipping water, and get changed and to your accommodation quickly and eat a full meal. You've done two stages but the challenge is only half over. The final stage is the hardest of all.

# ▍Directions

**Day Two**

▲ Head southeast from Somerton to Crane Hill and turn left on the A372, then take the first right to Ilchester. Turn left to Limington and ride through Draycott and Ashington to Mudford, where you turn right on the A359. Go around Yeovil on the ring road but turn left to Stoford. Turn left to Clifton Maybank then right to Yetminster. Head southeast through Leigh and Higher Totnell to join the A352 south. Turn left in Cerne Abbas then right to Piddletrenthide, where you turn right on the B3143 then left on the B3142 and continue

southeast through Puddletown and Tincleton to turn left after crossing the River Frome.

▲ Follow the river then turn right to Winfrith Newburgh and continue south then east to West Lulworth. Turn left on the B3070 then right and continue straight at East Lulworth to climb Whiteway Hill, then continue to Corfe Castle. Turn left on the A351 then go right at the roundabout then left into Wareham. Follow the A352 west but turn right on Puddletown Road and continue northwest.

▲ Turn right to Briantspuddle and head north over the A35 through Milborne St Andrew then Milton Abbas to go over Bullbarrow Hill. Go through Stoke Wake and Hazelbury Bryan, to cross the B3143 to Crouch Hill. Turn right and follow signs to Milborne Port. Cross the A30 and continue north through Charlton Horethorne to the A303, where you turn left and follow the westerly run of roads that shadow the A303 through Sparkford and Queen Camel to the B3151, where you turn left to Ilchester and retrace the outward leg to Somerton.

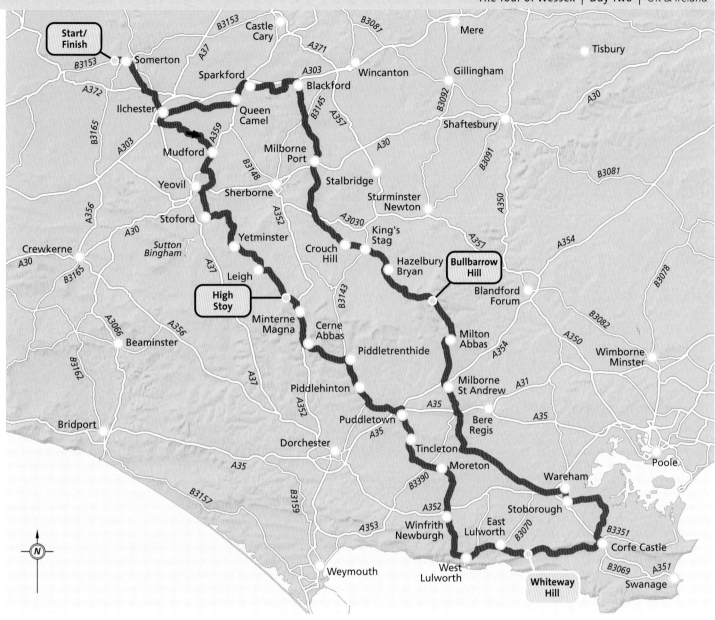

Start/Finish — Somerton
Castle Cary
Mere
Tisbury
Sparkford
Wincanton
Gillingham
Blackford
Ilchester
Queen Camel
Shaftesbury
Mudford
Milborne Port
Stalbridge
Yeovil
Sherborne
Sturminster Newton
Stoford
King's Stag
Crewkerne
Yetminster
Crouch Hill
Hazelbury Bryan
Bullbarrow Hill
Sutton Bingham
Leigh
High Stoy
Blandford Forum
Beaminster
Minterne Magna
Cerne Abbas
Milton Abbas
Wimborne Minster
Piddletrenthide
Bridport
Piddlehinton
Milborne St Andrew
Puddletown
Bere Regis
Dorchester
Tincleton
Moreton
Wareham
Poole
Stoborough
Winfrith Newburgh
East Lulworth
Corfe Castle
Weymouth
West Lulworth
Whiteway Hill
Swanage

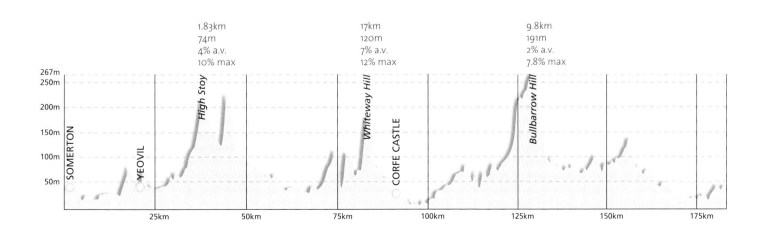

| | 1.83km | 17km | 9.8km |
| | 74m | 120m | 191m |
| | 4% a.v. | 7% a.v. | 2% a.v. |
| | 10% max | 12% max | 7.8% max |

High Stoy — Whiteway Hill — Bullbarrow Hill

267m
250m
200m
150m
100m
50m

SOMERTON — YEOVIL — CORFE CASTLE

25km   50km   75km   100km   125km   150km   175km

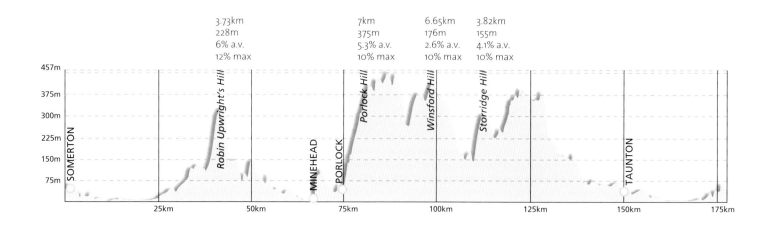

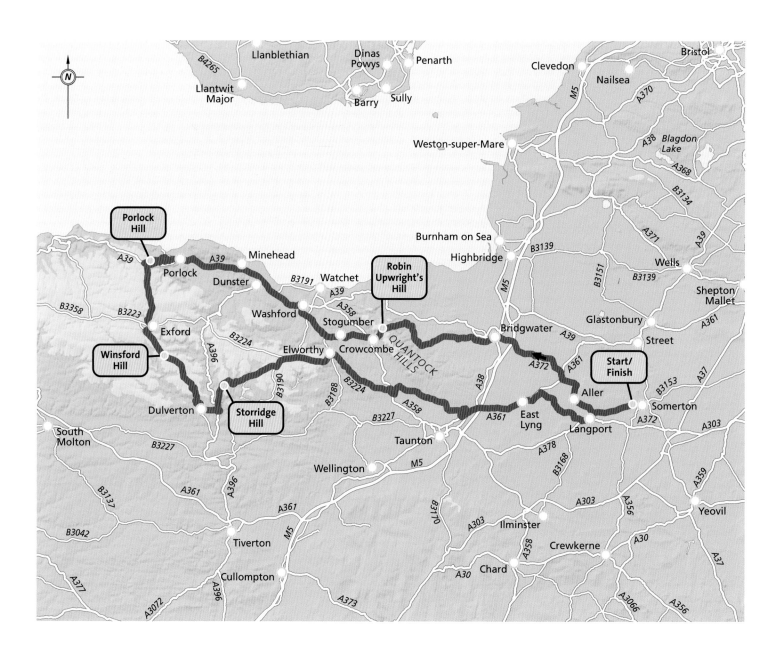

## Day Three

The hills kick in after 20 or so miles, just after Bridgwater. You continue west and climb into the Quantock Hills by Robin Upwright's Hill to Crowcombe Park Gate. Going up is steep enough but the descent to Crowcombe is fearsome. After that, you ride over some undulations at the bottom of the Brendon Hills, then there's a lull to Minehead, where the climbing starts again – and it's climbing with a vengeance.

The real Porlock Hill is one of the steepest in Britain, but the Tour of Wessex organiser, Nick Bourne, is a kind and humane man, so he uses the longer, less steep version of Porlock for the tour. It's still tough, but it's a nicer experience than the steeper version, although the steeper one should be on every cyclist's bucket list too.

At the top, the route heads across Exmoor to Exford, where there's a feed station in the event, then over Winsford Hill to Dulverton. Storridge Hill comes next, then you descend to Wimbleball Lake and cross it by the dam wall to climb Rugg's Hill, then on to the top of the Brendon Hills at Ralegh's Cross. You're nearly there now; the worst of Wessex is behind you.

A long descent leads to Bishop's Lydeard, then you use a back road to avoid Taunton and head across the Somerset Levels, where you started this journey two days ago, and finally ride back to Somerton.

**Descending towards Corfe Castle**

# ❚ Directions

**Day Three**

▲ Go west on the B3153 from Somerton to Langport, where you turn right on the A372 and follow this road to Bridgwater. Turn left where the A39 dual carriageway ends and go through Spaxton then past Hawkridge Reservoir to Over Stowey, where you turn left to climb over the Quantock Hills to Crowcombe. Cross the A358 and continue through Stogumber to Monksilver. Turn right on the B3188 to Washford, where you turn left on the A39 to Porlock.

▲ Turn right where the steep Porlock Hill starts and follow the shallower version just north of it to the top, where you cross the A39 and head south to Exford. Turn right on the B3224 then left to Chibbet Post, where you turn left then bear left to cross Winsford Hill to Dulverton. Follow the B3222 through Dulverton and turn right on the A396 then left off it, then keep right at the top of Storridge Hill.

▲ Descend over the dam at Wimbleball Lake and turn left on the B3190 to join the B3224. Follow this road over the A358 to Bishop's Lydeard. Turn left on Cothelstone Road then right to go through Yarford and Fulford then Cheddon Fitzpaine to Monkton Heathfield. Here, turn left on the A3259. Join the A38 then continue straight on the A361 over the M5. Turn right in East Lyng then left at Athelney, then take the first right to Langport. Retrace the outward leg from Langport to Somerton.

### Website
www.pendragonsports.com

### Date
March.

### Why the name?
Wessex was a Saxon kingdom, more correctly the Kingdom of the West Saxons. It comprised all of the southwest of England west of London and south of Oxford.

### Anything else?
The Tour of Wessex covers such a vast area that it passes lots of great cycling country. Exmoor and its coast are worth exploring fully. The same can be said for Purbeck and the Mendips.

### Don't forget
While one of the best ways to train is to ride hard one day then easier (or not at all) the next in order to recover, you should include some consecutive hard days in your training before trying something like the Tour of Wessex. Start building up the intensity and/or distance of your longest ride, which many cyclists do on a Sunday. Then, while keeping your Sunday mileage the same, increase the amount of training you do on Saturday as well. Finally, about three weeks before the event, do three consecutive days of hard training.

It's very important to eat and rest well when doing a challenge like the Tour of Wessex, so it's worth booking the best accommodation that you can. You can research hotels on consumer websites if you aren't familiar with the area.

Take plenty of spares for the bike and enough of whatever food you use while riding to last three days. You'll also need a variety of clothing because the weather can change over the course of three days. Compression tights can help you recover. And take your usual wind- or rainproof top with you during the rides.

**Riding the Dorset lanes, on a typical section of Day Two**

Somerset and Devon

**Distance** 160 kilometres | 100 miles
**Total climbing** 3,044 metres | 9,985 feet
**Route key** Four moorland climbs and coping with the wind and weather through long, exposed stretches

# 17 The Exmoor Beast

Exmoor is rugged, character-building country. It's a high table of moorland that rises steeply out of the Bristol Channel to just over 500 metres (1,640 feet), then spreads south, east and west as an undulating plateau that drops into foothills and valleys. The Exmoor Beast allows you to experience every aspect of Exmoor, from its high sea views through windswept moors and into ferny, moss-green valleys.

This ride is an older version of the Beast event, which starts in Tiverton on the south side of Exmoor in 2013, instead of Minehead on the north, but the new route is similar to the old, visiting many of the same places and giving participants the same Exmoor experience.

Dunkery Beacon is on both routes. It's the highest point on Exmoor, and when you start in Minehead it's the first challenge of the ride. There's nothing quite like a 500-metre climb from sea level in just over 10 miles, with some infuriating drops in altitude along the way, to get your body firing on all cylinders.

The exposed nature of the moorland tops is part of what puts the beast into Exmoor, and you encounter it for the first time after crossing the top of Dunkery. There's very little shelter up here. In 2009 the event was held during the first weekend in November, and the wind blew torrential rain in a 50mph jet wash across the route. The organisers closed the 100-mile option for safety's sake, but although 641 of the 1,728 listed to ride chose not to, only 76 of the 1,087 who did start dropped out, and there were no casualties. In fact, many who did it look back at their shared apocalypse with fondness. There's nothing quite like defeating the combined forces of nature and a tough route with your own leg power to give your self-esteem a boost.

The A39 section comes next. It's also called the Atlantic Highway and there are amazing views along this road, out over the Bristol Channel and right into Wales. It eventually drops right down almost to sea level in Lynmouth, then you climb back up onto the moor.

Riding over Brendon Common and down into Simonsbath, a village with a distinctly frontier feel, there's a steep climb followed by a complicated section of moorland roads that switches from one direction to the other, which at least means you aren't blasted by constant wind. Then the route straightens, making for Dulverton, where you cross the River Exe.

The next section is main road, but there aren't many main roads in England quite as pretty as the A396 at the point where it meanders north alongside the burbling River Quarme in a deep wooded valley to Wheddon Cross. There's a sharp climb away from the main road then you go south, tracing the same valley but on a higher route to Exbridge, where you start to climb Haddon Hill, which is the steepest on the route.

The hills come thick and fast now. There's a change in the scenery too, because you are riding towards the top of the Brendon Hills. They merge into Exmoor's eastern edge but they are cut by streams, so they are much more undulating, and there's more varied agriculture on the Brendon Hills than there is on Exmoor.

You reach the Brendon's ridge line at a three-way crossroads and turn sharp left to ride along the ridge, crossing its highest point of 409 metres (1,342 feet) at Wiveliscombe Barrow. Then there's an exhilarating plunge off the ridge from the crossroads at the top of Quarme Hill, going north now and back towards the sea, and back to the start in Minehead. The last five miles also go along the A396, this time next to the River Avil, and through Dunster with its fairytale castle.

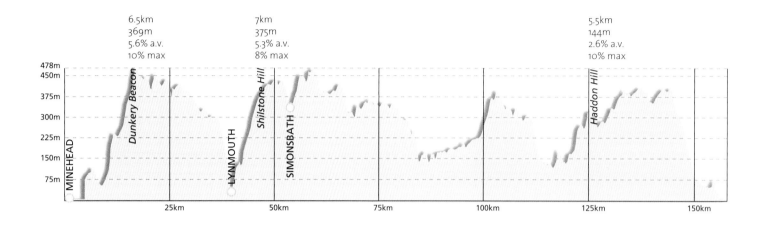

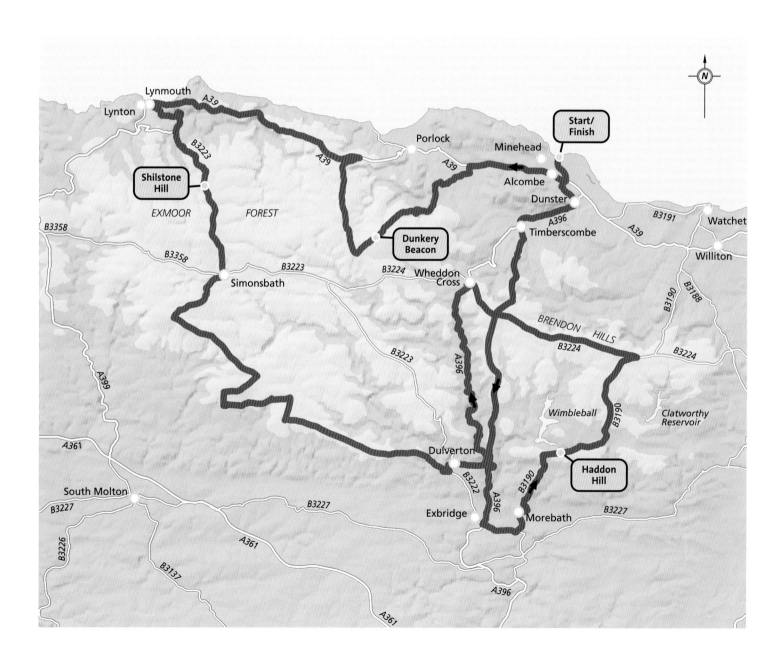

## ▌Directions

▲ Go west out of Minehead on the A39 and turn left to Blackford. Turn right just before the village and continue up Crookhorn Hill and fork right to climb Dunkery Beacon. Continue to Exford Common, where you turn right and head north back to the A39. Turn left and continue to Lynmouth. Follow the A39 through the town and back uphill to Hillsford Bridge, where you go straight at the hairpin bends on the A39 to join the B3223.

▲ Continue through Simonsbath, over the River Barle, and turn left at the crossroads on top of the hill. Follow this road to the Sportsman's Inn, where you turn right. Turn left at the T-junction, then take the first left to the crossroads, where you turn right. Turn left at the next crossroads and continue through Dulverton on the B3222. Continue east on the B3222 and turn left on the A396 to Wheddon Cross, where you turn right on the B3224. Turn right at the next crossroads.

▲ Continue to the A396, where you turn left. Turn left at the B3222 junction near Exbridge, then left on the B3190. Follow this road to the top of Haddon Hill then Brendon Hills ridge. Turn left on the B3224 then turn right just past the radio mast and descend to the A396 at Timberscombe, where you turn right then go left in Dunster to return to Minehead.

Steeper parts of Exmoor, including sections of Porlock Hill, require an energetic approach

**Website**
www.exmoorbeast.org

**Date**
Towards the end of October.

**Why the name?**
The beast implies the nature of the route, which is savage in places, but it also refers to the legend of a big cat living on the moor. Actually, it's more than legend; dead, half-eaten sheep have been found with injuries typical of a big cat kill, and there are eyewitness accounts from people who claim to have seen big cats on the moor.

**Anything else?**
You could ride the Dartmoor Classic route in a long weekend, or the Devon coast-to-coast or the nearby Tarka Trail. They are all brilliant cycling experiences.

**Don't forget**
Dress for the weather, take plenty of food and drink if you ride this route outside the event because villages are few and far between on the moor, and take the usual emergency top in case the weather changes en route. Training-wise, the Exmoor Beast is hilly, so include plenty of hills in your preparation. It's useful to ride as low and aerodynamically on your bike as possible anyway, but especially so on exposed rides like this. You need good core and upper body condition to hold a low position, so work on refining that.

Devon

**Distance** 171.2 kilometres | 107 miles
**Total climbing** 3,407 metres | 11,174 feet
**Route key** Several long climbs up to the centre of the moor and constant hilly roads around its edges

# 18 The Dartmoor Classic

Dartmoor is a vast, undulating plateau. Two roads cross at its centre and hundreds circle its steep sides. The Dartmoor Classic uses the two crossing roads and several of those on its edges to create a route that explores the very best of this beautiful and mysterious place.

In 2013 the event started at Newton Abbot racecourse for the first time. Previous start points have been just north of there, but towns on the route such as Ashburton and Moretonhampstead serve just as well if you want to ride the Dartmoor Classic outside the event. Having said that, starting and finishing in Newton Abbot ensures you get a delightful, easy and thoroughly enjoyable run to the finish as a reward for all your effort.

The rest of the route is challenging, make no mistake. The opening section climbs up to Hemsworthy Gate via Trendlebere Down and a difficult passage south past Hound Tor and Ripon Tor. Tors are rocky outcrops that look like piles of giant boulders. They are where the granite that formed Dartmoor pierces its thin skin of soil.

After a longish descent you follow the River Dart up its valley to Dartmeet, literally the meeting place of the West and East Dart rivers. It's a beautiful spot where sparkling water plays hide and seek through the trees, but the scenery becomes more spare, open and wild as you climb.

You continue across open moor, still climbing, to Two Bridges, where legend has it that a pair of unattached hairy hands have been known to attack unwary travellers in the dark. Dartmoor is full of legends like this.

Two Bridges is where the two trans-Dartmoor roads cross. The route swings left through Princetown to Yelverton, where a hard passage over the moorland-edge roads begins. You do

a loop west of the moor then head back to it, navigating by a rocky outlier, a distinctive peak called Brent Tor with a church perched on top.

The second long climb back to the centre of the moor, called Rundlestone, starts just outside Tavistock and twists through open scenery of boulder-strewn heather before passing the forbidding grey bulk of Dartmoor prison. The scenery, the sky – everything – is big when you cross the moor here. There are very few trees and the land slopes gently away to the north and south. This can be the fastest or one of the slowest parts of the ride depending on the wind direction, because it's so exposed.

If the wind is from the southwest, where it should come from in this part of the country, you will crack along at a rate of knots to reach the long descent to Moretonhampstead and then the last and best-looking climb of the ride. The locals call it Doccombe, after a village near the summit. The road wriggles upwards through a series of bends that are more like something you'd expect to find in Europe rather than England.

If hill climbs can have glory then Doccombe is glorious. It's also the gateway to the Dartmoor Classic's parting gift. In the event, or if you start this challenge from the Newton Abbot area, the last 15 miles are either downhill or flat. You also get the River Teign for company.

The river starts high up on the moor near Hangingstone Hill and splashes down to Dunsford, where the route crosses it, growing stronger and wider as it falls. The trend continues as you head south, with several tributaries joining the river, including one that topples over the Canonteign Falls near Whetcombe Barton.

Riders on a stage of the Tour of Britain crossing Dartmoor

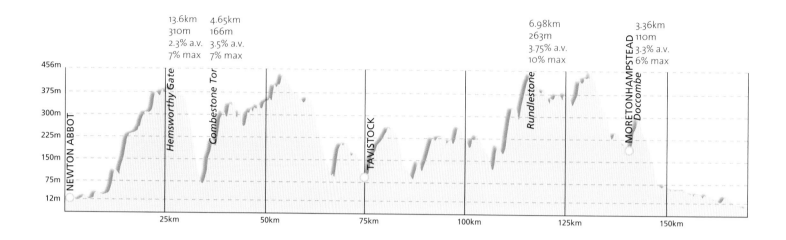

13.6km
310m
2.3% a.v.
7% max

4.65km
166m
3.5% a.v.
7% max

6.98km
263m
3.75% a.v.
10% max

3.36km
110m
3.3% a.v.
6% max

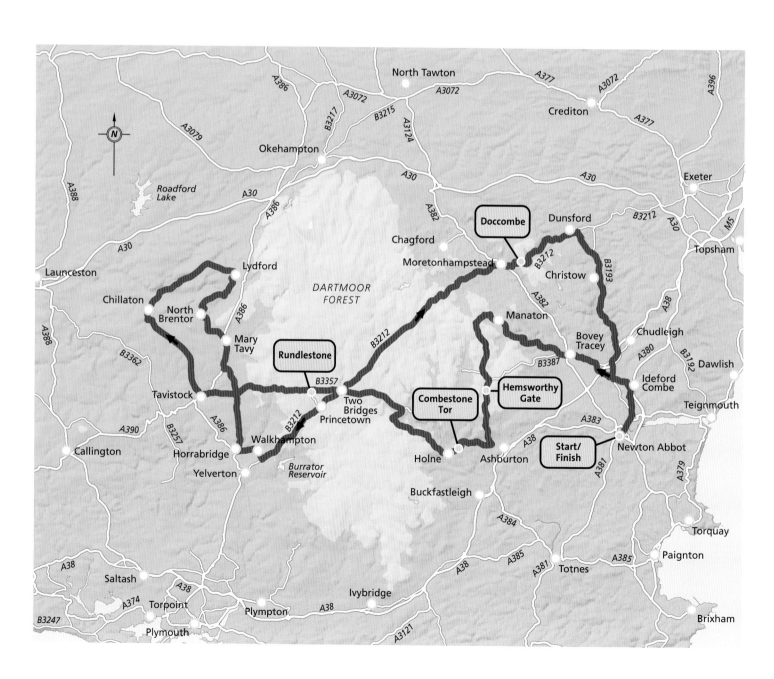

**Mark Cavendish climbing one of Dartmoor's hills**

# ▌Directions

▲ From Newton Abbot head towards Chudleigh then follow signs to Bovey Tracey. Go straight over the A382 roundabout and take the second right and follow this road through Manaton to go left at Langstone Cross then Heatree Cross. Continue south over Hemsworthy Gate summit towards Ashburton but go right at Hele Cross to Holne. Continue to Princetown, and bear left towards Yelverton.

▲ Turn right to Walkhampton then left to Horrabridge, where you follow a road due north out of the village then go left to Tavistock. Go straight through the town centre, following signs to Chillaton, where you bear right to Lydford then continue south to North Brentor to join the A386 at Mary Tavy. Turn left at Harford Bridge and at Moorshop go left on the B3357 to climb Rundlestone.

▲ Bear left at Two Bridges and follow the B3212 to Moretonhampstead, where you cross the A382 to climb Doccombe. Go right after Dunsford where the River Teign bends right and the B3212 bends left. Follow this road to join the B3193 back to Newton Abbot.

**Website**
www.dartmoorclassic.co.uk

**Date**
June.

**Why the name?**
Crossing Dartmoor's giant X of roads is the classic way to explore it on a road bike.

**Anything else?**
The South Devon coast is nearby, which is a lovely place to ride. So is Tarka Country, the valleys of the River Taw and the Torridge, which is north of Dartmoor and can be explored from Okehampton.

**Don't forget**
Pick a sunny day for this ride if possible. The sun shows Dartmoor and the Teign Valley at their sparkly best. This is a high-level route, so take the usual wind- and waterproof top in case the weather changes. You don't need to overload your pockets with food; there are plenty of village shops and cafes where you can replenish stocks.

Cornwall

**Distance** 145.6 kilometres | 91 miles
**Total climbing** 1,435 metres | 4,700 feet
**Route key** Lots of steep hills with hardly any flat riding in between

# **19** Cornwall Tor

The Cornwall Tor is a good old-fashioned hill-fest. It starts in the centre of this elongated county at the southwest tip of Britain, visits some of the cliffs and bays of the north and south coasts and wanders around a hilly hinterland of moors and valleys. There's also a short passage through some very unusual scenery that was created in Cornwall's industrial past.

The event starts at a National Trust property called Lanhydrock, but nearby Bodmin is a better base if you want to ride this route outside the event. The first section works its hilly way to the edge of Bodmin Moor, a wild and windy place that's one of the few British upland areas not managed as a national park. Perhaps because of this it has a rugged, unkempt look. It's a hard life for the locals farming up here, but the landscape has a quiet dignity because of it.

You come off the moor and head south past Liskeard, then descend through the trees into the steep-sided East Looe River Valley, where you follow the river to the sea. This section is lovely; the river fills its course and ebbs with the tide, creating two pictures – one a waterscape and the other a landscape of wide sandbars where snowy white egrets peck and forage.

Cross the river in Looe, where you catch a tantalising quick glimpse of the sea on your left, and climb out of the valley. There's a relatively flat run next, then you plunge into and out of the Lerryn Valley, a tributary of the Fowey, and continue to Lostwithiel, a town at the head of the Fowey Estuary. The climb out of Lostwithiel is hard, but the one that comes after it is even harder.

It goes from sea level at Par Sands, over Corn Hill and past the site of the Eden Project, then into a strange land known as the Cornwall Alps. The lanes here thread around a series of once white hills. They are being overtaken by vegetation now, but you can still see their white surfaces in places.

If you squint, it looks like snow, hence the alpine reference. The hills are in fact spoil heaps from the china clay industry that is still active here, albeit on a reduced scale.

A rare flat interlude comes next, as the route crosses the fragile ecology of Goss Moor, then it starts climbing again at St Columb Major as you approach the north coast. You see the sea from the top of the hill above St Mawgan, just across the valley from Newquay airport. This is the Atlantic Ocean now, and you descend to one of this coast's famous surfing beaches at Trenance.

There's a hard climb out of the bay then the road dips up and down for the next seven miles to Padstow. This section is one of the joys of the Cornwall Tor. There's a wide-open, cliff-top feel to this part of the ride, with lots to see. Bedruthan Steps, a group of rocks in Bedruthan Bay said to have been a giant's stepping stones, look spectacular, as does the idyllic Porthcothan Beach. And Padstow, known as 'Padstein' because of its association with celebrity chef Rick Stein, is no slouch in the good-looks department either. It stands on the west side of the wide Camel Estuary, which will be your last glimpse of the sea as you climb away from it to begin the final and much more rolling part of the Cornwall Tor. The steeper hills are behind you and the views are more open during the final section, but more open means more windy, and that can make the final leg tough. It's worth noting wind speed and direction before setting out, and if it's strong and not favourable then save something for this final section.

You know you are nearly home when the route meets the A30, Cornwall's main road connection with the rest of the country. If you've started from Bodmin, it's best to take the main A389 back into town from the big A30 roundabout. The Cornwall Tor event uses a lane that runs next to the A30 then rolls back into Lanhydrock.

Top left: Cornwall Tor sportive organiser Geoff Saxon (left) and Cornish pro racer Steve Lampier on a route recce.  Top right: Looe harbour
Above: The open landscape and big sky of inland Cornwall

### Website
www.kilotogo.com and click on 'Events'.

### Date
Usually the third weekend in April.

### Why the name?
Cornwall's upland areas have similar geology to Dartmoor, with the same rocky outcrops know as tors.

### Anything else?
The south and north coasts both warrant further exploration. If you like hills there's one on the north coast just south of Bude called Millhook that is one of the steepest in the country. Bodmin Moor is more for walkers than cyclists, but the lanes around its edges are worth exploring.

### Don't forget
It's wise to carry a light rain- and windproof top on any long ride, but other than that, Cornwall's climate is quite benign and this ride doesn't go too high. It does rain quite a bit down here though, so come prepared for a wet ride. Your legs need conditioning to the constant ups and downs, too.

**Mid-Cornwall Tor countryside**

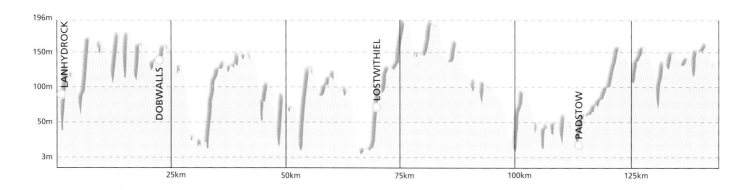

# Directions

▲ Go east from Lanhydrock and from Bodmin follow the Liskeard signs and turn left to Turf Down, then follow signs through Mount and St Neot to bear right and go through Dobwalls, over the A38. Continue south to Sandplace, where you bear right on the A387 to Looe.

▲ Turn right over the bridge then bear right on the B3359. Turn left at Lanreath and take the third left, then second right to go through Lerryn to Lostwithiel. Turn left on the A390 then left on the B3269 and go right on the A3082. Turn right through St Blazey Gate and continue north past the Eden Project to Bugle then Roche. Continue north then turn left on the A30. Take the first right and follow this road through St Columb Major past St Mawgan to Trenance.

▲ Turn right on the B3276 to Padstow. Go through the centre of town then up the hill to join the A389. Continue straight on the B3274 then continue straight off it where it bends sharp right at Pengelly. Take the third right then go left on the A30 and take the A389 back to Bodmin, or go under the A30 south and follow signs back to Lanhydrock.

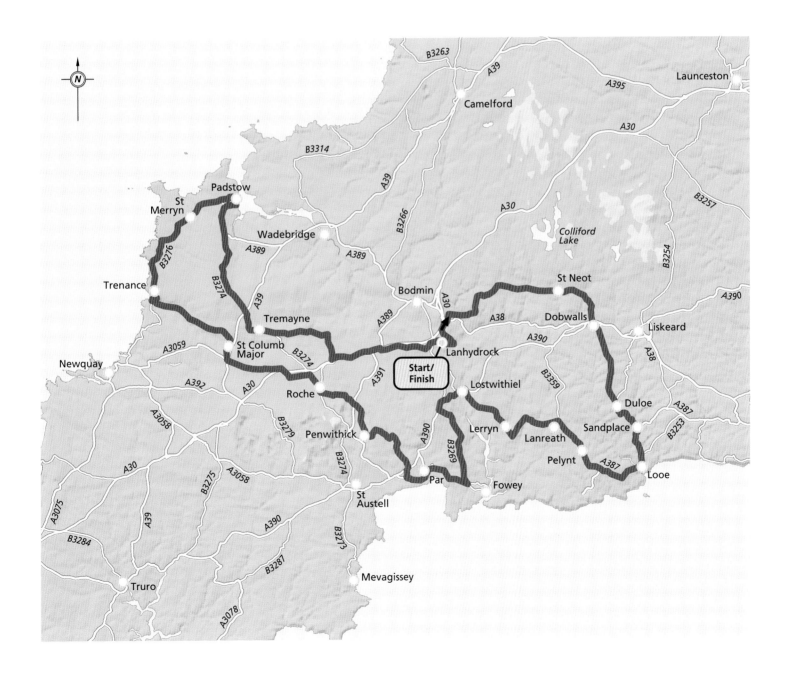

Wales

**Distance** 146 kilometres | 91 miles
**Total climbing** 1,970 metres | 6,480 feet
**Route key** Two major mountain climbs plus a lot of smaller but still very fierce hills

# **20** Etape Cymru

This ride has everything you would look for in a cycling challenge. It mixes a hard hill climb that only locals know with an historic mountain pass that is part of cycling history. It even starts and finishes with an easier stretch along some quiet, lower-lying country lanes.

The event starts at Bangor-on-Dee racecourse and meanders along a loop of lanes to begin its circuit of the hills between Wrexham and Rhosllanerchrugog. The ride gets hard now and will remain so until you return here. It tiptoes south along a delicate network of lanes on the east side of some mountains, part of the 8th-century Welsh border, then turns west to negotiate a tricky descent. This continues beneath a series of crags on which the border-maker, the Mercian King Offa, built his defensive dyke. The descent leads to the start of the ride's most famous climb.

The Horseshoe Pass is a beauty. There's nothing much to see at first and hardly any climbing, then you round a corner and see how it rises in a wide, sweeping horseshoe shape to the summit at 396 metres (1,299 feet). National hill climb titles have been decided here and two of British cycling's most famous races, the Milk Race and Tour of Britain, often used the pass in their routes.

There's a timed section up this climb in the Etape Cymru event. The fastest at the time of writing is the double Olympic gold medallist Geraint Thomas, with 14 minutes 22 seconds. Timings are taken on the climb from just after the place where the A542 out of Llangollen swings sharp right.

A short descent leads to the roundabout that's the centre of the cross-shaped main circuit of the Etape Cymru. The next leg goes along the side of Llantysilio Mountain, around its western end, and descends to Carrog, where you head west along the wide, flat-bottomed Dee Valley. Turning short of Corwen, you ride back to the centre roundabout parallel to

Llantysilio but on the opposite side of the valley. This section is harder than it looks, with a long climb that's heavy going.

Back at the roundabout again you head north alongside a chain of mountains called the Clwydian Range. You turn into them just north of Graig Fechan. Go through a pass between two peaks, then head south over the side of the last but one of the Clwydians, Moel y Waun.

The descent takes you to a main-road section that goes east past the mountain-bike paradise of Llandegla Forest. Head towards Wrexham but turn right before Coedpoeth to begin the most spectacular part of this ride, a climb called World's End.

You ride through a place called Minera, its name redolent of the mining that went on here, then there's a hairpin bend and you climb across the face of what is almost a cliff. World's End has a brutal first couple of kilometres but is much easier towards the top, as long as you don't get headwinds or crosswinds. It's worth stopping at the wide summit of World's End to take in the stunning views.

The descent of World's End must be respected. The first part is very steep and there's an extremely sharp right-hand bend in the short wooded section at the end of it. A stream runs through here and, except in times of drought (which aren't frequent in Wales), it runs over the road like a ford. It can be very slippery, so brake before you hit it and go slowly around the corner, keeping your bike as upright as possible.

Continue down under the crags of Eglwyseg Mountain to rejoin the outward leg from Bangor-on-Dee, with all arms of the cross and a real challenge completed. The section back to Rhosllanerchrugog is still tough – much tougher than on the outward leg because you will be tired by now – but you can relax afterwards and wind down in the country lanes of the final few miles.

**Welsh double Olympic gold medallist Geraint Thomas riding the Etape Cymru route**

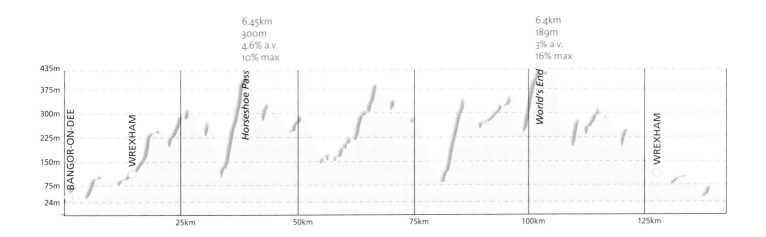

6.45km
300m
4.6% a.v.
10% max

6.4km
189m
3% a.v.
16% max

**Typical scenery at the heart of the Etape Cymru**

**Website**
www.etape-cymru.co.uk

**Date**
Early September.

**Why the name?**
Cymru is the Welsh-language name for Wales. It comes from a much older word, *Combrogi*, which means fellow countrymen.

**Anything else?**
A ride through the Clwydian range, criss-crossing from one side to another using the passes through the mountains is excellent. The bigger Berwyn Range is close by, too.

**Don't forget**
The usual kit you'd take with you on a mountain ride. No part of this one is far from places of habitation, but shops tend to be quite rare in the villages. There is an excellent cyclists' cafe at the Llandegla Forest Mountain Bike Centre, which also has a good bike shop. If you are doing this ride outside the event and are pushed for time, its essential character is the mountain section from Rhosllanerchrugog west and back.

# Directions

▲ Start in Bangor-on-Dee (Bangor-is-y-Coed) and head south then southwest to the A528. Turn right and then left onto the A539 then go right to Gyfelia. Continue north through Sontley, then turn left and go through Pentre Bychan and head west to turn left just before the Ty Mawr Reservoir. Turn right and then left to ride along the western edge of Rhosllanerchrugog village and continue around the mountain to Dinbren Isaf. Turn right on the A542 and follow this over the Horseshoe Pass.

▲ Turn left at the roundabout on the A5104 then fork left to Carrog. Turn right on the B5437 then right on the A5104. Turn left at the B5436 junction and follow this road back to the roundabout at the bottom of the Horseshoe Pass. Turn left on the A542 then go left on the A525 but continue straight where the A525 bends right. Turn right on the B5429 and turn right again where it bends sharp left, after Graig Fechan.

▲ Follow this road, keeping right at the fork after a left and right bend, then continue, crossing the B5431, to the A5104, where you turn right. Turn left on the A525, then turn right on the B5430. Turn right to Minera and follow the B5426 to turn sharp right at the four-lane junction to climb World's End. Continue down to the fork at Garth Wood just north of Dinbren Isaf and turn left to retrace the outward route.

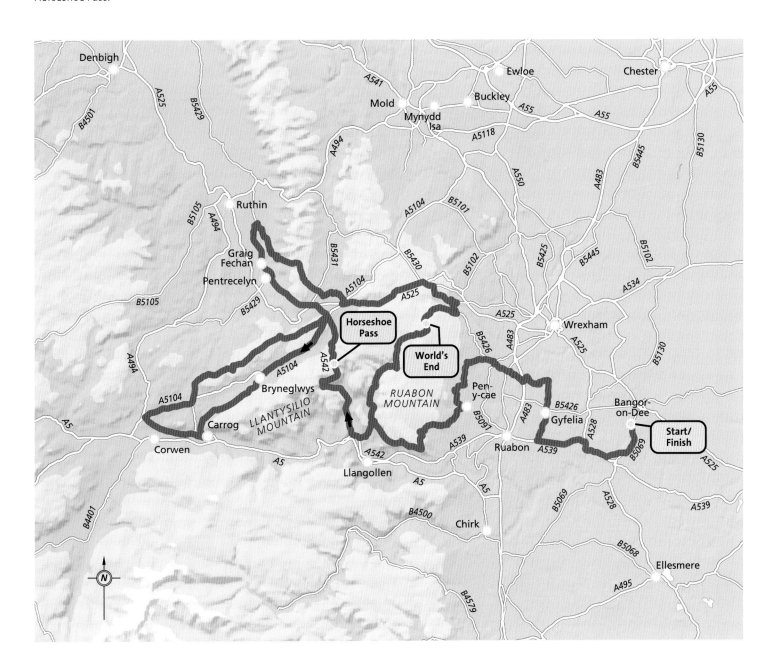

South Wales

**Distance**  206 kilometres | 128 miles
**Total climbing**  3,350 metres | 10,990 feet
**Route key**  Eight major climbs and very little flat road between

# 21 The Dragon Ride

The Dragon Ride is a market leader for UK cyclosportives. It's the only one to achieve UCI Golden Bike status, which means that it is part of a world series of similar events that the international cycling governing body, the UCI, recognises as having a shared excellence. It certainly has a compelling route.

Three distances make up the Dragon Ride event, but the true Dragon Ride challenge is the longest, the *gran fondo* distance. It's scenically stunning, a real mountain challenge that can hold its head up high with the other events in the Golden Bike series.

The opening and closing sections pass through some gritty, industrial landscape, but even that has a proud, work-ethic beauty, especially near Port Talbot where the steelworks' dark silhouette is set against the bright seascape of Swansea Bay. There's a steep climb over to the Vale of Neath, and another into the Swansea Valley. The hills serve as brief, green interludes in a long, built-up section, but the Dragon Ride totally changes character at Brynamman, where the first big climb begins.

At the western end of the Brecon Beacons lies the Black Mountains, a chain of mountains running east to west just north of the Welsh Valleys. The two areas are in complete contrast – where the valleys were once a hive of heavy industry, dotted with coalmines and steelworks, the Brecon Beacons is a tract of unspoilt, virtually empty land, which looks today as it must have done when the Romans built the first roads here.

The climbs come thick and fast now. There's a short, very twisting descent off Black Mountain before the exposed Roman Camp climb, then you descend past the Usk Reservoir to turn sharp right and begin the climb of Glasfynydd.

It's another tough customer: straight, exposed at the top, and with a dark forest section halfway up.

The summit gives way to a long, straight descent then a main-road climb called the Cray. You get almost all the way to Sennybridge then change direction again at Defynnog for another climb, one with a steep upwards kick in the middle. The passage through these hills is a lonely and wild one. There's very little shelter from any wind and nothing to see other than wild, grass- or heather-clad slopes with the occasional black crag peeping through.

The scenery changes in the Senny Valley, where the route follows a lovely little river, climbing steadily against its flow to what looks like a dead end. It's not, though – a short but brutal climb scales the steep side of Bryn Melyn mountain, with two hairpin bends making the way up possible. It's really hard but a long descent follows. Breathe deeply, eat, drink and compose yourself, because like every good challenge, the biggest and best of the Dragon is yet to come.

You slip under the Heads of the Valley road then go through Rhigos village to climb the spectacular mountain pass named after it. You pass one of the last working collieries in Wales, then two sweeping hairpin bends take you up the sides of a vast bowl hollowed out in the mountainside during the Ice Age.

The descent leads into the famous Rhondda Valley, where you pass through a landscape bearing the unmistakable signs of its industrial past. Terraced houses are strung like ribbons of bricks up the tiered valley sides, where the scars of pits and old spoil heaps are slowly healing over. Just one climb remains, the Bwlch, or simply 'the Pass' in English. After that, it's mostly downhill to Margam Country Park.

The British road race championships have used some of the Dragon Ride roads

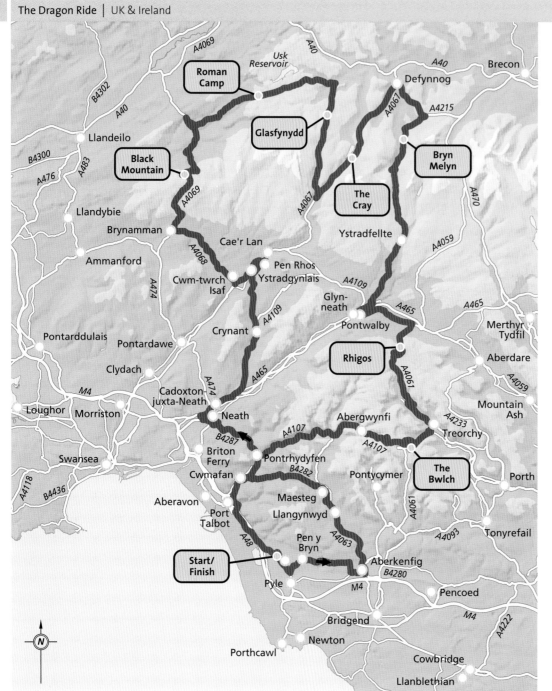

## Website
www.dragonride.co.uk

## Date
Early June.

## Why the name?
The Welsh Dragon, y Ddraig Goch, is the national flag of Wales.

## Anything else?
The rest of the Brecon Beacons are well worth exploring.

## Don't forget
A lot of this ride is high, so take a wind- and waterproof extra upper body layer in case the weather changes. There are plenty of places to buy food and drink if you need it in the Welsh Valleys sections, but very few in the Brecon Beacons. There will be a lot more traffic in the valleys, so take care.

**Right: Climbing the Bwlch**
**Far right (top): Dragon Ride organiser Lou Lusardi checks out the route**
**Bottom: Take care in wooded sections; roads may be damp**

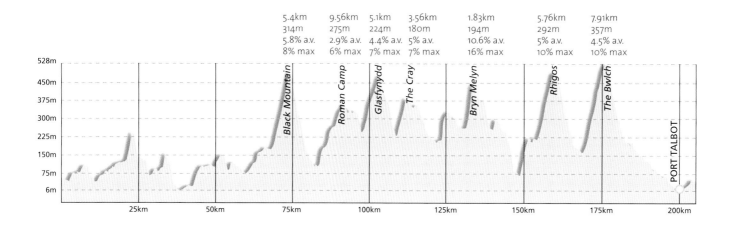

| 5.4km | 9.56km | 5.1km | 3.56km | 1.83km | 5.76km | 7.91km |
| 314m | 275m | 224m | 180m | 194m | 292m | 357m |
| 5.8% a.v. | 2.9% a.v. | 4.4% a.v. | 5% a.v. | 10.6% a.v. | 5% a.v. | 4.5% a.v. |
| 8% max | 6% max | 7% max | 7% max | 16% max | 10% max | 10% max |

# ▌ Directions

▲ Turn left out of Margam Country Park and follow signposts for Pen y Bryn and Aberkenfig, where you turn left on the A4063 and head for Maesteg. Turn left on the B4282 and go right in Cwmafan on the A4107, then left on the B4287 to Neath. Turn right and follow the main road then a minor one after Crynant to Ystradgynlais.

▲ Turn left on the A4067 then right on the A4068 to join the A4069 mountain road at Brynamman that climbs Black Mountain. Turn right at the Three Horseshoes pub to climb Bylchau Blaenclydach (also known as Roman Camp) then turn right after Pont-ar-Lechau, climb through Glasfynydd Forest and follow this road to the A4067, where you turn left to climb The Cray. Turn right in Defynnog on the A4215 then go third right to Heol Senni, where you turn left to climb Bryn Melyn. Continue through Ystradfellte and follow the Rhigos road, then turn right on the A4061 to climb Rhigos.

▲ Continue through Treherbert to Treorchy, where you turn right to climb Bwlch y Clawdd, then follow the A4107 towards Port Talbot. Turn left after passing under the M4 and follow the A48 back to Margam Country Park.

Northern Ireland

**Distance** 182 kilometres | 116 miles
**Total climbing** 2,615 metres | 8,575 feet
**Route key** The rollercoaster hills of the Torr Head road and a passage through the Glens of Antrim

# 22 The Giant's Causeway Coast Sportive

I love this ride. The organisers call it the Giant Killer, and it certainly is a major cycling challenge, especially since the hardest part comes very close to the end. But the solemn beauty of the countryside and coast will win your heart.

You start by the sea in Ballycastle in a picturesque bay where the Kintyre Peninsula of Scotland is visible 15 miles away over the water. Rathlin Island is even closer, like a stepping stone on the way. It's a wonderful view that gets better as you travel west along the northern coast of Ireland.

Look right as you climb towards Ballintoy and you see the islands of Islay and Gigha, and, in the far distance, Jura. Then the white cliffs of Antrim come into view, with wide sandy beaches in front of them where cattle laze like old ladies on holiday, taking the occasional paddle in the sea while keeping their coats on. And finally you arrive at the Giant's Causeway, a genuine world wonder and a World Heritage Site. You can't see much from the Causeway Road, so you need to either deviate off the route or come back another time.

Going inland through Bushmills, the route rolls through some pleasant farming country then turns down Bregagh Road towards Armoy and enters the Dark Hedges. These lines of 300-year-old beech trees running either side of a dead-straight road are like something from a fairytale. Their trunks are the buttresses of a leafy cathedral, their higher branches its vaulted roof. Ireland is a land of myth and legend and this is a magical place. A grey lady is said to haunt the Dark Hedges, gliding between the trees at dusk.

From Armoy you head back to Ballycastle for the second loop of the ride, which is longer and also more challenging. You ride around the back of the Antrim Mountains then directly through them, climbing a pass called Slieveanorra. The roads are higher here, but although the climbs are long, there's nothing too steep. The area has a lonely majesty.

The first pass leads to Cushendall on the coast. Turn away from the sea to climb again, through the forest, into Glenariff, beneath the peak of Trostan, the highest point in Antrim at 551 metres (1,808 feet). Glenariff is one of the nine Glens of Antrim that radiate out from the Antrim Plateau to the coast.

A couple of lower climbs follow, but eventually you reach the sea again at Glenarm, and the route hugs the coast almost all the way back to the start.

This section starts out easy but ends up brutal. You round two bays along a long, flat section with wonderful views across the sea. I thought I could make out the Galloway coast in Scotland from here, but it could have been a mirage in the mist. Then the route enters the pretty seaside village of Cushendall and starts a long climb up Layde Road.

There's a sharp descent to Cushendun, a short, flat stretch near the beach, then you hit the Torr Head road. There are three long, steep climbs, the hardest section of the whole route by far, and they come in the next 10 miles, when you already have 100 miles in your legs. It's not possible to overstate how hard this section is. Your legs and lungs will burn on the way up, and arms and fingers will hurt nearly as much from braking on the way down. Remember, though: always brake before a bend and brake earlier in the wet.

The Torr Head road can be torture but it has a saving grace, because the views are amazing and the dizzy exposure above the sea in places feels exhilarating. Eventually you reach Torr Head, where in days gone by a man sat noting the names of ships sailing through the narrow sound between Ireland and Scotland and reporting the information to Lloyds of London. It must have been a great job on a sunny day.

Finally it's downhill all the way to Ballycastle, a final rush of excitement before completing one of the best rides in this book. Just try to do it when the weather is on your side.

# ▌Directions

▲ Use the coast road from Ballycastle going northwest to join the B15 then the A2. Turn right on Causeway Road and follow this to join the A2 again, then continue to Bushmills. Turn left on Straid Road and follow the B17 to the B147, where you turn right. Turn left on Bregagh Road to go through the Dark Hedges, then turn left to Armoy, where you turn left and follow the A44 then Hillside Road to Ballycastle again. Turn right at the seafront then right on Glenshesk Road and follow it to a crossroads. Turn left and take the first left just before Bush River and climb into the Glens of Antrim. Continue on Glenaan Road then go right on the A2 to Cushendall.

▲ Turn right on the B14 then join the A43 going southwest. Turn left at Cargan then keep right and go left again on Longmore Road, then turn left on the A42 and right on the B97 to Glenarm. Turn left at the seafront and follow the coast road all the way back to Ballycastle.

Sometimes it rains in Northern Ireland: be prepared

## Website
www.giantscausewaycoastsportive.com

## Date
September.

## Why the name?
The Giant's Causeway is a major tourist attraction, which the organisers pinned their sportive event to in order to attract participants. The Causeway itself is located north of Bushmills and is a vast array of basalt columns that drop down from the cliffs into the sea. There's a modern interpretive centre on site that explains how it was formed, both the legends and the geological processes.

## Anything else?
Northern Ireland has a lot to offer cyclists. The Mourne Mountains are spectacular, for example. Visit www.cycleni.com for details of what's on offer.

## Don't forget
Take a rainproof top with you, some full-fingered lightweight gloves, and plenty of food and drink. The route goes through villages with cafes and shops, but there are none in the Glens of Antrim. The route doesn't climb much above 1,000 feet but you are quite far north and the weather is changeable.

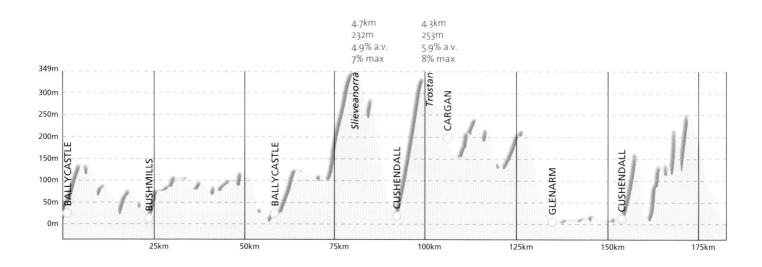

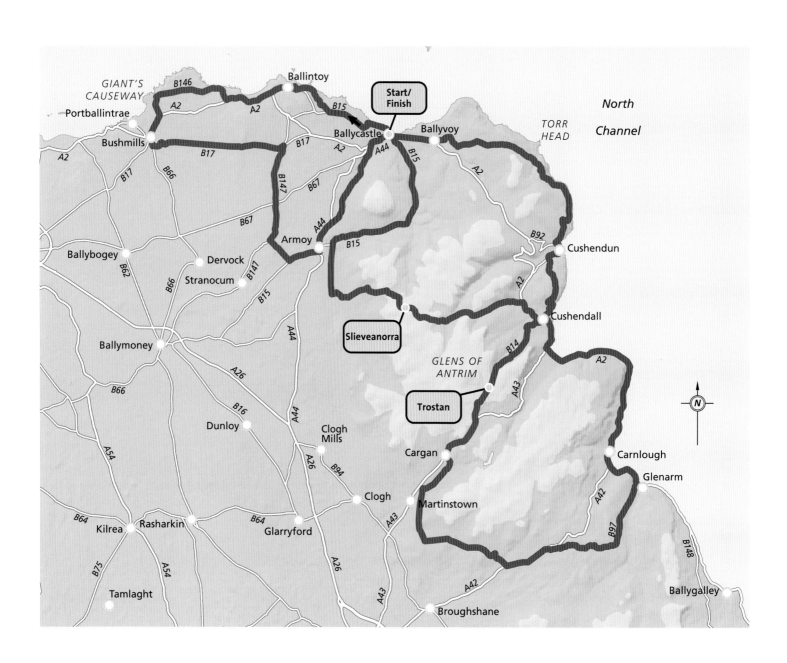

Sligo, Ireland

**Distance** 160 kilometres | 100 miles
**Total climbing** 1,450 metres | 4,757 feet
**Route key** Two significant climbs on an undulating route

# 23 Tour of Sligo The Ox Mountain Challenge

The Tour of Sligo is a two-day festival of cycling sponsored by the Irish post office, An Post, which does a great deal to support cycling in Ireland. They sponsor home events and also a team based in Belgium that works with one of Ireland's greatest cyclists, Sean Kelly, to develop Irish road-racing talent.

The festival breaks down into a family day on Saturday and three challenge rides on Sunday. The Ox Mountain Challenge is the longest and hardest of the challenges. It's also a riotous mix of sea and mountains in a place, County Sligo, that is one of the most beautiful in Ireland and has been an inspiration for a number of literary figures, including the poet W B Yeats.

The first section of the ride goes west along the coast, where you get a good view of the Atlantic, the original Coney Island set in it, and further across the bay to a mountain called Ben Bulben. The route then loops around a distinctive, dark, flat-topped hill called Knocknarea, on top of which is a cairn, Maebh's Cairn, or Queen Maeve's Tomb in English.

You follow the outline of another bay, then the route heads towards Ladies Brae, a significant climb rising 256 metres (839 feet) above sea level. If it's clear you can see where you've been from the top of this climb, right down into the bays and over Knocknarea to Ben Bulben, but this is the west of Ireland so it might not be clear. Still, stories about the soft rain of Ireland are true. Even the rain is special.

A long descent off Ladies Brae leads to a long but steady uphill section that goes through the middle of the Ox Mountains. The route then swings southwest to run along their southern edge, then north past Lough Easkey to return to the coast.

This is much more open than the previous coastal stretch, so you get something approaching the full Atlantic effect. The wind can be troublesome here, but it is counterbalanced by the sound of crashing waves and the rugged splendour all around you.

A second climb of Ladies Brae, which starts at around 60 miles, leads to the last third of the ride, away from the Ox Mountains that have been the focus so far, and around Lough Gill to follow the circuit that makes up one of the other rides happening on the same day in the Tour of Sligo event.

The Lough is a deep blue jewel surrounded on its north shore by green hills and fields – a sapphire in an emerald setting – while the south side, where the route passes, is more rugged. You slip into County Leitrim for a short stretch of road before returning to County Sligo at Dromahair. This signifies the start of the last leg: the run home to Sligo past a string of three small loughs – Doon, Anelteen and Colgagh.

**Irish roads can be tough but the scenery makes up for that**

Looking down on Sligo and out towards the sea

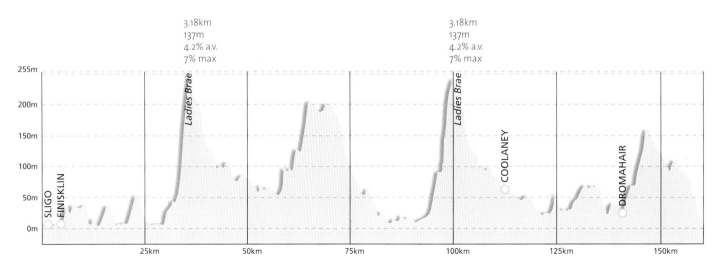

3.18km
137m
4.2% a.v.
7% max

3.18km
137m
4.2% a.v.
7% max

# Directions

▲ Start in Sligo and head west towards Finisklin and follow the R292 towards Strandhill. Turn left towards Ransboro and Ballysadare, where you join the N59 west then turn left at Beltra post office to climb Ladies Brae. After the descent, turn left towards Cloonacool. Turn right towards Masshill. Head north towards Dromore West then cross the N59. Follow the coast road back to the N59, where you go left.

▲ Take the first right and go over Ladies Brae again then turn left at the T-junction and ride through Collooney. Continue towards Sligo then join the R284 near Ballysadare and turn left at Ballygawley. Follow the R290 to the junction with the R287 and turn right to Dromahair. Turn left then right to Ballinode and go left there to head back to Sligo.

## Website
www.tourofsligo.ie

## Date
First weekend of May.

## Why the name?
It's a tour of Sligo.

## Anything else?
Sligo is full of good bike rides. This ride explores the mountains south of the city, but there are even more to the north.

## Don't forget
You'll be well looked after in the event with aid stations at 40, 80, 105, 114 and 136 kilometres. Food and water is available at alternating stations. Check the weather forecast and dress accordingly. Take an extra thin layer in case the weather changes. If you do this ride outside the event, you need to take plenty of food and drink because the villages here are quite spread out.

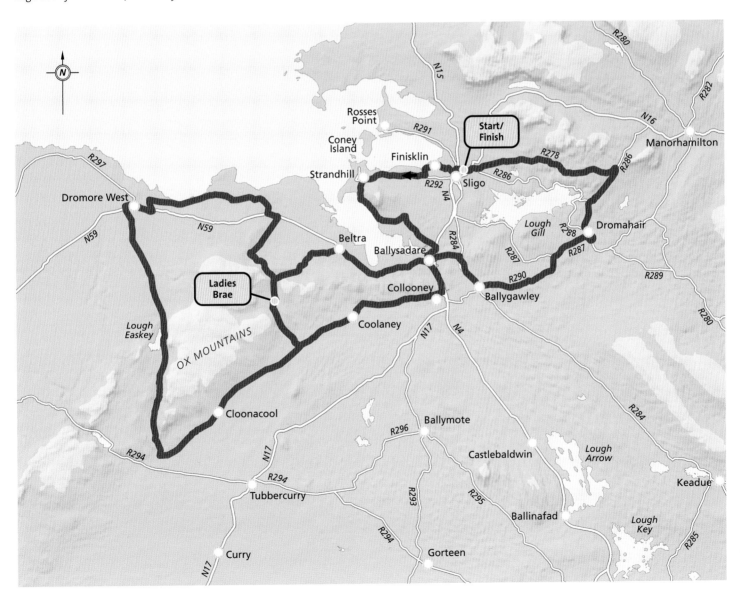

Ireland

**Distance** 654 kilometres | 408.75 miles
**Total climbing** 2,000 metres | 6,560 feet
**Route key** The ability to recover on a daily basis so you can keep going over this extended route

# **24** Malin to Mizen

I wanted to include a route that went across a whole country in this book, because crossing a country by bike is a special kind of challenge – exactly what bikes were made for. Bikes are unique human-powered vehicles, and represent one of the most efficient ways in which a human being can convert muscular power and energy into forward motion. With relatively little training any averagely fit person can ride much further than they can run, and with much less effort.

Malin to Mizen is Ireland's Land's End to John o' Groats, but the roads it uses are much quieter, it's shorter and has some organised events you can take part in, which is why I chose it instead. Its full title is Malin Head to Mizen Head: both names you could have heard on the shipping forecast. Malin Head is the northernmost point of Ireland and looks out over the stormy Atlantic Ocean, and Mizen Head is the country's southernmost point on the mainland, looking out over the Celtic Sea down in County Cork.

It's a challenge attempted by walkers and runners but more often by cyclists. Marie Curie Cancer Care charity provides logistics support for any cyclist who can pay a fee and raise a certain amount of money for them, while CLIC Sargent promote a Malin to Mizen Cycling Challenge. There are other organised events and supported holidays between the two ends of Ireland, and of course you can do the route independently at any time.

Alex Barry set a record time of 19 hours 3 minutes in 1993 for a non-stop Malin to Mizen, while in 2012 Ricky Geoghegan rode there and back again, Malin to Mizen and back to Malin (773.2 miles) in 2 days, 7 hours, 37 minutes. He was the first person ever to do it.

Those times are benchmarks for the ambitious and the super-fit, but most people set themselves five to seven days to do the ride; the CLIC Sargent event is held over seven. A six-day route breakdown would be to do the 49 miles to Letterkenny on day one, then go to Sligo (75 miles), Athenry (86 miles), Kilrush (68 miles) and Kenmare (80 miles) on successive days, leaving a final stage of 46 miles from Kenmare to Mizen for the sixth day. Some cyclists do the end-to-end ride the other way around, Mizen to Malin, which theoretically takes advantage of prevailing southwest winds.

Going north to south, you slice between some mountains through Donegal, then there's a lovely section beside Lough Swilly. The section to Sligo crosses bogs and runs by the sea, then the leg to Athenry goes mainly through farmland. The next leg is through more mixed terrain in County Clare, where limestone crags jut out from thin moorland cover. The Limerick section covers more farmland, with the town of Limerick itself the only really urban area you ride through.

Then, as the route strikes off in the most southerly direction so far and heads southwest, it becomes hillier and wild-looking before reaching the sea at Bantry Bay. You then ride out onto a narrow peninsula between Dunmanus Bay and Roaring Water Bay to Mizen Head.

**Malin to Mizen passes through lovely County Clare**

# ▌Directions

▲ This is a long and complicated route, but there are plenty of internet resources to download it from. Basically you head to Malin, then Buncrana, then follow the R238 coast road, then turn right on the R239 and shadow the N13 past Letterkenny to Ballybofey. Continue south to the east of Meenagarranroe Bog Reserve, then follow the N15, L2195 and R231 to Ballyshannon.

▲ Head west to Bundoran and turn left on the R280. Go west, then south to Sligo. Head south on the R284 to Ballygawley, turn right on the R290 then left to Ballymote. Follow the R293 southwest to join the L1398 south towards Kilmovee. Turn right just before Kilmovee, go right on the R328, then left on the N83 to Ballyhaunis. Continue south through Drumbaun to the R327, turn left then second right. Turn right on the L6618 and follow this road south to the N17 and Tuam.

▲ Continue south on the R347 then turn right to join the N17 and do a left-hand loop to cross it 5 miles later. Follow the L3102 south past Athenry and continue to Sixmilebridge, then go through Limerick. Follow the R511 south then go southwest at Charleville, then south through Kanturk to turn right in Banteer. Turn left in Mill Street, then go right and head southwest to Bantry. Follow the R591 southwest to Mizen Head.

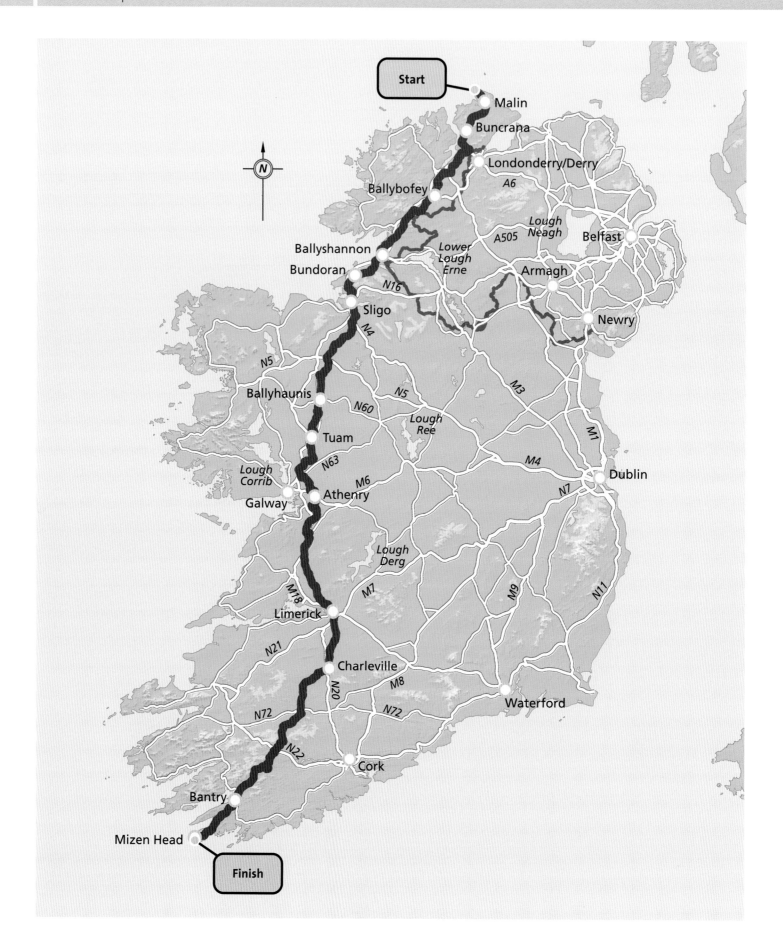

**Riding the route close to Galway Bay**

## Website
www.clicsargent.org.uk/event/malin-mizen-cycle

## Date
The CLIC Sargent Malin to Mizen takes place in May.

## Why the name?
End-to-end challenges are always named after their place names.

## Anything else?
Ireland is a superb cycling destination with some amazing terrain. The Clare coast is worth exploring, so are the mountainous areas of Kerry, Waterford, Connemara, Donegal and Wicklow.

## Don't forget
You'll need enough clothing to get you through the number of days you decided on for this challenge, or the number of days of an event. Bear in mind, too, that the Irish weather is changeable and rain is a fact of life, so go prepared with enough kit for your needs and all weathers.

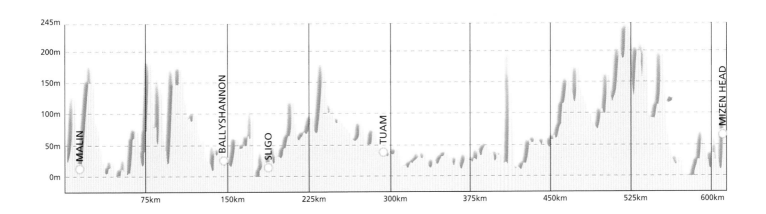

France

Region du Nord

**Distance** 170 kilometres | 106.25 miles
**Total climbing** 470 metres | 1,540 feet
**Route key** 27 sections of cobblestone roads called *pavé*, the same number as in the professional race

# 25 Paris–Roubaix Challenge

Paris–Roubaix is one of the oldest and most prized races in professional cycling. It's one of five single-day races known as monuments of the sport, a true classic of cycling with a classic route. The professional race runs from Paris to Roubaix, a distance of 257 kilometres (159 miles), but almost every year the battle to win it is fought out over the final 170 kilometres (105 miles). This is where all the cobbled roads are: roads built for cartwheels, not tyres. Roads that are referred to collectively in the sport as the Hell of the North.

The cobbled roads split up the race. They suit strong, fast riders and Paris–Roubaix's winners' list contains some legends. Men like Fausto Coppi, Eddy Merckx, Roger de Vlaeminck, Bernard Hinault and, coming right up to date, the best classics racers of their generation, the Belgian Tom Boonen and Fabian Cancellara of Switzerland.

The cobbles of Paris–Roubaix are part of the fabric of cycling, and the Paris–Roubaix Challenge is the perfect way to experience them. It covers all 27 sections, starting with the stretch between Troisvilles and Inchy, which comes 20 kilometres (12.5 miles) after the challenge start in Busigny.

The cobbles are rated according to how rough they are. Troisvilles to Inchy is a three-star stretch; the hardest sections get a five-star rating. The first of those is the most famous of all, the Trouée d'Arenberg. There are 10 sections before it, ranging from two to four stars.

This part of France used to be mining country. The deep coal mines are gone but the spoil heaps remain, as do some of the pitheads and the rows of miners' cottages. They are the backdrop to Paris–Roubaix, and one of the most iconic pitheads stands at the gateway to Arenberg.

The cobbles here are horrendous. *Trouée* means trench, and the Arenberg is a trench of rough stones that goes dead straight for 2,400 metres through a forest of spindly birch trees that look like they never get enough light. You ride Arenberg like all the other cobbled sections, seeking the smoothest line, which is often at the edge, and avoiding the cambers. But sometimes that means riding right along the middle of the road, its crown, which can be rough.

The technique for riding cobbles is simple: hold the tops of the handlebars, let your arms and legs soak up the bumps, and guide rather than steer your bike. Stay seated, keeping as much weight as possible over the rear wheel to give it traction. Pushing a higher gear than you would normally use also helps you to make better progress, but don't overdo it.

The other five-star sections are at Mons-en-Pévèle with 47 kilometres (29 miles) to go, which is 3,000 metres long, and the Carrefour de l'Arbre with 15 kilometres (9.5 miles) to go, which is 2,100 metres long. They are both awful, with missing cobbles and a battered surface. They require total concentration, but so do all of the cobblestone sections.

Paris–Roubaix is an extreme challenge but it's also extremely rewarding. By riding these famous roads (so famous that they have preservation orders on them), you are riding in the history and across the landscape of cycling. You'll see the sights recorded in thousands of pictures in hundreds of magazines from a unique perspective, one that can only be had by riding the Hell of the North yourself.

Eventually you reach the final cobblestones, a man-made sector along the central reservation of one of the main boulevards in Roubaix. It's called the Espace Charles Crupelandt, named after the only man from Roubaix ever to have won the classic, which he did in 1912 and 1914. It is just outside the open-air velodrome, the traditional finish of the race where challenge participants are sometimes allowed to do one lap of the pink concrete bowl to celebrate the end of their day in hell.

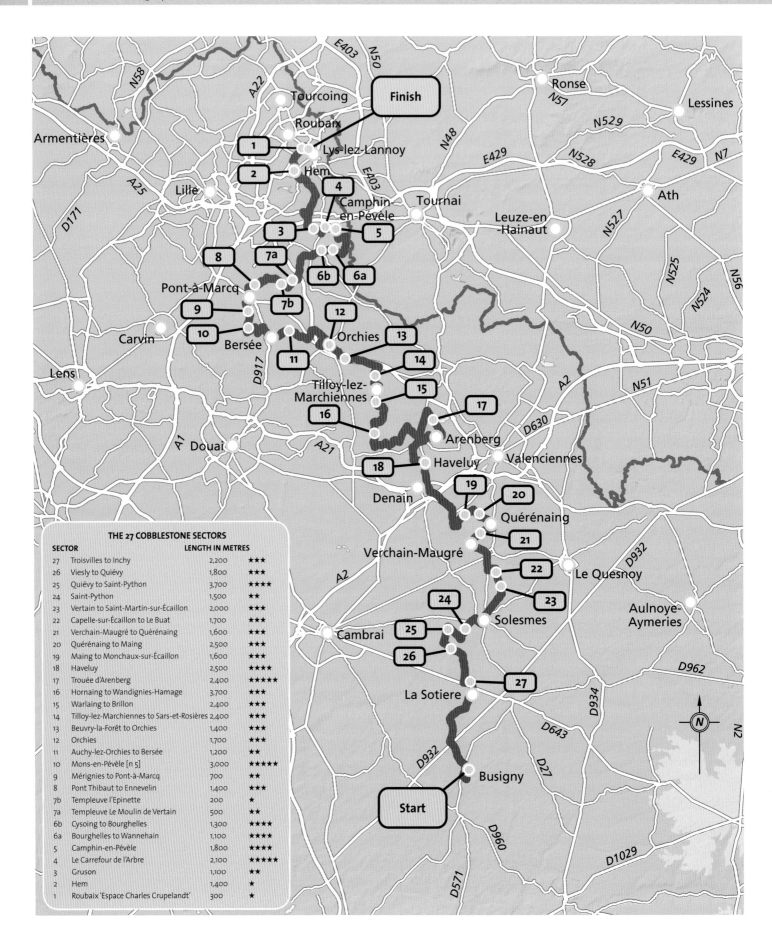

Finish

Tourcoing
Roubaix
Armentières
Lys-lez-Lannoy
1
2
Hem
Lille
4
Camphin-
en-Pévèle
Tournai
3
5
7a
8
6b
6a
Pont-à-Marcq
7b
9
12
10
Orchies
13
Bersée
11
Carvin
14
Tilloy-lez-
Marchiennes
15
Lens
16
17
Douai
Arenberg
18
Haveluy
Valenciennes
19
Denain
20
Quérénaing
21
Verchain-Maugré
22
Le Quesnoy
23
Aulnoye-
Aymeries
24
25
Solesmes
Cambrai
26
27
La Sotiere
Busigny
Start

Ronse
Lessines
Ath
Leuze-en-
Hainaut

### THE 27 COBBLESTONE SECTORS

| SECTOR | | LENGTH IN METRES | |
|---|---|---|---|
| 27 | Troisvilles to Inchy | 2,200 | ★★★ |
| 26 | Viesly to Quiévy | 1,800 | ★★★ |
| 25 | Quiévy to Saint-Python | 3,700 | ★★★★ |
| 24 | Saint-Python | 1,500 | ★★ |
| 23 | Vertain to Saint-Martin-sur-Écaillon | 2,000 | ★★★ |
| 22 | Capelle-sur-Écaillon to Le Buat | 1,700 | ★★★ |
| 21 | Verchain-Maugré to Quérénaing | 1,600 | ★★★ |
| 20 | Quérénaing to Maing | 2,500 | ★★★ |
| 19 | Maing to Monchaux-sur-Écaillon | 1,600 | ★★★ |
| 18 | Haveluy | 2,500 | ★★★★ |
| 17 | Trouée d'Arenberg | 2,400 | ★★★★★ |
| 16 | Hornaing to Wandignies-Hamage | 3,700 | ★★★ |
| 15 | Warlaing to Brillon | 2,400 | ★★★ |
| 14 | Tilloy-lez-Marchiennes to Sars-et-Rosières | 2,400 | ★★★ |
| 13 | Beuvry-la-Forêt to Orchies | 1,400 | ★★★ |
| 12 | Orchies | 1,700 | ★★★ |
| 11 | Auchy-lez-Orchies to Bersée | 1,200 | ★★ |
| 10 | Mons-en-Pévèle [n 5] | 3,000 | ★★★★★ |
| 9 | Mérignies to Pont-à-Marcq | 700 | ★★ |
| 8 | Pont Thibaut to Ennevelin | 1,400 | ★★★ |
| 7b | Templeuve l'Epinette | 200 | ★ |
| 7a | Templeuve Le Moulin de Vertain | 500 | ★★ |
| 6b | Cysoing to Bourghelles | 1,300 | ★★★★ |
| 6a | Bourghelles to Wannehain | 1,100 | ★★★★ |
| 5 | Camphin-en-Pévèle | 1,800 | ★★★★ |
| 4 | Le Carrefour de l'Arbre | 2,100 | ★★★★★ |
| 3 | Gruson | 1,100 | ★★ |
| 2 | Hem | 1,400 | ★ |
| 1 | Roubaix 'Espace Charles Crupelandt' | 300 | ★ |

N

# ❙ Directions

▲ From Busigny, go north on the D21 then continue north on the D98B and D98 through Viesly and northwest through Quivey to Solesmes. Turn left and follow the D109, D958 and D40A to Verchain-Maugré, where you turn right to Quérénaing. Go north on the D958 then turn left on the D59. Turn left on the D88 then right on the D40A and follow this road through Denain. Go left in Haveluy, take the first right, then the third right through Wallers to Arenberg.

▲ Turn left on the D313 and follow the cobblestone road through the forest, then turn left on the D40. Turn right just before Wallers then left on the D955 to Hélesmes. Turn right, ride through Hornaing, and go right on D81 to turn right in Wandignies-Hamage. Follow the D81 north to Tilloy-lez-Marchiennes, then pick up the D158B north.

▲ Turn left on the D953 Route Nationale and go northwest over the A23 to turn left after Beuvry-la-Forêt, following the cobbled section to rejoin the D953 in Orchies. Turn left then take two rights and follow two cobbled sections of road through Bersée. Turn right and right again on the D917 then left, right, left to go right on the D120. Follow the cobbled lane on your left in Mérignies. Then join the D94C to Pont-à-Marcq and go right to Ennevelin then Templeuve. Go northeast to Cysoing and go right to Wannehain, then left to Camphin-en-Pévèle. Go left to Gruson then go north through Chéreng, then Hem and into Roubaix.

**Website**
http://sport.be.msn.com/parisroubaix/2013/eng/

**Date**
April.

**Why the name?**
It comes from the race, and the race was created in 1896 to publicise the velodrome that two textile manufacturers had built in Roubaix.

In Paris–Roubaix, the cobbled sections of road cut the race field down into small groups, each one fighting to catch the one in front

**Anything else?**
Once you've ridden the challenge you should go back and watch the pros race over one of the cobbled sections you have ridden. You'll be amazed by their speed and hooked for life by the atmosphere. The race is usually held one week after the challenge, and as it's in the north of France it's very accessible from the UK.

**Don't forget**
This is a place-to-place challenge, so outside the official event you need someone to drop you at the start, pick you up at the end and act as a support vehicle. Your bike must be in perfect working order and you should use fatter tyres than normal. New ones are best but if they are a bit older they shouldn't have too much wear. Finally, you will need to be fit and strong. As well as your normal training, do some seated over-geared efforts on your bike to help you get used to pushing the bigger gears needed to make progress on cobblestones. Just shift into a higher gear than is comfortable now and again and push hard for five minutes.

Centre Val de Loire

**Distance** 230.5 kilometres | 144 miles
**Total climbing** 1,450 metres | 4,766 feet
**Route key** The distance

# 26 Paris–Tours

This is definitely a DIY challenge because there is no Paris–Tours cyclosportive at the moment. Paris–Tours is one of the races they call the classics in Europe, and as such it has a classic history and a classic route.

All the other classic races (and there are only seven that really warrant classic status) have a sportive with the same name over more or less the same route, so it's probably just a matter of time before someone organises a sportive on this one. Not only is Paris–Tours a great and historic race, it runs through some lovely cycling country in the Centre region of France and into the Loire Valley.

The race is called the sprinter's classic because it very often finishes with the whole field sprinting it out along the wide, straight Avenue de Grammont in the centre of Tours. It's one of the most famous finishes in cycling, along with the Champs-Élysées in Paris, which since 1975 has hosted the end of the final stage of the Tour de France.

Paris–Tours has been won by some of the greatest road sprinters in cycling, but you will wonder how they did it when you ride this route, because it's not flat and sprinters don't usually like hills.

The roads in this part of France undulate across a patchwork of arable fields, and there are some sharp little climbs when you get into the Loire Valley proper. It's tough going for a solo rider or for small groups, especially given the distance of Paris–Tours, but the route crosses the sort of terrain where pro-racing teams can control the peloton and set things up just right for their sprinters. It's happened many times in the past, although not always.

Paris–Tours used to run from the French capital directly to Tours, the capital of the old region of Touraine, but the restrictions of modern traffic have forced the race start further south to Eure-et-Loire. The 2011 start was in the town

of Voves, but the Eure-et-Loire authorities move it around to get as much exposure as they can for their *département*.

This route goes south, then west through Bonneval, start point of the final time trial of the 2012 Tour de France, which was won by Sir Bradley Wiggins. Let patriotic thoughts spur you on as the route heads south once more, this time towards Amboise, a beautiful town on the River Loire.

Tours is only a few miles to the west of Amboise going directly alongside the river, but after crossing the Loire the Paris–Tours route does a sweeping circuit of the little hills on the river's south side.

Short, sharp climbs, such as the Côte de Crochu, 28 kilometres (17 miles) from the finish, the Côte de Beau Soleil with 10 kilometres (6 miles) to go, and the Côte de l'Épan, just 7 kilometres (4 miles) from the line, will test your legs as much as they provide an exciting finale for the race.

This is a glorious area for cycling. The villages and towns are made of a local stone that is the colour of butter, and the small fields and orchards have led it to be known as the Garden of France. You also pass the world famous Touraine vineyards. The Loire River is the longest in France at over 1,000 kilometres, and it is historically a dividing point in the country between the north and south.

If the final climbs don't break up the field then the deciding factor of the Paris–Tours race is the Avenue de Grammont in Tours. This is a true test of a sprinter and his team – their nerve, judgement, resilience and, above all, their speed. The Avenue is wide and well-surfaced, with beautiful buildings on either side, and riders can see the finish line from a long way out. It's so easy to get this one wrong and peak too early. It's something to think about as you ride into Tours. Having seen the finish and its approach, it's much easier to appreciate the race next time you watch it on TV.

Riders crossing the River Loire with the Château d'Amboise in the background

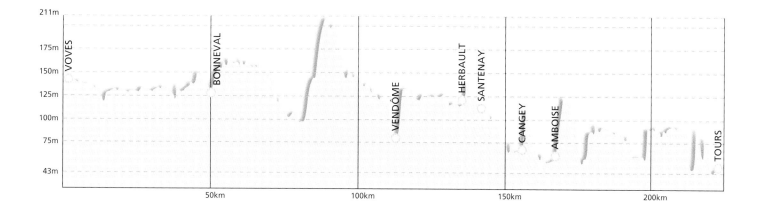

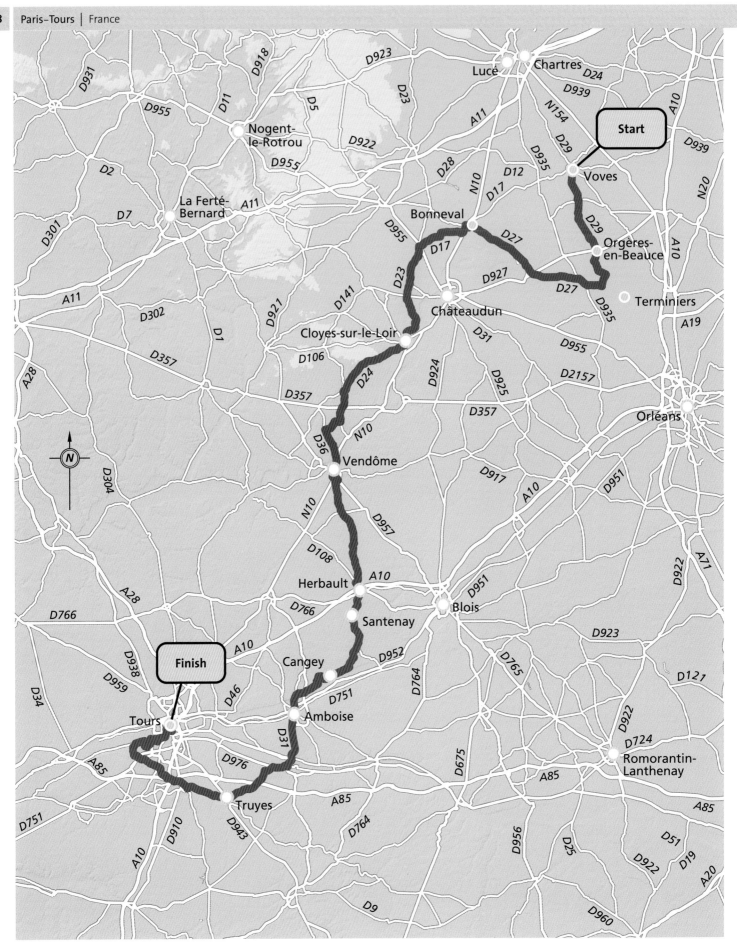

# ▌Directions

▲ These directions are for the 2011 race. The route changes slightly each year so if you wish, you can follow the latest one on the race website instead. It doesn't matter because the nature of the event stays the same.

▲ Head south from Voves towards Terminiers, then take the D27 right to Bonneval. Follow the D17 southwest, turn left on the D23 and continue south to Cloyes-sur-le-Loir. Follow the D24 then D141 south, turning right then left on the D36 through Vendôme to Herbault. Follow signs to Santenay, where you pick up the D1, then the D65, then the D58 south to Cangey.

▲ Turn right on the Rue de Saint-Ouen-les-Vignes, follow this up the hill, then turn left at the summit and left again on the D201. Turn right on the D1 through Limeray and continue to Amboise. Take the D431 then the D31 south out of town then go right through Athée-sur-Cher and follow the D45 southwest to Truyes to go right on the D943. Go left on the D17 to turn right at the D50 junction and descend into Tours on the D127.

▲ Turn right on the D7, then go right towards the Lac des Bretonnières. Turn left along the Avenue des Aubépines, then go right then left at the roundabout and sharp right on the Rue de l'Epan. Take the first exit at the roundabout, then the first right, then go sharp left on the Rue de Beaulieu to the next roundabout, where you take the first exit and join a dual carriageway to go across the River Loire. Turn right along the Boulevard Jean Royer then left onto the Avenue de Grammont.

**The pro peloton heading towards Tours in the Paris–Tours classic**

**Website**
www.letour.com/us/homepage_coursePAT.html

**Date**
The race is in early October, but because there is no Paris–Tours cyclosportive it's entirely up to you when you attempt this one.

**Why the name?**
Many of the classics are place-to-place events. In the early days of cycling, professional riders were sponsored by bike manufacturers, all of whom wanted to show how durable and dependable their bikes were. That's why many of the oldest races are from one place to another, so that they were identifiable journeys that the man and woman in the street could equate with being long-distance. In 1901, when the first ever Paris–Tours race was held, it would have made a big impression because back then covering such a distance involved a full day's train ride.

**Anything else?**
The hills south of Tours, the Touraine vineyards and the Loire Valley are all great for cycling.

**Don't forget**
Because there is no organised event, you have to do Paris–Tours on your own or with a group of friends. You'll need a support vehicle because it's a long way to carry all the food you'll need, and you won't be able to carry enough liquids to stay well hydrated. You also need somebody to pick you up at the finish.

**Distance** 120 kilometres | 75 miles
**Total climbing** 3,100 metres | 10,168 feet
**Route key** Three major Tour de France mountain climbs

# 27 Megève Mont Blanc

Megève Mont Blanc is an ingenious cyclosportive because the event is composed of three distances, and you don't have to specify which one you want to do when you enter. If you want to stop at the end of the first distance, 80 kilometres (50 miles), you can do so and still be near the start. But if you feel good and have made the required time, you can carry on and do the middle distance event of 120 kilometres (75 miles). Then, finally, if you've made the cut for that and want to continue, you can carry on to do the full distance, of up to 150 kilometres.

The Megève Mont Blanc routes change slightly each year, so if you take part in the event you will do a slightly different route to this one. It's the middle distance route from the 2010 event, so that makes it ideal for someone wanting to try a high mountain challenge but who is concerned about lasting the distance.

The route starts and finishes in Megève, right under Mont Blanc. The first section leads down the valley to Flumet, where you change direction to climb the Col des Aravis by its shorter side. It's the first of four climbs on this route, so take it easy. A long descent follows, which goes through La Clusaz to Saint-Jean-de-Sixt. The town stands at the bottom of another famous Tour de France climb, the Col de la Colombière, but you turn left, away from the Colombière to ride through a gap in the mountains created by a tiny river called Le Nom, which is French for name.

It leads to Thônes, where you head south and swing slowly through 180 degrees to reach Manigod on the Col de la Croix Fry climb. This is an exquisite little climb that starts in Thônes but gets steeper here with a series of hairpin bends, and lies like a ladder resting on the north side of the Col des Aravis. According to local legend, the climb was a secret route on which Aravis liqueur was transported, along with Reblochon cheese, a delicacy invented by crafty farmers

who didn't fully milk their cows when their landlords' agents called to take their bosses' share. Once that business was done each day, and the agent gone, the farmers started milking again, and with this richer milk they made delicious Reblochon cheese.

After the Col de la Croix Fry's short descent you have to negotiate the north side of the Aravis, but it's the section with the best hairpin bends in it, and they provide spectacular views down into the valley below. The Aravis ridge above you and to the left is pretty spectacular too, as is the glimpse of Mont Blanc you get as you summit the Aravis.

The Aravis' descent starts with a very technical section, and there have been crashes here during the Megève Mont Blanc event, so take care. The twisting, turning way down straightens out shortly after passing through La Giettaz. Then speed build-up is your main worry; brake early before hitting the streets of Flumet.

The next climb is the last one, but the Col des Saisies is long, and you climb it by the Crest-Voland. This area is very Pyrenean in character, even though it's in the heart of the Alps. The first 3 kilometres (1.8 miles) gains 200 metres (656 feet) then loses half of it in a 1-kilometre descent. After that, the road wriggles upwards at between 6.5 and 8.5 per cent for 6 kilometres (3.7 miles), then continues almost flat for a while. Take this bit nice and easy, because the final kilometre rises at 7 per cent to the summit, this ride's turnaround point. Go back to the Saisies ski resort, and fork right where you climbed up earlier for the main road back down the Saisies. This is part of the Route des Grandes Alpes, a famous tourist route through the mountains, so traffic can be heavy. The descent ends on the edge of Flumet. You head back to Megève along a steadily rising road, with a taste of the Megève Mont Blanc in your legs.

# Directions

▲ Start in Megève and head southwest along the D1212 to Flumet. Turn right on the D909 and climb over the Col des Aravis then keep following the D909 through La Clusaz and Saint-Jean-de-Sixt to Thônes. Turn left on the D12 then left again on the D16 to Manigod.

▲ Follow the D16 over the Col de la Croix Fry then turn right after a short descent onto the D909 and go back over the Aravis. Descend to Flumet and turn right on the Avenue de Saisies then turn left where you see the Col de Saisies direction sign. Retrace your route at the top of the climb and descend on the D218B to Flumet, then go right to Megève.

**A breakaway in the Tour de France with Mont Blanc in the background**

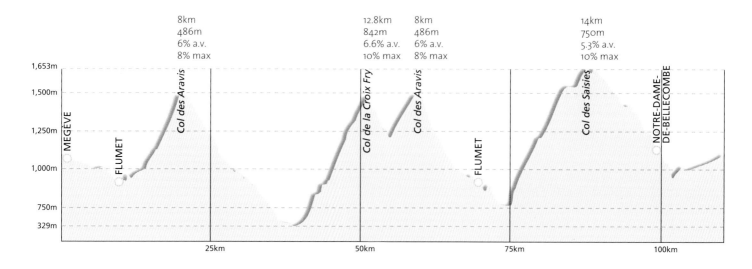

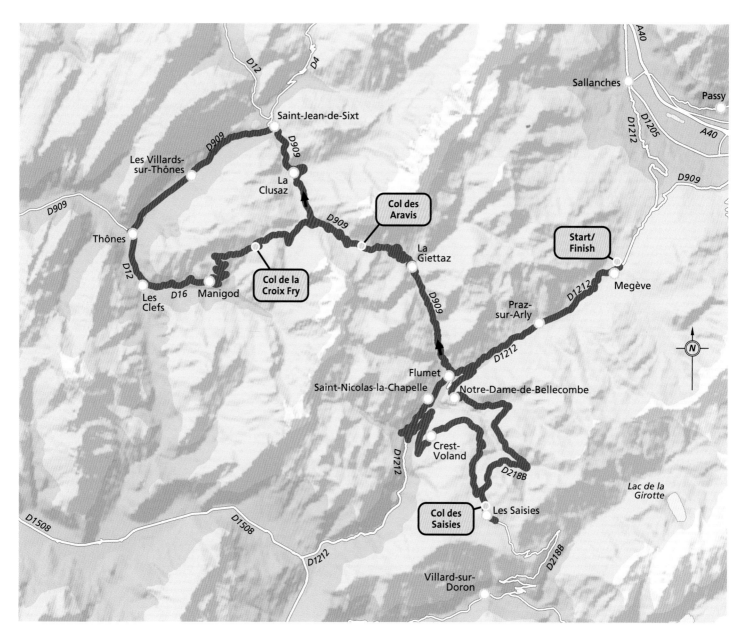

Descending mountains is a skill that improves with practice. Always keep your speed down to where you are comfortable, and be aware of traffic around you. You might not be able to use the whole road like these Tour de France riders

**Website**
www.csportsmegeve.com

**Date**
Early June.

**Why the name?**
It's not just because of the obvious domination of Mont Blanc in this part of France, it's also because the total climbing of the long route is exactly the height of the great mountain.

**Anything else?**
Lots of Tour de France climbs. Just south of the Saisies is the Cormet de Roselend. Get over that and you are in Bourg Saint-Maurice, where three famous Tour climbs start, including the Petit Saint-Bernard and the mighty Col de l'Iseran, which is one of the highest ever climbed by the Tour. Brits might like to visit Cordon, a village just above Sallanches where Barry Hoban became the first British racer ever to win a mountain stage in the Tour de France.

**Don't forget**
Take the usual high-altitude survival kit of light wind- and waterproof clothing. Thin gloves can be a godsend too on descents on chilly days. Eat and drink throughout the ride, erring on the side of more rather than less.

Massif Central

**Distance**  278 kilometres | 172 miles
**Total climbing**  5,310 metres | 17,417 feet
**Route key**  14 significant climbs, and it can be very hot here during the summer

# 28 L'Ardéchoise Marathon

This is the biggest cyclosportive in Europe. Around 16,000 people take part in a four-day festival of cycling, with various events of different lengths including multi-day tours and the mighty Ardéchoise Marathon, a huge undertaking, billed as the hardest cycling challenge in Europe with good reason.

The start and finish place, and the hub of the whole cycling festival, is a village called Saint-Félicien. It's right on the eastern edge of the Ardèche, where you can look across the wide Rhone Valley and see the jagged snow-capped Alps in the hazy distance. The Ardèche is a land of plateaux and deep gorges. It is limestone country, full of ragged peaks and shaggy cliffs.

The Ardéchoise route is long, hard and hilly, but the climbs are nowhere near as big as those in the Alps and Pyrenees, or even further into the Massif Central for that matter. The Ardèche is quite far south and a long way from the cooling effect of the sea, and the highest point on the route is 1,506 metres, so it can get hot here. It's a factor you have to consider should you decide to do this one on your own.

It's not likely to be a problem in the event though, because there aren't many places along the route where you'll be alone, and refreshment is nearly always to hand. Cycling is big anyway in France, but 16,000 extra customers for four days make the Ardéchoise a massive deal for local businesses. It's good for the community, and there is a strong sense of community in rural France. Everybody gets involved with the events, many of them in fancy dress, handing up food and drink or just cheering anything or anybody that moves on wheels. The Ardéchoise is a party for the locals, but it's a serious challenge for those taking part.

The climbing starts almost immediately. There's just a short descent out of Saint-Félicien then you are on the Col du Buisson, and there is not much respite until the end. The next climb, Col de Mézilhac, is tough, then after a couple of lower peaks there's a block of climbing. You go up Col de la Baricaude, a section comprising eight short but hard hills inside 70 kilometres (43 miles), with the highest point of the ride, the Col de la Croix de Boutières, right in the middle.

A long descent leads to the Col de l'Ardéchoise, whose 1,184-metre (3,884-foot) summit is at around the 190-kilometre (118-mile) mark. There's some respite then, with a long descent down through Arcens to Saint-Martin-de-Valamas, where a castle is half sculpted, half built into a rocky pinnacle that stands above the village. With 10 climbs and 210 kilometres (130 miles) behind you, four climbs remain. The Col de Clavière is hard, the Rochepaule is quite easy, but the Col du Lalouvesc is nasty. It's steep in places and the French hill-running championships have been held here several times. However, it's only 25 kilometres (16 miles) to the finish from the summit, nearly all downhill.

Challenges in cycling are a combination of distance and the severity of the route – the Ardéchoise Marathon has both. It is something you need to plan for, train for and take on only when you're confident, and all of those things are even more relevant if you attempt it outside the event. But how satisfying it must be to do it.

# Directions

▲ Because the 278-kilometre Marathon route is a huge undertaking to do outside the supported Ardéchoise event, this shorter sportive route is better suited to solo or unsupported group rides. Start in Saint-Félicien and head west through Pailharès then south over the Col du Buisson to Lamastre, where you take the D578 southwest through Nonières then go through Mézilhac.

▲ Turn right on the D122 then right again on the D116 to head northeast and join the D237 to Saint-Martial. Continue to Saint-Martin-de-Valamas, where you turn left on the D120 and go through Saint-Julien-Boutières to Saint-Agrève, where you pick up the D9 and go north. Take the D214 left fork to Rochepaule. Follow this road towards Lalouvesc, but turn right on the D228 to the top of the Col du Buisson. Turn left at the summit and follow the D273 back to Saint-Félicien.

## Website
www.Ardéchoise.com

## Date
Mid-June.

## Why the name?
The cycling festival is a celebration of this beautiful part of France. L' Ardéchoise was the only name for it.

## Anything else?
The Auvergne is just to the northwest of the Ardèche, a fantastic place to ride, with some classic Tour de France climbs. The region was once dominated by volcanoes and their remains create a gaunt and singular landscape.

## Don't forget
The full marathon is a big undertaking. There are shorter events, including a sportive that is still well over 200 kilometres, if you want to try it out before the big one. The Marathon is a long day out no matter how fit and experienced you are.

Use your training to condition your body to long rides with lots of hills. Focus on doing one really long and hilly ride each week, taking a couple of days easy before and after it. The rest of your training should consist of making hard efforts uphill, harder than you will make on the day of the challenge.

L' Ardéchoise is a challenge where you must have your nutrition strategy well organised. You will burn a lot of calories, probably around 8,000, maybe more. That's a lot of food you need to eat on the move, and a lot for your stomach to process. Work on nutrition during your long training rides, and stick rigidly to the pattern you develop throughout the challenge. You will need support if you do this ride outside the event, but there is some useful information on the event website about where you can buy food en route.

**Below left: View from Saint-Félicien with the Alps in the distance**
**Below right: Competitors in the Paris–Nice event racing through the Ardèche**

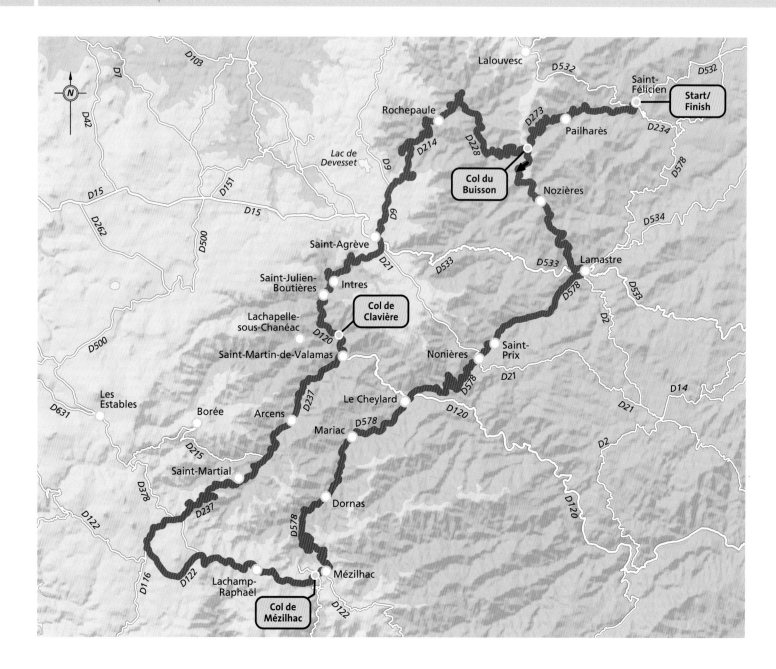

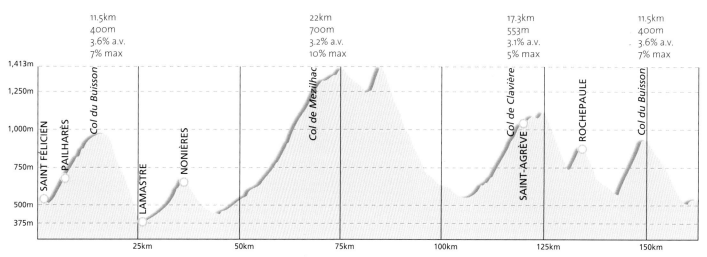

## The Alps

**Distance** 155 kilometres | 97 miles
**Total climbing** 5,180 metres | 16,990 feet
**Route key** Three of the hardest and most famous mountain climbs in the Tour de France

# 29 La Marmotte

In many respects La Marmotte is the ultimate cyclosportive event. It was first held in 1982, so it's one of the oldest sportives, but it's also one of the most beautiful. An elegant circuit of three mountains steeped in Tour de France history, when you ride La Marmotte you ride the path of champions.

The climbs are the Col du Glandon, the Col du Télégraphe, the Col du Galibier and Alpe d'Huez, where La Marmotte ends on the Avenue du Rif Nel at 1,860 metres (6,102 feet) above sea level. It starts in Le Bourg-d'Oisans, the town at the foot of Alpe d'Huez, and the first leg rolls gently down the Romanche Valley to Rochetaillée, where the fun starts.

The southern ascent of the Col du Glandon shares a road with the Col de la Croix de Fer, which splits only when close to their summits. A short, sharp pull up a hydroelectric dam leads to a lake, where the gradient eases before slowly racking up to 10 per cent. There's a steep descent after Rivier d'Allemont, then a brutal stretch of 12 per cent climbing. This is hard, but there's a lot worse to come.

Eventually the gradient settles and you leave the tree-lined ascent to enter a wide-open world of turquoise lakes, lush green meadows and snowy peaks. The surroundings are spectacular, but it's a long slog to the junction where the left fork leads to the top of the Glandon and the way straight ahead leads to the top of the Croix de Fer.

The final uphill part of the Glandon is steep, but so is its descent. It's frighteningly fast, especially near the top and bottom. Take extreme care here. The descent was neutralised during the 2010 Marmotte event to prevent people taking risks to improve their time. It ends in the Maurienne Valley, where you turn right, and you should take time to eat and drink while heading for the start of the Col du Télégraphe.

This is one of the oldest Tour de France climbs. First used by the race in 1911, when the road over its summit was little more than a goat track, the Galibier is really two climbs in one. First you climb the Col du Télégraphe, then there's a very short descent to the ski town of Valloire, and then you begin the Galibier proper. Together they represent nearly 30 kilometres (18.6 miles) uphill and you will reach 2,626 metres (8,613 feet) on top of the Galibier.

It's a really grounding experience. The Galibier is vast. You ride along a huge valley towards what looks like a solid wall of jagged rock, then, after an age of going upwards, in front of you the road swings right in a fierce hairpin bend to begin the final slog. It's hard and it's high. The Galibier's summit hosted the highest ever finish in Tour de France history in 2011, and the first part of the descent is exposed and scary. In 1935 a Spanish racer called Francisco Cepeda plunged to his death off this road.

The narrow and really steep part of the descent leads to the summit of another pass, the Col du Lautaret, which carries the main D1091 road between Briançon and Grenoble. You turn right to follow this road down the valley, where it still twists and turns and goes through a number of tunnels. Eventually the road straightens somewhat and flattens out just before you reach Le Bourg-d'Oisans. Use this section to eat and drink ready for the final climb, but not too much because it's just around the corner.

Alpe d'Huez begins with a long upward ramp to the first of its famous 21 hairpin bends. Each one is numbered, counting down your progress to the top, and each has a plaque bearing the name of a Tour de France stage winner on the climb. Riding here provides both a history lesson and inspiring views of the extravagance of nature. Alpe d'Huez is amazing; the road winds so the straights pile on top of each other like rungs of a wonky ladder up what is virtually a rock face. Reaching the top is one of the finest feelings in cycling.

# ❙ Directions

▲ From Le Bourg-d'Oisans head northwest on the D1091. Turn right in Rochetaillée and follow the D526 then D926 to turn left on the D927 over the Col du Glandon. At the end of the descent turn right on the D1006 and follow it to Saint-Michel-de-Maurienne.

▲ Turn right on the D902 to climb over the Col du Télégraphe. Descend through Valloire and climb the Col du Galibier. Descend to the Col du Lautaret summit, where you turn right on the D1091. At Le Bourg-d'Oisans, take the first exit at the roundabout to join the D211 and continue to the top of Alpe d'Huez.

## Website

www.sportcommunication.info. Click on the Union Jack symbol for an English translation, then 'Events', then on La Marmotte on the interactive map.

## Date

July.

## Why the name?

*Marmottes* are buck-toothed gofer-like creatures that live high up in the Alps and seem to survive on nothing.

## Anything else?

There's almost too much. This is the centre of the Alps, playground of the Tour de France for over a century. There are famous Tour de France climbs on both sides of the Romanche and Maurienne valleys.

## Don't forget

This ride goes high, well over 2,000 metres in places. Even in summer it can be cold. Study the weather forecast before you ride and dress accordingly, and even in hot weather take a top that you can put on at the peak of climbs to take off the chill on the descents. Make sure you eat and drink during the ride, and eat plenty before it. La Marmotte is one of the most demanding cycling challenges you'll face, so prepare for it accordingly. Hone your cornering skills. Brake before a corner, not in it, and only go at the speed you are comfortable with.

**Tour de France riders on Alpe d'Huez**

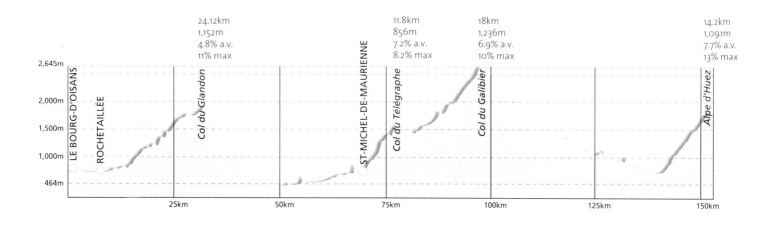

24.12km  
1,152m  
4.8% a.v.  
11% max

11.8km  
856m  
7.2% a.v.  
8.2% max

18km  
1,236m  
6.9% a.v.  
10% max

14.2km  
1,091m  
7.7% a.v.  
13% max

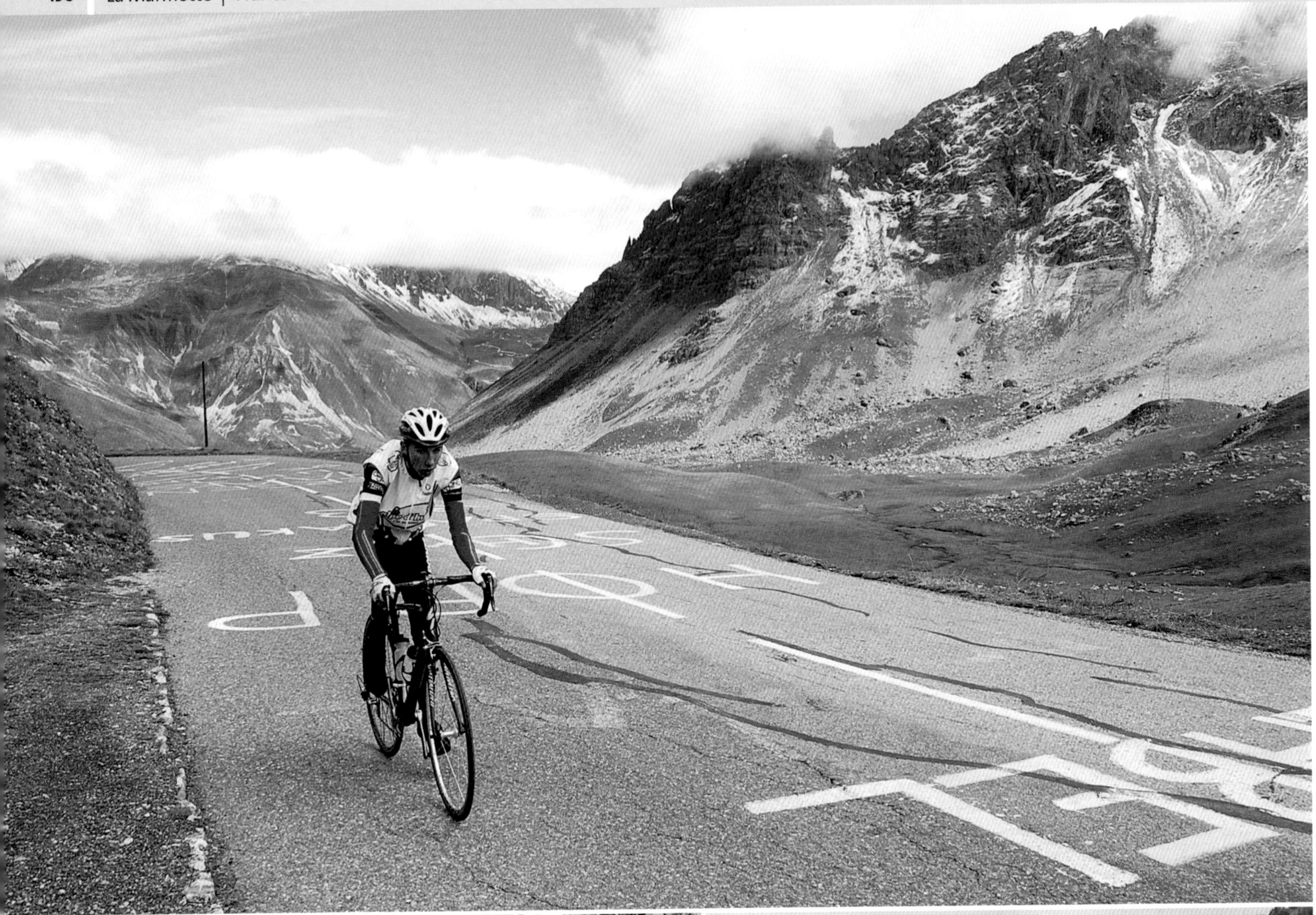

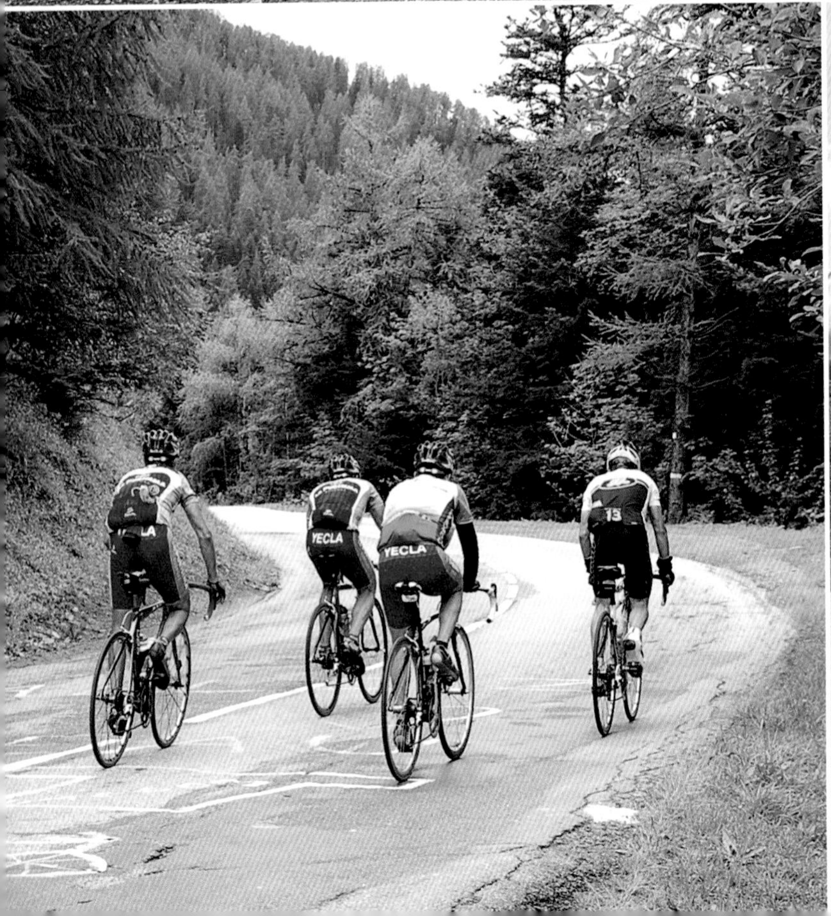
YECLA
YECLA

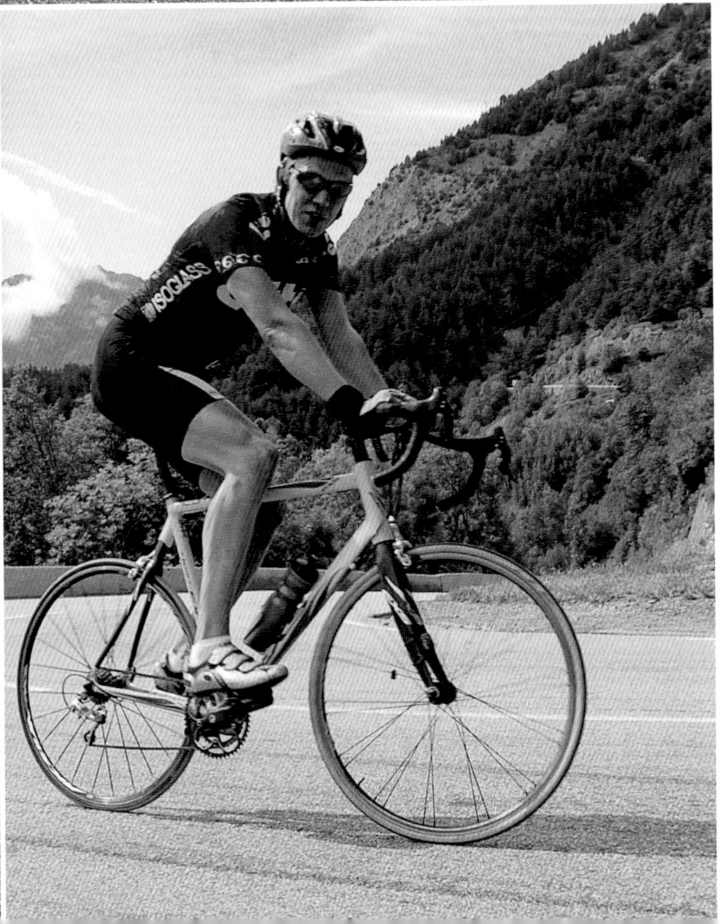

Provence

**Distance** 137 kilometres | 85.62 miles
**Total climbing** 4,400 metres | 14,432 feet
**Route key** Three ascents of one of the hardest mountain climbs in cycling

# **30** Cinglés du Ventoux

Mont Ventoux dominates the landscape for miles around the Vaucluse. Its white peak is the highest point by far, and it's a mountain of mystery that has provoked fear and fascination over the centuries. The first ever recorded mountain climb done for recreation was accomplished here in the 14th century by the Italian poet and scholar Petrarch, and it set the scene for centuries of physical endeavour on the mountain.

The Ventoux is part of cycling folklore now, although the Tour de France didn't visit here until 1951. When it did, though, the mountain quickly captured the imagination of cyclists all over the world, because it inspired some epic struggles on its uncompromising, sun-bleached slopes. Then the Ventoux's place in cycling history was sealed when British rider Tom Simpson collapsed and died just a mile from its summit during the 1967 Tour de France.

Cinglés du Ventoux is a simple but very testing challenge. There are three paved roads to the top of Mont Ventoux, and the Cinglés challenge is to climb all three in a day. You can do it at any time you like, provided the roads are open and not blocked by snow.

You need to obtain a route control card from the Club des Cinglés du Mont-Ventoux (their website explains how to do this) and the card must be stamped in the town you choose to start from: Bédoin, Malaucène or Sault. I think it's best to do the challenge in that order, but you can do it any way you want; all you do is ride to the summit from each town in turn.

The Bédoin ascent is probably the hardest, although it doesn't feel any easier from Malaucène, and the average gradients of both are identical. But Bédoin is potentially the route that will be highest in temperature, because it climbs from the south. For that reason it's good to get it out of the way early. Another point in Bédoin's favour is that it's the side the Tour de France always uses, so it's the most historic.

Get your card stamped in a shop or by the tourist office and off you go. The first few kilometres are relatively easy, then you turn left in a village called Saint-Estève and the road rears up to 10 per cent and stays that way for the next 7 kilometres (4.5 miles). It's hard and unrelenting, and the best way to cope is to gear low and spin your legs, staying seated as much as possible. Towards the end of this steep section the trees thin out and you break clear of them just before a cafe called the Chalet Reynard.

You can see the white summit now for what it is, a mass of bare, shattered white rock that reflects the sun's light and heat and seems to magnify both. Thankfully the gradient lessens a bit until you are past the Simpson memorial stone, then the last kilometre and a half, especially the last bend, are really steep.

Get your card stamped at the souvenir or sweet shop at the top then descend to Malaucène, where another merchant must stamp the card, then turn around and ride back to the top. This side has a steeper start than the south side and the gradient varies a bit, although it averages out as the same. The road changes direction more often than on the south side, so the upward slog is less intimidating. The treeline is higher, so there is more shelter, and it's cooler because you are on the north side of the mountain.

With your card stamped at the summit again, you descend at first on the same road that you came on from Bédoin, but then you turn left after Chalet Reynard and continue down to Sault.

Another stamp at a local shop (although it's worth noting that the Club des Cinglés does allow photographic evidence that you were at a destination on the mountain, provided that the date and time certifies the photograph, which is useful if you want to start really early in the morning), then

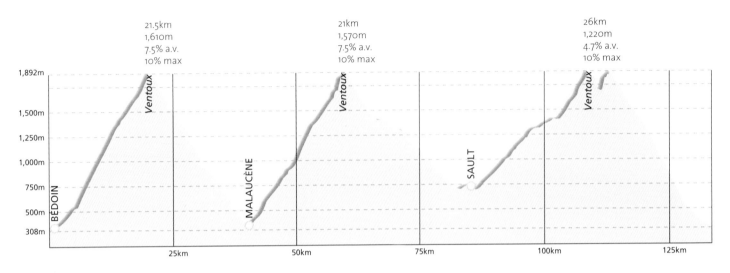

21.5km
1,610m
7.5% a.v.
10% max

21km
1,570m
7.5% a.v.
10% max

26km
1,220m
4.7% a.v.
10% max

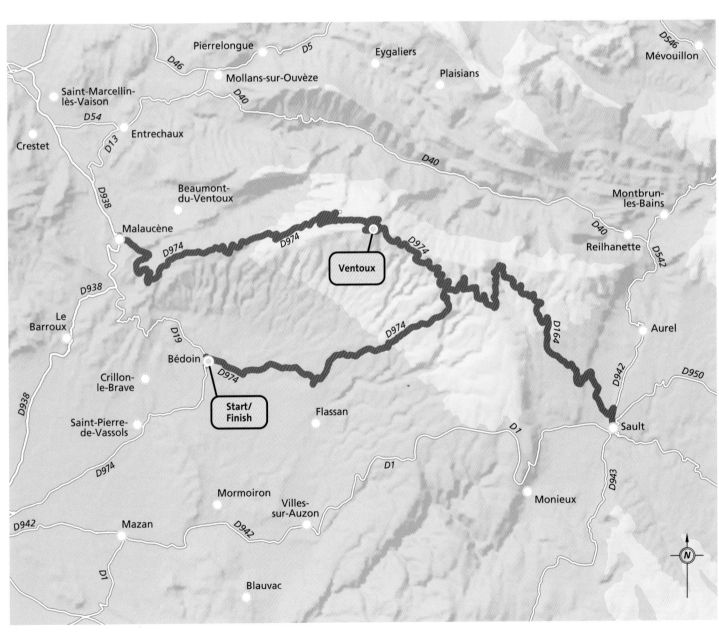

you climb back to the top from Sault, which is the longest ascent but by far the easiest. This side has the least height gain and the gradient doesn't exceed 6 per cent until past Chalet Reynard, where you climb the last part of the way as you did from Bédoin.

There's just one descent left now, back down the side you started going up, but it isn't over until you get there. Take care on this descent because tiredness creeps up on you and your attention can wander. If you are descending the Bédoin side, there are a lot of long, steep straights, so watch your speed.

Above: Nearing the summit of Mont Ventoux. Above right: The final corner

# Directions

▲ From Bédoin, follow the D974 over the summit and down into Malaucène. Turn around and ride back up the Ventoux following the D974 over the summit. Turn left at Chalet Reynard on the descent and follow the D164 to Sault. Turn around and ride the D164 to the summit for a final time, then return to Bédoin.

**Website**
www.clubcinglesventoux.org and click on the English version.

**Date**
Any time, but the Club des Cinglés recommends restricting attempts to between early April and late September.

**Why the name?**
*Cinglé* is the French word for crazy, so completing the challenge qualifies you as a member of the Ventoux Crazy Gang. The challenge has been going since 1988 and there are well over 5,000 members now.

**Anything else?**
Once you've done three, why not four? There's a fourth way up the Ventoux by a loose-surfaced forestry road. Add that to the three surfaced ascents in one day and the Club des Cinglés will make you a Galérien, or 'Galley Slave'. If you do the three ascents twice each in a day, they make you a Bicinglette. It's only 171 miles, half of it uphill and 8,800 metres (28,864 feet) of climbing. Only 56 people had done it at the time of writing, but if you think they are

inspiring then consider Jean-Pascal Roux: in May 2006 he climbed the Ventoux 11 times in 24 hours.

**Don't forget**
Check the weather before you start and dress accordingly. Carry a thin rain top or gilet that you can put on at the top for the descents if it's chilly. There can be huge temperature differences between the bottom and top, even in summer, and there can also be very little difference too. As with all long mountain climbs, ride within yourself, spin rather than push your pedals, and keep eating and especially drinking. Heat exhaustion can be a factor in this part of France.

The Pyrenees

**Distance** 174 kilometres | 108.75 miles
**Total climbing** 3,750 metres | 12,300 feet
**Route key** Three major Tour de France climbs

# 31 Etape du Tour 2010

The Etape du Tour is a full stage of the Tour de France. It changes each year and is usually one of the hardest stages in that year's race. It's a chance for anyone to ride the full course, over the full terrain and distance that the Tour racers negotiate on one day in their three-week journey around France. The Etape turned 21-years-old in 2013; not the oldest cyclosportive, but for many it is the gold standard of cycling challenges.

It's very rare for the Etape not to be a mountain stage of the Tour, and the one I have picked to represent the challenge comes from the 2010 Tour de France. The stage was set in the Pyrenees, and it celebrated the first time, 100 years before in 1910, that Tour de France riders climbed mountains of this scale.

This Etape challenge goes from Pau to the summit of the historic Col du Tourmalet, the highest pass used by the Tour de France in the Pyrenees, and the climb that has featured in more editions of the race than any other. It debuted on that day back in 1910, and when you climb now it will leave you in awe of the heroics that were involved on that journey into the unknown 100 years ago.

The stage route is quite flat for the first 45 kilometres (28 miles) to Oloron-Sainte-Marie. It's quite busy, so as you won't be doing this route in an event, where the course must be followed precisely, a quieter alternative can be had by following the main road to the Gan village turn-off then picking up the D24 to Oloron. You rejoin the N134 there and continue south to Escot, where the day's first climb starts. Again, there are quieter roads that run almost alongside the main one, which are more suitable for cyclists.

The Col de Marie-Blanque begins in Escot. It's 9.5 kilometres (6 miles) long with an easy start and a very difficult top part. There are quite a few gradient changes in between too. The Pyrenees are older than the Alps and their worn topography doesn't lend itself to the constant gradients you find on Alpine climbs. The top part of the Marie-Blanque is a real test, with gradients well over 10 per cent. Trees hide the summit to prolong the agony, so other than the occasional signpost you never know how far you are from it until the final 100 metres (328 feet).

Keep a lookout for bears on the Marie-Blanque. The indigenous species that used to live in these mountains gave the Tour organisers sleepless nights when they came here 100 years ago. Bear attacks on humans weren't common back then but they happened, and because the Tour wasn't yet a big sporting event, and the field spread out over many hours on these roads, the organisers worried that a lone cyclist could be at risk. Many of the riders covered long sections of that first Pyrenean stage in isolation, and in the dark. Indigenous bears have since been hunted almost to extinction; the bears you might encounter today are ancestors of a few Slovenian bears that were released here several years ago.

There's a twisting descent from the top of Marie-Blanque to Bielle, then the road trends downhill for 20 kilometres (12.5 miles) towards Asson. The route turns sharp right and you enter the Ouzon Valley, where the Col du Soulor begins. This is a 13-kilometre (8-mile) climb with an average of 7 per cent, but it has two distinct halves. The first 5 kilometres (3 miles) from Etchartes rise steadily from 2.5 to 7 per cent, then the gradient changes every kilometre after that, jumping between 7 and 9 per cent all the way to the top.

The first part of the Soulor's descent is quite tricky and technical, but it straightens out after around 3 kilometres (2 miles) and you can really get up some speed during the next stretch to Argelès-Gazost. Still, don't overdo this section because the hardest climb is still to come.

Belgian world champion Tom Boonen on the Col du Tourmalet during the 2006 Tour de France

The Tourmalet starts in the Gorge de Luz at Luz Saint-Sauveur after a steadily rising trek south from Argelès-Gazost. You turn sharp left just after the town centre and the climb starts with a quite manageable section, but the rest is horrible. It's 10 miles to the top from here, 10 miles where the gradient bounces between 7 and 9 per cent until the final kilometre, when it jumps to 10 per cent with some short sections higher than that.

The summit of the Tourmalet is unforgettable. The road goes through a tight V-shaped notch in a low, rocky wall and over a knife-edge. One minute you are going up, the next down. But into this tiny space they've crammed a cafe and a giant metal sculpture of a cyclist riding out of the saddle. The surreal feeling of the place is further reinforced if you venture over the top because a large herd of llamas live on the threadbare meadows around the ski station of La Mongie below.

The route ends at the summit, but because this is a place-to-place challenge you'll need someone to meet you at the end to take you back to your base. La Mongie is the best base to choose because it's easy to find and there are places where you can get a meal.

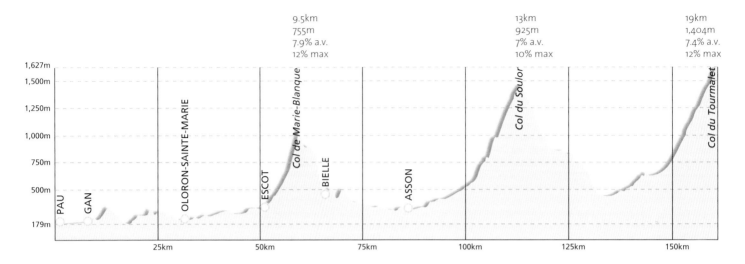

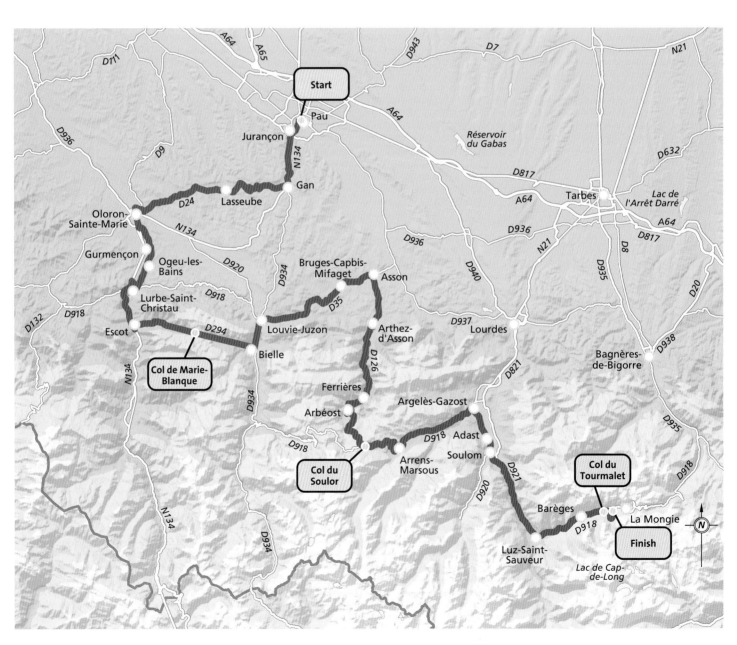

Above: The Etape switches mountain ranges from year to year.  Top right: Every cyclist wants to ride the Etape, even track sprinters like Sir Chris Hoy, who did it in 2006.  Bottom right: The finish attracts a huge crowd

# Directions

▲ Head south out of Pau on the N134, either direct to Oloron-Sainte-Marie or following the D24 from Gan to the same place. The 2010 Etape followed the busy N134 further south, but there are quieter roads that shadow this one. Whichever you choose, continue south to Escot, where you turn left to begin the Col de Marie-Blanque.

▲ Descend to Bielle then turn left on the D934 to Louvie-Juzon, where you go right on the D35 to Asson. Turn right on the D126 to climb the Col du Soulor. Go left at the summit and follow the D918 to Argelès-Gazost, then turn right on the D921 to Luz-Saint-Sauveur. Follow the signs for the Col du Tourmalet, following the D918 to the summit.

**Website**
www.letapedutour.com

**Date**
Always during the Tour de France and usually the middle week, so the second week of July.

**Why the name?**
*Etape* is French for stage, as in the stage of a race.

**Anything else?**
The Pyrenees are a cyclist's playground. There are mountains that have featured in the race everywhere you turn. But for a novel challenge that hasn't featured in the Tour, just follow the N921 south from Luz-Saint-Sauveur. Climb

through Gavarnie to the Cirque de Gavarnie and follow the road up to the top of the 2,270-metre (7,447-foot) ridge that is the border with Spain. It's a wild, high-altitude experience.

**Don't forget**
You need someone to meet you at the finish for transport. Ideally they should also drive part of the route to support you with drinks and food. However, there are some towns and villages with shops, so you could manage without that as long as you take plenty of food and drink with you and keep some of it back for emergencies. You need to carry a rain/wind top, and gloves can help. There can be huge temperature differences between the valleys and mountains of the Pyrenees.

Belgium

**Distance** 249 kilometres / 155.6 miles
**Total climbing** 1,250 metres / 4,100 feet
**Route key** 17 short but steep climbs, the majority of them paved with cobblestones

# 32 Tour of Flanders

Cycling has never been more popular than it is in Britain just now, but it has always been popular in continental Europe. However, even on the continent there are some cycling hotspots, and none are hotter than Flanders. Many people in the Dutch-speaking half of Belgium follow bike racing with an almost religious zeal, and even those who don't try to watch the Tour of Flanders.

The Tour of Flanders is not only a celebration of Flemish cycling and the unique terrain that helps to make it so exciting; it also serves to usher in the spring for the whole country. Flemish children are taught that the racers' colours are a metaphor for spring flowers. The race is so important that it's very hard for an outsider to win it, all the more so because Flanders has produced many more world-class road racers than is warranted by its size.

The first Tour of Flanders was held in 1913, and there have been many different routes, although they all include some of the short steep hills that are arranged along a ridge in East Flanders called the Flemish Ardennes. For many years the organisers settled on the route described here, which is the route from 2011. It changed in 2012, quite controversially, and cycling fans have yet to warm to the new one. Somehow the new route seems to have taken the edge off the excitement.

The full-length Tour of Flanders cyclosportive (there are shorter options on the same day) runs over the new full course. But if you do the Tour of Flanders challenge at any other time it's best to follow this old route; it's the one with the most history and the one that climbs the most iconic hill in Flanders, which the new one doesn't.

The iconic climb is the Muur van Geraardsbergen, which in English means the Geraardsbergen Wall. And that's what it is: a wall – not literally, of course, but it may as well be for

the effect its twisting, cobbled super-steep surface has on the strongest legs. It used to be the penultimate climb, the decision-maker that decreed who could or who couldn't win the race, but more of the Muur later.

The route starts on the outskirts of Brugge and heads south across the flat plain of West Flanders, then turns east through the city of Kortrijk into East Flanders and towards the ridge. The route hits the hills in Anzegem with the Tiegemberg. *Berg* is the Flemish word for hill. You will have completed 100 kilometres (62 miles) by now, but the ride has just started. It goes up one side of the ridge, along the top, down the same side, then back up and along the top again.

On and on it goes, sometimes going from one side of the ridge to the other, sometimes doubling back on itself, but all with the three recurring rhythms of the race; up and along, down and back up again, or up and over. There are 18 significant hills and many more changes of direction, all on tiny farm roads punctuated occasionally by flat stretches of concrete slab road called *betonweg*.

It's hard. Your body will be rattled by the cobblestones, your legs and lungs burned by the uphill slogs, your nerves tested by the steep downhills and sharp bends, while the concrete roads pound the base of your skull, bump, bump, bump, as you roll over the regular joints in them.

But even in the tough, uncompromising landscape of Flanders, there are some sections that stand out. The Oude Kwaremont, a cobbled road that just goes on and on. The Koppenberg, so steep and so rough that even great pro racers have had to walk part of it, pushing their bikes in solemn silence, sad as grounded eagles.

Then there's the Muur, or Muur-Kapelmuur to give it its race name. The *kapel* is a chapel on top of the hill, and fans came here each year to watch the race as pilgrims do

Above: Sculpture on the Muur van Geraardsbergen dedicated to the fans who stand by the roadside during Belgian bike races. They and it are called 'Wielervolk': cycling people

Above: Race-deciding action near the summit of the Muur

to a shrine. The town of Geraardsbergen spreads up this hill, and the road switches this way and that through its streets. The pavements are lined 10-deep on race day, with every vantage point snaffled up in the early morning. As well as hitting a wall of a hill, the racers hit a wall of sound as they throw themselves at this climb. And every year, no matter how many were still in contention at the bottom of the Muur, very few are left 475 metres (1,558 feet) later at the top.

Then finally there's the Bosberg, which means wooded hill, and it is just that, a hill in the woods. It's not very steep, the cobblestones aren't too rough, but with well over 200

kilometres (124 miles) done on this switchback, sawtooth route, the Bosberg feels like Everest. There have been some great moments at this point in the race, some epic attacks that left everyone for dead; they should be your mental image. The fact that it's nearly all downhill from the top to the finish helps too.

When you've finished the race, to appreciate how big a part cycling and the Tour of Flanders play in Flemish society, take a walk up the Muur. Its slopes are littered with references to the Tour of Flanders, and the great Belgians who have won it, expressed through works of art, photographs and even poems.

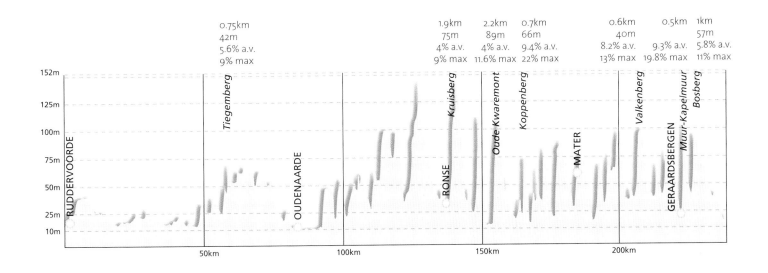

0.75km
42m
5.6% a.v.
9% max

1.9km
75m
4% a.v.
9% max

2.2km
89m
4% a.v.
11.6% max

0.7km
66m
9.4% a.v.
22% max

0.6km
40m
8.2% a.v.
13% max

0.5km
57m
9.3% a.v.
19.8% max

1km
57m
5.8% a.v.
11% max

152m
125m
100m
75m
50m
25m
10m

RUDDERVOORDE
Tiegemberg
OUDENAARDE
RONSE
Kruisberg
Oude Kwaremont
Koppenberg
MATER
Valkenberg
GERAARDSBERGEN
Muur-Kapelmuur
Bosberg

50km    100km    150km    200km

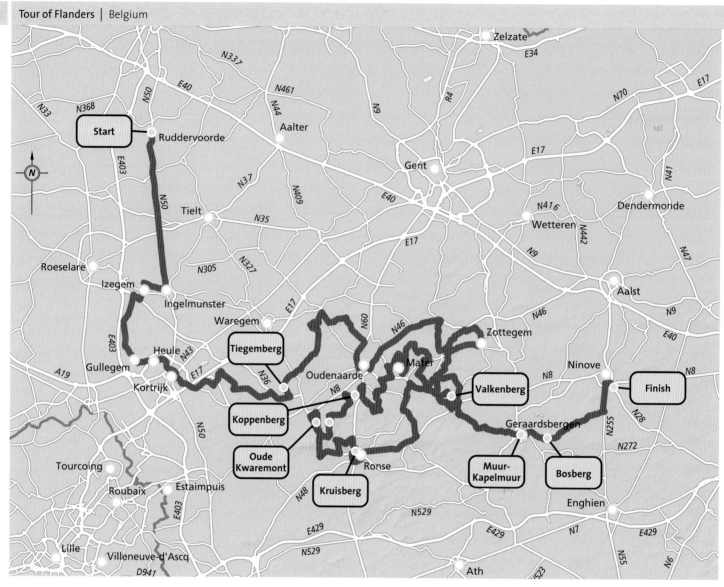

# ▌Directions

▲ Start in Ruddervoorde on the N50 south of Brugge. Turn right in Ingelmunster then left to Izegem. Turn right on Rijksweg then left to go through Gullegem, Kortrijk and Zwevegem to Tiegem. Turn left to Anzegem and follow the N494 to Kruishoutem. Turn right then left towards Huise, go right through the centre of Oudenaarde, left through Eine, over the river then left along the N46. Go through Nederzwalm, then go right onto the N415. After Munkzwalm turn left to Velzeke-Ruddershove, right to Zottegem and right onto the N454.

▲ Turn south through Rozebeke. Head for the N415 where you turn left. Turn right on the N8 then left on the N454. Turn left to Bossgat then right to La Houppe, where you turn right

and follow the N48 to Ronse. Turn right on the N60 then left on the N425, then go left to Russeignies. Turn right and head north towards Berchem. Turn right before entering Berchem, then right through Kwaremont, left on the N36, and first left towards Melden. Turn right at the bottom of the hill then right again after the Koppenberg, then first left on the N60 through Markedaal, following signs to Taaienberg then Etikhove. Turn right on the N457 then left up the Eikenberg, then right on the N8 and left on the N441. Turn right towards Mater and go left on outskirts. Head north to the Zwadderkotmolen and turn right. Take the first right and go through Mater, branching left on Keirestraat, then turn left along Jagerij. Continue north and turn right

then left to Sint-Blasius-Boekel. Turn right on the N454 then left on Meersestraat. Turn left in Sint-Kornelis-Horebeke, then left up the Leberg. Turn right on the N415. Follow the N8 but go straight along Kleistraat. Take the second right, then first left after the N48. Go left again into Brakel, turn right on the N493 and follow this into Geraardsbergen. Follow signs to the Muur. Cross the N495 after the top, then go right on Brusselsestraat and go through Atembeke, then though woods (Bosberg) to Denderwindeke. Turn left on the N255 to Ninove, right on the N8, then right on the N28 into Meerbeke, where the Tour of Flanders finishes. Continue right on Sint-Peitersstraat then left on Leopoldlaan. Follow the N8 and go right to Centrumlaan for the sportive finish.

The Tour of Flanders field with a clear view of the ridge of hills behind them where the race is decided

## Website
http://sport.be.msn.com/classicchallenge
and click on 'Ronde van Vlaanderen cylco'.

## Date
The day before the professional race, which is usually held on the first Sunday in April.

## Why the name?
Belgium is a country divided by language. The south is French-speaking and in the north they speak Dutch. However, many Flemish people feel more of an affinity with the old County of Flanders. This included part of northern France and a bit of southwest Holland. The Tour of Flanders began because Flanders wanted to state its own identity, something it already had done, and has continued to do, through the number of top cyclists it has produced. The Flanders flag, a back lion with red tongue and claws on a yellow background, can be seen all round the route, often waved and flown as a political statement as much as in support of the race.

## Anything else?
There are hundreds of bike races each year in Flanders. Every village fete has a race, called a *kermesse*, which does multiple laps up the main street and along surrounding side roads. They have a unique atmosphere and details of where they are held are published in newspapers. If you do this challenge outside the event, then it's well worth trying to watch a *kermesse*.

## Don't forget
Even if you do the full race distance as part of the organised event, you must provide your own support vehicle. And since the race is held in early April, you will start in the dark, so take lights that you can detach easily from your bike and put in the vehicle when no longer needed. You need to be fit for this one, plus you need to be as agile as you are strong on your bike. It's a complicated route, so downloading it onto a GPS is almost essential.

West Flanders

**Distance** 236 kilometres / 147.5 miles
**Total climbing** 1,845 metres / 6,051 feet
**Route key** Several short but hard climbs and wind blowing in from the coast

# **33** Gent–Wevelgem

This is one of Belgium's two other classics. It's not held in quite the same esteem as the two most legendary races, the Tour of Flanders and Liège–Bastogne–Liège, but it's still a career-making race to win, and many of the best ever bike racers have won it. The route is long and hard, and the crosswinds along the coast and short hills in a part of Flanders called Heuvelland always ensure a worthy winner.

There is a Gent–Wevelgem cyclosportive, but this race has a different first section. In order to minimise the participants' logistics problems, the sportive starts and finishes in Wevelgem, not further north in Deinze like the pros do. The sportive is also shorter, but if you do this one outside the event you may as well go for the whole thing, which is the spirit of this book anyway. We've featured the pro route, but the sportive version also contains most of what Gent–Wevelgem is about.

The first leg goes west to the Belgian coast then turns left to run along the coast road towards France. This is the first difficulty of Gent–Wevelgem; some ferocious winds can blow in off the North Sea. The cyclosportive misses this section out but it's worth doing it if you ride this one outside the event to get the full Gent–Wevelgem effect.

Without doubt, the key to this route is the hills that rise out of the Flanders plain on either side of the French–Belgian border. The route turns towards them and away from the sea just south of Veurne, where the prevailing wind helps the race accelerate towards the first hill, which is over the border in France. It's tempting to hammer this section, but just use the wind to up your pace a bit, keeping something back for what's to come.

You can see Mont Cassel for miles; the flat-topped, conical hill with a walled town on top looks like it comes from a fairytale. The route climbs up past newer houses then goes through a gate called the Porte de Dunkerque before entering the old town. You turn sharp right, clatter along the cobbled main street, then the route descends back down onto the plain. After that, you return to the summit by an even smaller road. Cassel is a great place to stop at a cafe; there are some lovely ones along the main street. Otherwise, press on, because there are more hills to come.

The Mont des Cats is still in France, although this area was once part of the County of Flanders, which is why you see village names here like Godewaersvelde and Steenvoorde. You enter Belgium just past the 100-mile point and climb the Rodeberg, which is where the Gent–Wevelgem race starts a circuit that it repeats twice. You should too, if you want the full effect.

There's a big hill with communication masts on top of it in front of you now, and you keep to the road that goes around the left side of it, heading for Kemmel village. The hill is the Kemmelberg, the most famous climb in this race but a place also made famous by the death and destruction that occurred here during World War I. At 159 metres (521 feet) high, the hill was a key strategic point, and it came under attack during the 1918 spring offensive by the German army. It was held by the Allies but later lost, and in the fighting more than 120,000 died. The memory of so many dead cannot be separated from the Kemmelberg, and the hill is littered with stark reminders of their passing.

It's a tough climb, going up a concrete road out of Kemmel village that turns to cobblestones after a sharp right turn. It also gets much steeper here, and it's a real slog to the wooded top. Take care now because the first part of the descent is 20 per cent, and you are still riding on cobblestones. You pass the Kemmel Ossuary, where the remains of 5,000 unidentified soldiers are buried.

Gent–Wevelgem is notorious for the crosswinds that make the racers fan out across the road in echelons so they can shelter from it. The wind is blowing from your right in this picture

The route then climbs the Rodeberg again and traces the same way as before between that hill and the Kemmelberg for a second ascent of that, too. After that, you come off the circuit, over another climb, then head for Ieper (Ypres). There is a lumpy section of road around Zanvoorde to negotiate before the flat final leg to Wevelgem.

Gent–Wevelgem is always a finely balanced and fascinating race: a battle between the hard men who can rip the peloton to shreds in the crosswind and blast their way up the cobbled climbs, and the sprinters, who, if they find themselves at the finish with the leaders, will fly past everyone to take the victory.

# I Directions

▲ From Deinze head west through Tielt and Pittem, taking the N35 to Lichtervelde then the N32 north to Torhout. Follow the N33 to Oostende and turn left on the N341 and follow the N318 to Nieuwpoort. Pick up the N39 to Veurne then Adinkerke and turn inland to go through Leisele and Oost-Cappel, then over the French border through Herzeele to Wormhout.

▲ Head south for Cassel and turn right at the top of the hill to do a circuit through Oxelaëre back into Cassel. Turn right at the top of the hill again, this time in the opposite direction through Eecke, crossing the A25 to Godewaersvelde, where you turn right. Climb over the Mont de Cats then Mont Noir to turn right in Westouter and climb the Rodeberg, turning right on the N304 to Kemmel.

▲ Climb the Kemmelberg, then turn left at the next three crossroads and right at the fourth. Turn right on the N322 then left on Gildestraat to climb the Rodeberg the way you did previously. Follow the previous route through Kemmel over the Kemmelberg but carry straight on at the fourth crossroads, where you turned right after the last ascent of the Kemmelberg. Continue to Ieper. Go right on the N37B then right to Zillebeke and continue to Zandvoorde, where you turn left, head northeast over the N8 and go right just after the motorway bridge. Turn left on the N8 and follow it through Menen into Wevelgem.

Top: Riders take to the paths to avoid rough cobbled roads where they can
Bottom: Gent–Wevelgem winner Nico Mattan (right) rides the Kemmelberg with British pro Dan Lloyd

**Website**
www.gent-wevelgem-cyclo.be

**Date**
The end of March.

**Why the name?**
The original race went from the centre of the city of Gent to Wevelgem. Increased traffic has made starting in Gent impractical, so the start point was moved to Deinze, just south of the city.

**Anything else?**
The part of France just south of this route, an area inside the triangle of Calais, Boulogne and Saint-Omer, is fantastic cycling country, a mix of wooded hills and marshes that is way off the tourist track.

**Don't forget**
If you do the place-to-place route from Deinze, a support vehicle would be a great help. Don't go too hard on the long, flat section at the start of this route, because the hills at the end are quite demanding. In training it's a good idea to make some hard efforts in a high gear of about three to four minutes' duration to simulate the hills of this challenge.

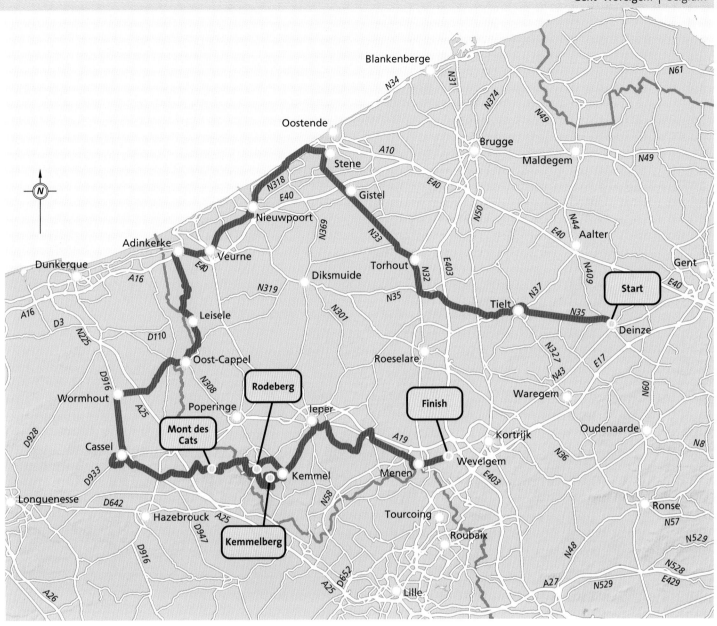

0.7km   1.7km   3km   1.7km   3km
80m     136m    153m  136m    153m
4.3% a.v.  4.8% a.v.  4% a.v.  4.8% a.v.  4% a.v.

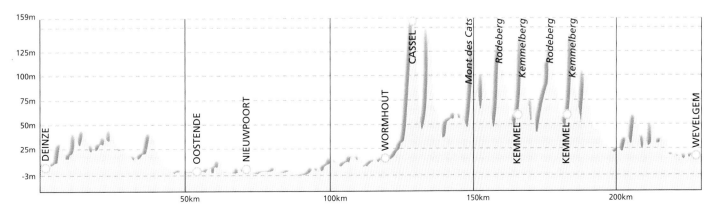

**Distance** 100 kilometres / 62.2 miles
**Total climbing** 525 metres / 1,722 feet
**Route key** Several hills from the Tour of Flanders, but you have to ride them on an old bike

# **34** Retro Ronde

The Retro Ronde is a very different challenge. It's a two-day festival of cycling that culminates with a big ride out on Day Two, the Sunday. You could do this route on your own, but it's definitely one where participation in the event is recommended, and there are activities over the two days for every level of cyclist. Not only that, the route is so off the beaten track that it's very difficult to follow without the direction signs of the event or without downloading it into a GPS.

The key to this challenge is retro. The longest of the Sunday rides is a circuit of some of the Tour of Flanders hills, but it has to be done on retro bikes and dressed in retro kit. The organisers define retro as a vintage bike manufactured before 1987, or a single-speed bike with a steel frame. If there are gears on your bike, the shifters must be on the frame, where they used to be, and no modern pedals are allowed; you must use old-fashioned pedals with toe clips and straps.

The idea is to recreate an era when bikes and cycling were simpler. Some regard these as the golden days of cycling, a time before modern tactics and training raised the standard of professional racing, which means racers have to time their efforts better now. That tends to make racing quite conservative, at least compared with what it used to be like. It might be a rose-tinted view but many older racing fans talk longingly about the 1950s, '60s and '70s, and before, if they can remember, when the tactic was often 'attack until you can attack no more'. Then somebody won and the rest were strung out in a long, broken line behind them.

Anyway, the Retro Ronde is based in Oudenaarde at the Tour of Flanders museum, which is fascinating to visit in its own right. In the evening of Day One there are street races around the town centre, or criteriums to give them their cycling name. There are three races: one for fixie bikes, one

for single-speeds, and one for multi-geared retro bikes. If any British city cycle couriers are reading this, that fixie race has your name on it: go and have a go.

Next day there's a cyclosportive that starts and finishes in Oudenaarde. The imaginative route combines little-known hills, hidden dirt roads and stretches of cobbled track that only the locals know and use, including one known as Rampe, a Flemish word for disaster. It's the very antithesis of a modern road race, and a modern cyclosportive for that matter. The first section ends with a flat stretch along the River Schelde cycle path.

The Tiegemberg comes next, a Tour of Flanders hill. Then you climb the long, cobbled Kwaremont, which is no joke on an old bike, and the older the better is the theme of the day. The Retro Ronde website (see right) contains a short film that explains the ethos and atmosphere of the event. It looks jolly, quite quaint, a bit like a vintage car rally, but doing the whole 100 kilometres (62 miles) is a tough challenge on an old or a single-geared bike.

The second half of the route is much like the first. It steers clear of roads where motor vehicles reign supreme and even runs through what looks like a farmyard at one point. There are plenty of hills.

A live band plays at the finish and the whole town comes out to cheer and to marvel at the durability of the old bikes, some of which date back to the 1920s and '30s. And by the look of them, so do some of the participants.

Have a go! The Retro Ronde is a bona fide cycling challenge but one that doesn't take itself too seriously. If you don't own an old bike they are quite easy to pick up at car boot sales or over the internet, and it can be interesting tracking down components for a renovation project; websites such as www.classicrendezvous.com are a big help.

# ▌Directions

▲ Go west out of Oudenaarde on the N453 then turn right on Kortrijkstraat then first left. Head north through Ooike, where you go right to Mullem then left to Ouwegem and left to Huise, where you go right, right again, left and then right towards Waregem. Turn left towards Wortegem and head south to pick up the River Schelde cycle path going west. Do a loop north towards Anzegem but go left to Tiegem then climb the Tiegemberg and follow directions to Kluisbergen and Berchem. Follow the Ronse road but turn left near a lake to climb the Oode Kwaremont. Follow directions to Lamont and turn right on Kalverstraat, then right on Zeekstraat, left on the N60 and right on Dieriksstraat and left towards Maarkedal. Keep east of Maarkedal and head for Brakel but turn left in Steenberg to go over the N8 then left again and loop back across the N8 to go left and join the N46 into Oudenaarde.

Top and bottom: The Australian pro racer Allan Peiper loved this part of the world so much he stayed here after his racing career ended
Right: Old bikes form an artwork in the centre of Brakel

**Website**
www.retroronde.be

**Date**
Usually held in May.

**Why the name?**
*Ronde* means tour in the bike-racing sense of the word. The Tour of Flanders is the Ronde van Vlaanderen in Flemish.

**Anything else?**
If you have a taste for retro riding, the Strade Bianche in Italy is a retro ride that is thriving today, and it spawned a pro race using the famous white roads of Tuscany that is fast becoming a classic.

**Don't forget**
Although single-speed bikes are welcome, the No Mountain Bike rule means you cannot use a single-speed mountain bike. That preserves the retro feel, as the very first race bikes were dropped-handlebar single-speed bikes. If it has gears it must be pre-1987, and it must have old-fashioned gear shifters mounted on the frame and old-style pedals with toe clips and straps. Clothing can be either original pre-1987, or a copy in modern materials. A number of manufacturers make such things: www.prendas.co.uk is a good place to look.

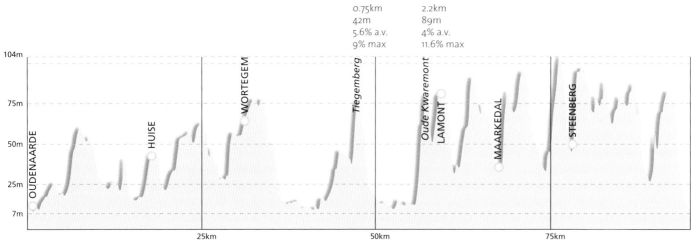

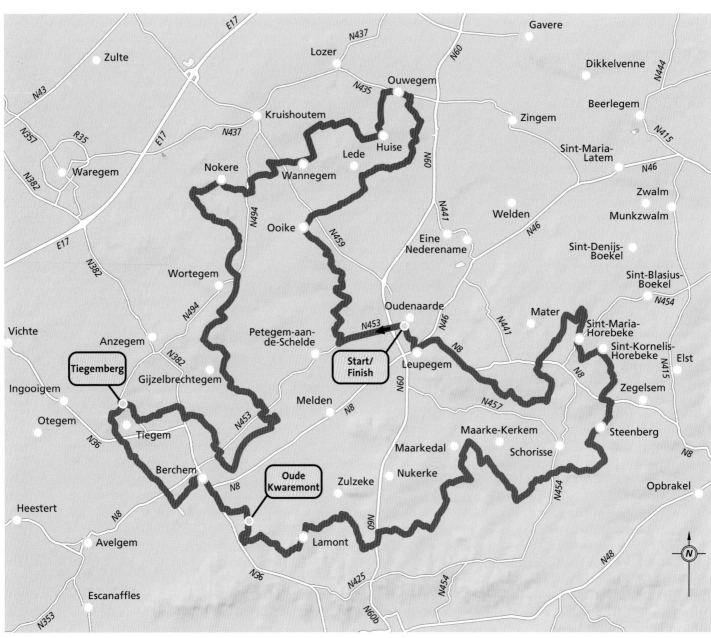

**Distance** 175.4 kilometres / 109.62 miles
**Total climbing** 2,808 metres / 9,210 feet
**Route key** Several tough hills including a super-steep climb to the finish

# 35 Gran Fondo Eddy Merckx

Not only does this ride celebrate Eddy Merckx, the best road racer the world has ever seen, it also celebrates Belgium's fourth classic race. Flèche Wallonne, or the Walloon Arrow to give it an English name, isn't a monument like Liège–Bastogne–Liège or the Tour of Flanders, but it is a classic race, one that shares the status of Gent–Wevelgem in cycling.

Have you spotted a pattern yet? Belgium is divided by language into Dutch-speaking Flanders and the French-speaking Walloon region, and everything the Walloons have the Flemish have to have too, and vice versa. The Tour of Flanders was created to counter the growing status of Liège–Bastogne–Liège, and when Flèche Wallonne graduated to classic status, so did Gent–Wevelgem.

This happens in everyday life too. If a new university opens in Flanders, it won't be long until another one opens in the other half of the country, and so on. You can imagine then that the regional allegiance of the most famous Belgian ever is very important, but in fact it's every bit as complicated as his country. Eddy Merckx was born in Flanders but moved early in his life to a French-speaking suburb of Brussels. (Brussels is technically a third region.) In a way, Merckx is the truest Belgian, a bilingual who won't state an allegiance to either region. I asked him once if he was Flemish or a Walloon, and he said, 'I'm a Belgian.' Unfortunately for the country's unity, not many Belgians think the same.

The Gran Fondo Eddy Merckx starts in Huy and finishes on top of the infamous Mur du Huy, the Huy Wall, just like the Flèche Wallonne race does. Its route is hilly – not quite as hilly as Liège–Bastogne–Liège, because the hills around Huy are a scale down in length and height from the true Ardennes climbs further east, but they are still as steep.

The first climb comes after 10 kilometres (6 miles) through the Bois des Dames. There's an undulating section then a long descent before climbing to the town of Sprimont, which is on the Liège–Bastogne–Liège route and marks the furthest east the Eddy Merckx route goes. The Côte de Chambralles comes next at 65 kilometres (40 miles), and it's vicious. Then there's a long descent followed by a section that climbs steadily for the next 22 kilometres (14 miles).

You're in Maffe, almost due south of Huy, with 107 kilometres (67 miles) done now. The next 40 kilometres (25 miles) trend down but there are 15 steep little hills, each one with a slightly longer descent, that take you to Andenne and the start of a longer climb. You then descend to the River Meuse, skirt the edges of Huy and climb back up into the woods almost to where you just came from. The two last climbs ensure your legs will be really tested by the Mur de Huy, which is a bit vindictive because the Mur is a test for the freshest legs on any day. Buckle up, because it is really tough.

You descend almost to the river then turn right into the Avenue de Condroz, where the Mur begins, but the climbing is a manageable 7 per cent. After 100 metres (328 feet) the road flattens to almost nothing then rises again at 5 and then 6 per cent. It's tough but not that tough; you'll probably be wondering why people make so much fuss about the Mur. Don't get complacent; the worst is yet to come.

It begins as the route flicks right from wide main roads into the Chemin des Chapelles, named after the seven chapels that stand along its length. There's no time to offer up a prayer, as the sensation of climbing switches in the legs from just about tolerable to truly painful. A road sign says 19 per cent, but I don't know why because 19 is neither the average gradient nor the steepest part of the climb.

The first steep section is straight and averages around 11 per cent. A right and left bend maintain the gradient, then as the road straightens the terrible truth of this climb comes

**Riders tackle the feared S-bend of the Mur de Huy**

into view. As if an aid to location were necessary at this stage, stencilled letters mock you from the road – 'Huy, Huy, Huy'. The vicious S-bend that is the crucial part of this climb is at this point.

Kim Kirchen, the Luxembourg winner of Flèche Wallonne in 2008, reckons that the S-bend is where most race riders get the Mur wrong. 'You have to have something left for after the S-bend,' he says. It's good advice for everyone; just making it around the 25 per cent gradient of the formidable S-bend requires a huge effort, and one that is very difficult to judge. But don't spend all your energy here or you could end up walking the last bit.

The S-bend is about 40 metres (131 feet) long, then the gradient relaxes a bit, but not much. The road curves gently

to the left for 300 metres (984 feet) at around 14 per cent. Avoid hitting maximum effort until as late as possible. On the left of the road there's a short terrace of stone houses, the first a house height below the last. Their front steps mark out the gradient. On the right is a cobbled path and a roadside shrine, just in case seven chapels are not enough for you. But you are nearly there and can give it everything now.

Suddenly the black wall of tarmac that has been your focus all the way up the climb is replaced by blue sky. The last chapel rises into view on the right. You've reached the top. You feel like a spider climbing out of a bowl. The world comes back into view after being nothing but a tunnel of pain since that 19 per cent sign way back down the hill. The Mur is done. It's over – at last.

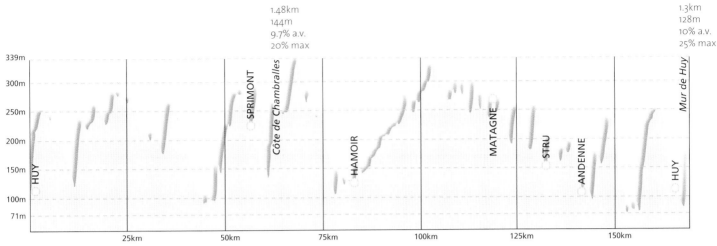

1.48km
144m
9.7% a.v.
20% max

1.3km
128m
10% a.v.
25% max

**This route is hilly, and where it isn't the course undulates constantly**

## Website
http://sport.be.msn.com/granfondo

## Date
June.

## Why the name?
It's named after Belgium's Eddy Merckz, the world's best male road racer.

## Anything else?
In 2013 the Gran Fondo was one of the qualifying events for the age-group world championships held on the Charly Gaul route based in Trento in Italy. It is likely that the Gran Fondo Eddy Merckx will remain a qualifier and could even be the title race one day as it is part of the UCI's World Cycling Tour that is aimed at encouraging age-group competition.

## Don't forget
The Gran Fondo Eddy Merckx is a challenging event and you will need to be fit to take part as you are up against those racing to qualify for the age-group world championships. Your training should be a mix of long hilly rides and shorter interval sessions. It's also a good idea to do some group training and work on your cornering, climbing and descending skills. Some race experience helps too. Racing in the UK is very accessible, and there is lots of advice on how to get started on British Cycling's website at www.britishcycling.org.uk

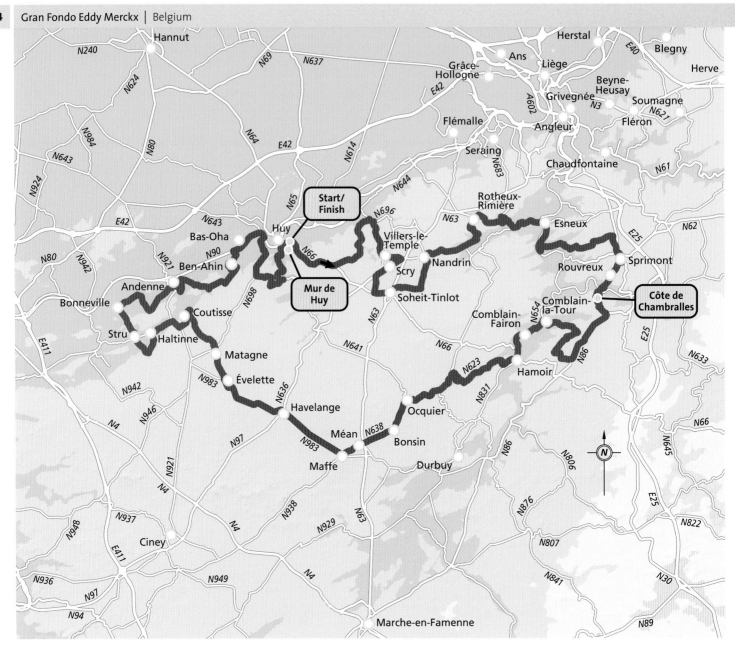

# Directions

▲ This route is based on the 2011 challenge. Start in Huy, go southeast on the N66 then turn left and follow this road to turn right on the Route de France. Turn right on the N636. Take the second left, then go left on the N66 and left in the centre of Soheit-Tinlot, then turn right on the Rue de l'Eglise. Go right in Nandrin and through Rotheux-Rimière, turn right again and cross the river in Esneux, and continue to Sprimont. Go south through the town, then turn right on the Rue de la Liberté and follow this road over the N633 to the N86, where you turn right.

▲ Turn right after 7 kilometres, then right on the Route de Hamoir, then left on the Rue de Comblain. Continue through Comblain-la-Tour. Go over the river then left alongside it to Hamoir, where you turn right on the Rue du Néblon. Follow the N623 to the N638, where you turn left. In Maffe, turn right on the N983 and follow it through Havelange to turn right just past Évelette. Go northwest through Matagne then turn left to Sainte-Begge and follow the N941 to Haltinne, where you turn left then take the second right, then the first right to go north through Stru. Continue to

Bonneville, where you turn right, then right at the T-junction, then right again, then left to Groynne, then to Andenne.

▲ Turn right as you enter the town and climb the hill, then descend to the river in Huy where you follow the N90, then the N698, then turn right to go through Bellegrade, which is at the top of the hill. Turn left, then left on the N641 to descend into Huy, where you turn right on the Avenue du Condroz, then right again on the Chemin des Chapelles to climb to the top of the Mur de Huy.

**Distance** 255 kilometres / 159 miles
**Total climbing** 4,700 metres /  15,416 feet
**Route key** 11 steep and quite long climbs that are characteristic of the Ardennes region of Belgium.
The distance and sometimes the weather are problematic

# 36 Liège–Bastogne–Liège

This is the oldest classic race in cycling. First run in 1892 as a race for amateurs, it's been a pro race since 1894 and it has become one of the five monuments of the sport; the five one-day races that are bigger, harder, older and simply more prized than the rest. Win a monument race and a pro is set up for life. They are that important.

There are several organised challenges on variations of this route, including one the day before the pro race. There are three distance choices, including one over the full route that the pros ride. None of the routes are easy. The Ardennes is an enormous region that stretches from northeastern France through southern Belgium and into Germany.

Liège is just north of the Ardennes, and the race goes south into them to reach Bastogne, then returns north by a different route. Basically, this is a hard ride south that gets harder, in places a lot harder, going north. Ardennes' hill size is similar to the sort of thing you find in upland Britain, in Wales, Scotland and the Lake District. The route peaks at around 550 metres (1,804 feet), with longer climbs over more generally rolling terrain going south, and much steeper, sometimes shorter, climbs going north. Overall, it's brutal.

The character change comes at around 100 miles, going north and just after Vielsalm on a short steep climb called the Côte de Wanne. It's like Mr Hyde turning into another Mr Hyde – but this one is nastier and really angry. Next up is one of the hardest climbs in cycling.

It's in the town of Stavelot and it's called Stockeu. You descend into town and do an almost 180-degree right, then the hill climbs dead straight, up through the town past a staircase of front doorsteps outside the terraced houses, and into the woods. There's a statue of Eddy Merckx at the top: a Belgian national hero, the greatest men's road racer ever, and the Liège–Bastogne–Liège record holder with five wins. The statue is awful, by the way; it looks nothing like Merckx.

The race, however, should have 'Made for Merckx' stamped on it. He was called the Cannibal because he ate races and the competitors in them. He was at his very best when he had a hard route to help him.

The Côte du Rosier is next, 4.5 kilometres (3 miles) long with sections of 12 per cent. It started raining here in the cyclosportive event in 2012. Not gentle April showers but Ardennes rain: cold, constant rain that chills you to the bone. The Ardennes has a microclimate. It can be hot and humid here in April, and it can snow. It did in 1980, when another force of nature, Bernard Hinault, won the race by almost 10 minutes from a field of 174 that was whittled down to 21 by the finish.

The Haute Levée comes next, and it's cobbled, just in case you aren't suffering enough by now. Then there's Mont-Theux, which leads to the most famous climb in the race, La Redoute. It's long and it's hard but it's no longer or harder than many of the others. What makes La Redoute special is it's 226 kilometres (140 miles) into the race, so the ideal place for the favourites to launch their attacks.

Time after time La Redoute has been the springboard for victory. The top riders play a waiting game, covering the breaks with teammates and pulling them back while the route takes its toll at the back as those in contention are whittled down. Two hundred kilometres in cycling is like 'the wall' in a marathon; it's an invisible, maybe psychological barrier that saps most people's strength, but not the best. This is where they ride harder.

There's a long descent off La Redoute, then there are three climbs left, including La Roche-aux-Faucons and the last

Straight sections of road are rare on this route

climb, the Côte Saint-Nicholas, which is right in the middle of Liège and climbs through the working-class areas of this old industrial city.

Liège was Belgium's Sheffield, a centre for steel manufacturing surrounded by coalmines. Many Italians came to work here during the 1940s and '50s, and they stayed. This is where a lot of their families live; they love cycling and Italy has provided 12 Liège–Bastogne–Liège winners over the years. The atmosphere here on race day is electric.

But just like the Tour of Flanders, this race is more a celebration of Belgian cycling. Italy's 12 winners put them second in the overall victory standings, way ahead of third-place Switzerland with six and France with five, but the Belgians are overwhelming winners with 59. That says a lot about the ability of Belgian cyclists, but a lot more about what the sport means in this country.

**Website**
http://sport.be.msn.com/classicchallenge and click on 'Liège–Bastogne–Liège'.

**Date**
Usually the second-to-last weekend in April.

**Why the name?**
Liège was chosen as the start point because it was the richest and most influential city in Wallonne, the French-speaking part of Belgium. The first organisers wanted to take the race into the Ardennes to make it spectacular and Bastogne was chosen as the turnaround point because it was the furthest they could get by train to check all the riders through, then still be back in Liège in time to record them through the finish.

**Anything else?**
The other Ardennes classic is Flèche Wallonne, and it has a dedicated cyclosportive. There is also scope in this part of the world to get a map, make up your own routes and explore. The Ardennes is superb mountain bike country with thousands of trails.

**Don't forget**
Not only does the Ardennes have its own climate, the weather can change from one hour to the next. It's a real four-seasons-in-one-day place. Take a rain- or windproof top with you even if it's sunny, and some thin gloves that you can fold and carry in a pocket. There are plenty of refuelling stations on the organised event, but if you do this on your own you will find many shops and cafes in the towns and villages along the way, as the Ardennes is a popular tourist destination.

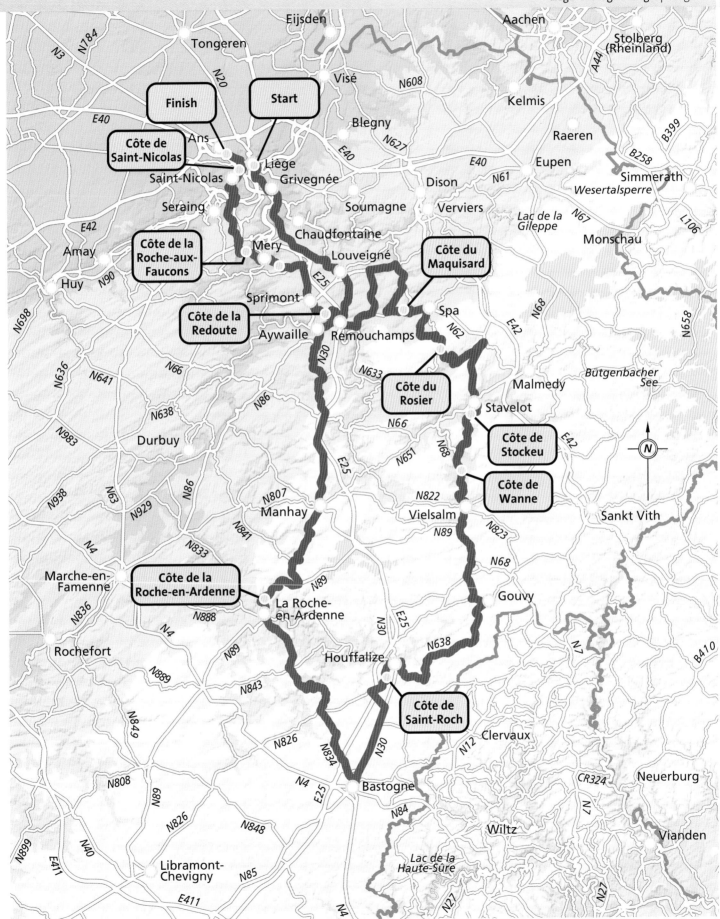

# ▌ Directions

▲ Head south out of Liège on the N30. Go through Louveign to Remouchamps and follow the N666 to Aywaille. From there head south on the N86 and N30 to Manhay, then go right through La Roche-en-Ardenne, where you turn right on the N834 to Bastogne. Turn left on the N30, then left on the N847, then right on the N826 to Houffalize, where you turn right on the N30. Turn left to go through Cowan and Tavigny, where you turn left on the N638 to Gouvy. Turn left on the N827 then the N892, then left on the N68 through Vielsalm, then fork right to Stavelot.

▲ Turn right near the river, then left at the top of the Stockeu hill, then left on the descent to go back through Stavelot. Follow the N622 north to Francorchamps, where you take the first left to Ruy, then turn right, then left to Spa. Turn left on the N62 to Marteau. Turn left by the river, then take the first right to La Reid, where you turn right. Turn left on the N62 and follow this through Theux. Turn left on the N606, then right on the N697 and go through Remouchamps, but keep to the right side of the river, then turn right on the N662, then left to Sprimont.

▲ Follow the N30 north, turn left on the N674 and follow this to Mery, where you turn left over the river and climb the Roche-aux-

**An Ardennes descent**

Faucons. Turn right on the N63, then left at the big crossroads to come back down the other carriageway. Take the first right, then the first right again to join the N663 north into Liège. Turn right on the Rue Ferdinand Nicolay under the flyover then onto the Ougrée Bridge. Turn left after the Liège football ground, then take the first right and follow this road up through Tilleur, then go right under the E25 motorway. Turn left on the Rue Bidaut then left on the Rue de Hesbaye and follow this road to the finish on the Rue Jean Jaurès.

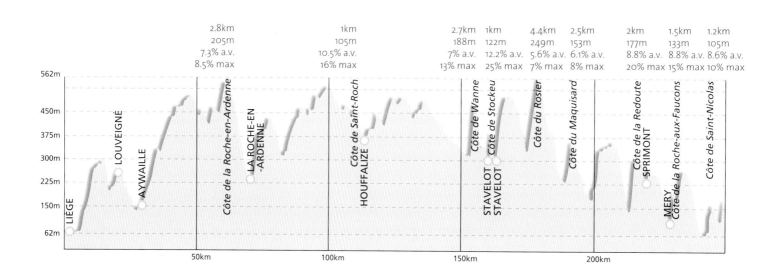

A mass of colour as the professionals climb Stockeu

Holland

Limburg

**Distance** 242 kilometres / 151 miles
**Total climbing** 3,137 metres / 10,289 feet
**Route key** Coping with over 30 hills, hundreds of changes of direction and a thousand speed bumps

# 37 The Amstel Gold Race

Holland isn't flat. Limburg is full of short, sometimes steep hills, and this ride seems to visit all of them. It follows the route of Holland's only classic bike race, a race that started in 1966 as a publicity stunt for the Amstel brewery, with a course that ran past every one of their offices. However, the organisers quickly realised that to gain classic status the race needed a classic route, and they found that in Limburg.

It's a complicated route, but that adds to its challenge and to the quality of the Amstel Gold Race winners over the years. To seek out every hill in the southeast corner of Holland, the Amstel Gold Race twists and turns all over the place. There are hundreds of corners, and each one will break your rhythm, requiring you to slow down then accelerate to pick it back up again. Add in an unusual feature of Dutch roads – speed bumps everywhere – and this event is a toughie.

The race starts and finishes in Valkenburg, the centre for two convoluted loops. Valkenburg and its surrounding area have hosted the world road cycling championships five times, and there's no better way to underline how big a challenge the Amstel Gold Race is than that. The first hill comes after 2 miles, then there are 10 miles of flat road by the River Maas, then it's up or down almost all the way to the finish.

The hills aren't too much of a problem until the route passes Heerlen, another Dutch town that has hosted the 'Worlds', then they come thicker and faster. It's the cumulative effect of the Limburg hills that hurts your legs and lower back muscles. This is one ride where core conditioning and the ability to cope with climb after climb, acceleration after acceleration, are absolutely crucial.

Through Valkenburg for the first time at 55 miles you transition into the second half of the route, and it's harder. You start to notice the other feature of this route: the traffic calming that litters Dutch streets. Get out of the saddle,

put the cranks parallel to the floor, keep your elbows and knees loose, and use your arms and legs as shock absorbers, allowing your bike to move up and over the bumps by flexing your elbows, knees and hips. There are thousands on the Amstel Gold route, so you will hate them by the end.

Once through Valkenburg, the rate at which little hills appear increases as they count you down to the finish. In the race there are six climbs in the first 55 miles, then 25 in the following 100. But the crunch comes right at the end, with eight climbs in the 25 miles to the finish. That's one every three miles, or every 10 to 15 minutes. The climbs average just under a mile going up, so that makes eight sets of one-mile hill intervals to round off the 126 miles already ridden.

Expressed in hard numbers or in words, they beat out a cruel rhythm. Wolfsberg, Loorberg, Gulperberg, Kruisberg, Eyserbosweg, Fromberg and then the steepest of them all, the Keutenberg. They all soften you up nicely for the long, gradual descent into Valkenburg to the foot of the Cauberg for the classic finish of the Amstel Gold Race on top of the climb, although the race organisers are talking about changing it in the future. I hope they don't; the changes they made to the Tour of Flanders should be a warning.

Two bridges take the main road, the Wilhelmlaan, across the River Geul. There's a sharp right bend, then the Cauberg begins. Rising gently at first, taking 400 metres (1,312 feet) to increase to just over 6 per cent, the real climb begins abruptly: 9 per cent for 100 metres then 200 metres forming an 11 per cent crux. Finally the road eases from 8 to 4 per cent before the final 500 metres of dragging road to the top.

There will be spectators. The Dutch love a party and the Cauberg is lined with cafes. During the Amstel Gold Race, the riders say they smell the hill from miles away. Twenty thousand people drinking beer on one street has that effect.

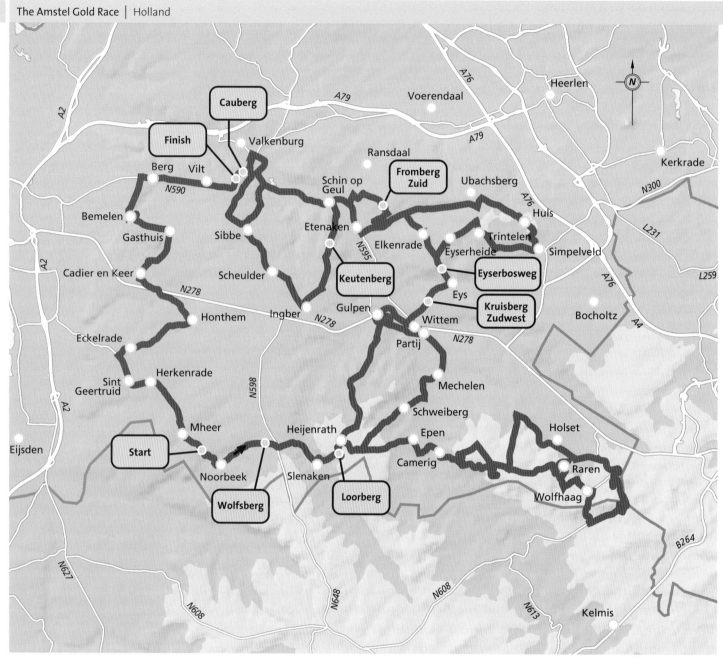

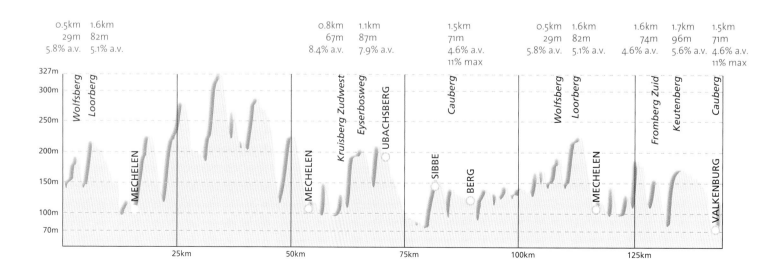

# Directions

The full Amstel Gold route is complicated, so this route reflects the final 150 kilometres.

▲ Start in Mheer, go southeast to Noorbeek then east through Hoogcruts and Slenaken. Head northeast through Heijenrath and Landsrade to Gulpen. Head east before entering the town, go south through Mechelen then southwest to the junction with Julianastraat. Go left to Epen. Turn right then second left to pick up the Epenerbaan east to the junction with Rugweg. Turn left, go right to Raren, left past the golf club, skirting the southern edge of Vaals to go south, then turn right at the Drielandenpunt to Gemmenich. Turn right and go through Wolfhaag then left on the Epenerbaan. Go right on the Zevenwegenweg, then left, then right through Camerig. Continue west through Epen to turn right and go through Schweiberg, then left through Mechelen, then north to Partij.

▲ Turn left on the Oude Heirbaan, then right on the Gulperbergweg then right on the N278. Go left to Wittem then first right to Eys. Turn left, then right, then second right through Trintelen then Bosschenhuizen to Simpelveld. Turn left, go through Huls, then go left then right in Ubachsberg to Fromberg. Turn right to Valkenburg then left to Sibbe, then right, and right back into Valkenburg, where you turn left and follow the N590. Turn left in Berg, left in Bemelen then right in Gasthuis and left in Cadier en Keer to cross the N278 southeast to Honthem. Turn right then first left after Eckelrade and go through Sint Geertruid and follow the Julianaweg southeast then south through Mheer to repeat the first 7 kilometres of the ride, then turn right in Heijenrath. Turn left to Schweiberg then repeat the earlier section through Mechelen, Gulpen and Eys but go straight on at the Eyserheide junction through Elkenrade. Turn left on the Vrakelbergerweg then first right and second left to go left to Schoonbron and turn right. Turn left to Engwegen and go through Berghof. Turn right to Lemmensstraat and go through Ijzeren to turn right in Sibbe then left into Valkenburg, where you follow the road to the top of the Cauberg.

**The pros racing up one of Limburg's short, steep hills**

## Website
www.amstel.nl (you have to enter your birth date because Amstel make alcoholic drinks), then click on 'English' and 'Events'

## Date
Mid-April.

## Why the name?
Amstel Gold was a beer brewed by Amstel.

## Anything else?
The Amstel Gold Race often gets lumped in with Liège–Bastogne–Liège and Flèche Wallonne: together they are called the Ardennes Classics. The pros ride all three in a week, so why not try that as an extra challenge?

## Don't forget
You'll be well looked after in the event, and there are plenty of shops and cafes on the route if you do it independently. Your training should focus on making hard efforts on short hills, and on longer rides with plenty of hills in them. Daft as it might sound, it's not a bad idea to practise riding over traffic-calming strips if there are any near you, so it becomes second nature. You need a GPS for this route outside the event, or a map with the route marked on it and a good sense of direction.

Germany

## Hamburg

**Distance** 156 kilometres / 97 miles
**Total climbing** 780 metres / 2,558 feet
**Route key** Short, sharp hills in western Hamburg

# 38 Vattenfall Cyclassics

This challenge is best done as part of the official event as much of it goes through the streets of Hamburg, including the historic and notorious Reeperbahn. The other highlights are a loop south through the spectacular Lüneburg Heath, and a traverse of the Köhlbrandbrücke, Hamburg's highest bridge.

The all-comers event is called the Jedermann-Rennen, a cyclosportive inspired by the Vattenfall Cyclassics professional road race. It started in 1996 as an attempt to provide Germany with a pro race that would eventually become a classic, but that's not always easy. The UCI has given it top-level status, but becoming a classic takes time. Still, the race is gathering momentum and there have been some great winners. The Jedermann-Rennen is regarded as a big deal in Germany, so it's well worth taking part. Not only that, it provides a unique opportunity to ride through a large and busy city, which is rare in cycling; it's certainly rarer than in running, where big city marathons are well established.

There are three rides: 55 kilometres (34 miles), 100 kilometres (62 miles) and a 156-kilometre (96-mile) circuit that takes in both, so it follows the pro route. The only difference is that the professionals do several circuits of the Hamburg Hills to make up their 250-kilometre (155-mile) distance, whereas the Jedermann-Rennen does only one.

And the event is enormous: 20,000 signed up in 2005 to ride the three distances. The long-distance group traces the 100-kilometre loop, and the 55-kilometre city route is a circuit of the Altona district, including the most famous hill on the route, the Waseberg, and ending back in the city centre with a ride down the Reeperbahn.

This used to be called the sinful mile because it was Hamburg's red-light district, but it has become a lot more respectable recently, although not entirely. The Reeperbahn is known throughout the world as the place where The Beatles honed their craft, and, in the words of Sir Paul McCartney, 'became a good little rock and roll band'.

The Altona circuit is the last part of the longer-distance Jedermann ride, which starts by crossing the Elbe to the island of Wilhelmsburg then heads south into the Lüneburg Heath. This is the largest ecosystem of its kind in northern Germany. It's lovely open, rolling countryside with a fascinating ecology based on sandy moorland dotted with clumps of birch, pine and oak trees, and occasionally wild juniper. The route does a short stretch through the beautiful Lüneburg National Park before swinging north to return to Hamburg.

In the event, you cross back onto Wilhelmsburg via the Köhlbrandbrücke. This huge cable suspension bridge is normally not open to cyclists and it gives fantastic views of the city, so many Hamburg residents participating in the Vattenfall Cyclassics pause here for a while so that they can appreciate the city where they live in a way they don't normally get a chance to. And Hamburg has a magnificent skyline.

If you tackle this ride outside the event you cannot use the Köhlbrandbrücke, so you need to turn right after 75 kilometres (47 miles) to Harburg then retrace the first few kilometres back into the city centre, before picking up the Altona loop. The Waseberg is in Blankenese, and the Reeperbahn is between Altona and Hamburg city centre.

The Vattenfall Cyclassics is a city cycling challenge with just a short rural loop, but it doesn't feel too urban as Hamburg's suburbs are leafy, light and airy. The Waseberg climbs, for example, feel like you are out in the countryside, and certainly nowhere near a busy, modern port, which is where you are in reality. I wanted to include a city cycling challenge in this book, and there isn't a better one than this.

**The pro peloton speeding through the streets of Hamburg**

# Directions

▲ From the city centre head south over the Freihafenelbbrücke, go around the edge of the docks, then south through Wilhelmsburg and Harburg. Continue south through Jesteburg and head to Dierkshausen. Turn right on the K55 then go right after Schierhorn to head north through Holm-Seppensen. Continue north over the A1, through Langenrehm and Ehestorf, then head back into the city via the Köhlbrandbrücke. Outside the event turn right in Hausbruch to miss out Köhlbrandbrücke and retrace the first part of the route back into the centre of Hamburg.

▲ Cross the Alster Lake by the dam and head northwest towards Eimsbüttel then on the Fruchtallee, then the Holstenkamp to turn right at the Mennonitenfriedhof. Go north then northwest over the motorway and into Lurup, where you turn right on the L103 towards Pinneberg, then go left on the L105 then right on the K15 to Holm. Turn left and follow the B431 to the River Elbe. Turn left and follow the Tinsdaler Weg east around the north of Blankenese to climb the Waseberg, then descend to continue east alongside the Elbe through Altona and along the Reeperbahn back into Hamburg.

## Website
www.vattenfall-cyclassics.de

## Date
Towards the end of August.

## Why the name?
The event is sponsored by a Hamburg power plant called Vattenfall Europe.

## Anything else?
Explore the gently rolling landscape of the Lüneburg Heath. It's peaceful, bewitching countryside, perfect for a day on a bike.

## Don't forget
There are plenty of feed stations on the event, so just take enough with you to fuel an average ride. It can be quite warm here in summer, and it can also be chilly, so pay attention to the weather forecast before the event and dress accordingly. As ever on a long ride, the weather can change, so carrying a thin wind- or waterproof top is a good idea.

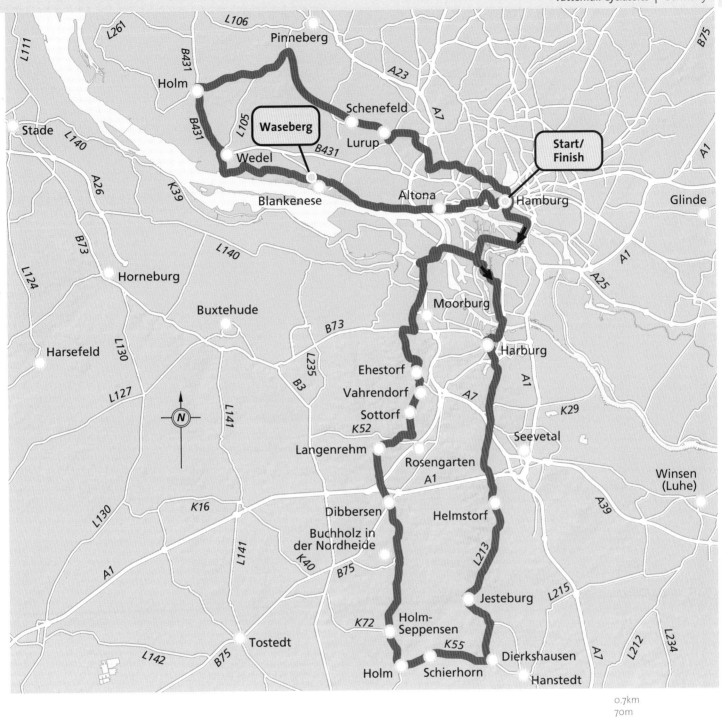

Stade
L111
L261
L106
Pinneberg
B431
Holm
B431
Schenefeld
A23
A7
B75
**Waseberg**
L105
Lurup
L140
Wedel
B431
**Start/Finish**
A7
Blankenese
Altona
Hamburg
Glinde
A1
L140
Horneburg
A26
B73
Moorburg
A25
A1
Buxtehude
B73
Harburg
A1
L124
L130
Ehestorf
A7
Harsefeld
L235
Vahrendorf
L127
B3
Sottorf
K52
Seevetal
K29
L141
Langenrehm
Rosengarten
A1
Winsen (Luhe)
L130
K16
Dibbersen
Helmstorf
A39
L141
Buchholz in der Nordheide
L213
A1
K40
B75
Jesteburg
L215
K72
Holm-Seppensen
K55
Dierkshausen
A7
L212
L234
Tostedt
L142
B75
Holm
Schierhorn
Hanstedt

0.7km
70m
10% a.v.
16% max

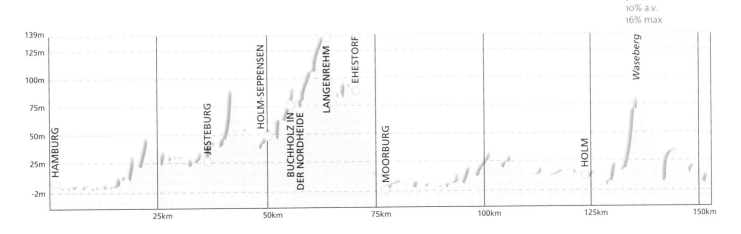

139m
125m
100m
75m
50m
25m
-2m

HAMBURG
JESTEBURG
HOLM-SEPPENSEN
BUCHHOLZ IN DER NORDHEIDE
LANGENREHM
EHESTORF
MOORBURG
HOLM
*Waseberg*

25km    50km    75km    100km    125km    150km

Switzerland

Berner Alps

**Distance** 125 kilometres / 78 miles
**Total climbing** 1,900 metres / 6,232 feet
**Route key** Three mountain climbs

# **39** Gruyère Cycling Tour

This ride is worth doing as much for its beauty as it is for the challenge. It is a challenge, make no mistake, but it's a lesser one than some of the others in this book and ideal if you want an introduction to the scale of mountain climbs they have in Europe. In Tour de France terms, the climbs of the Gruyère Cycling Tour would be classed as medium mountains.

The countryside is certainly not as wild as the terrain you have to contend with in the Alpenbrevet. You start the Gruyère Cycling Tour in Bulle, where Switzerland looks like the Switzerland everyone imagines it to be: a country of mountain meadows studded with wild flowers and wooden chalets, set against a grey and white backdrop of jagged mountains, under a blue sky. It's not sunny every day in Switzerland, but it seems like it is.

After wandering up a valley, the first climb, the Mittelberg, is probably the hardest. It's classified as being 11 kilometres (7 miles) long and starting in Jaun, but in reality you begin climbing towards it 5 kilometres (3 miles) after the start, so that makes it more like 25 kilometres (15.5 miles). The two toothy peaks on the right side of the road at the summit are the Dent de Savigny (2,252 metres) and Dent de Ruth (2,233 metres).

The Mittelberg's descent has quite a technical start, with several hairpin bends, but the road straightens out and gravity takes over in a big way. Control your speed carefully here, because you could end up going faster than you feel comfortable with.

You descend to ride through Saanen, then the jet-set ski holiday town of Gstaad and into the Gstaad Valley, where you begin to climb the Col du Pillon. If you look left at the summit of this climb, following the line of the cable car, you get glimpses of the Transfleuron Glacier. The mountain just west, which looks like a regular mountain with a mini Matterhorn on top of it, is called Scex Rouge (2,971 metres/9,747 feet).

A short descent leads to Les Diablerets, then you follow a river through a gap in the mountains to just outside Le Sépey, where the final climb, the Col des Mosses, begins. The headquarters of the International Cycling Union (UCI) are just a few miles the other side of Le Sépey in Aigle. They have a race school there so the Col des Mosses often gets used by the pupils for training rides. The climb is also a regular feature of a famous stage race in this area, the Tour of Romandie, and it has featured in the Tour de France.

A sharp right takes you onto the climb, which is long, but the gradient isn't too harsh and it's constant. That allows you to get into a good rhythm. Rhythm means getting your breathing under control and keeping it steady, and matching it to a fast pedal cadence – it's the key to success on long climbs like those in the Alps and Pyrenees.

The road from the top of the Col des Mosses down to Bulle is one of the glories of the Gruyère Tour. The road switches from fast, straight sections to technical, twisting ones, some with tight bends and others with huge, sweeping curves connecting straights that seem to cross the sides of whole mountains. The views are incredible. The Lac de l'Hongrin fills a valley on your left soon after the summit, its sapphire-blue surface contrasting sharply with the steel-grey scree slopes that rear up out of it. The road squeezes itself between two mountains, then after L'Etivaz you plunge into the Châteaux-d'Oex Valley. There's a short climb, then you go down the Sarine Valley for the final delightful 20 kilometres (12.5 miles) in chocolate-box Switzerland.

Lac de Gruyère

12

180

A12

12

Bulle

Charmey

Jaun

Start/
Finish

Montsalvens

Broc
Epagny

Gruyères

190

**Mittelberg**

Neirivue

Albeuve

190

11

Saanen

Gstaad

Montbovon

Rossinière

11

142

190

11

Lac de
l'Hongrin

L'Etivaz

Feutersoey

**Col des
Mosses**

11

Gsteig

Le Sépey

142

**Col du
Pillon**

142

11

Ormont-
Dessus

Les
Diablerets

147

N

# Directions

▲ Start in Bulle and head southeast then take the left turn through Broc to Jaun, where the Mittelberg starts. Continue south then southeast through Saanen and Gstaad to begin the Col du Pillon. Descend through Les Diablerets then continue west to Le Sépey. Turn right to climb the Col des Mosses and descend to L'Etivaz, where you turn left and go through Rossinière and Montbovon to Gruyères, where you bear left in Epagny to return to Bulle.

### Website
www.gruyere-cycling-tour.ch

### Date
End of August/beginning of September.

### Why the name?
Most of the ride is in the Gruyère area, a place world famous for its cheese.

### Anything else?
From Le Diablerets, the next valley to the south is that of the Rhone before it flows into Lac Léman, then out again and into France at the Geneva end. Martigny is a town at the elbow in the young river where it changes direction from flowing west to north. Martigny is also at the foot of the Col de la Forclaz, a famous Tour de France climb scaling a lower shoulder of the Mont Blanc Massif. Sion is further east, where you can ride up Val d'Hérens to Arolla at the foot of the Matterhorn (4,478 metres). They are both great adventures.

### Don't forget
The usual high-altitude support kit of a light wind- or waterproof and gloves that fit in your pocket or in a bag on your bike. If you do this ride unsupported outside the Gruyère Tour event, you need to take plenty to eat and drink with you as the villages get quite sparse in places.

Switzerland's meadows and mountains

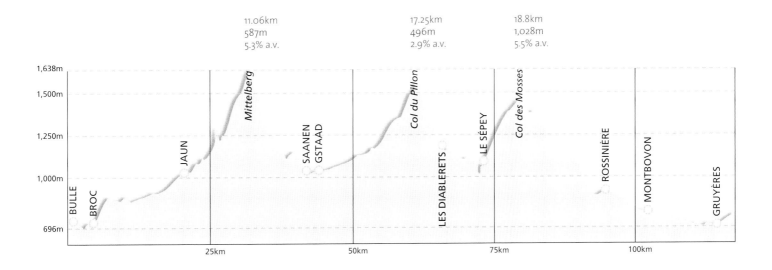

| | 11.06km | 17.25km | 18.8km |
| | 587m | 496m | 1,028m |
| | 5.3% a.v. | 2.9% a.v. | 5.5% a.v. |

**Distance** 270 kilometres / 169 miles
**Total climbing** 7,031 metres / 23,067 feet
**Route key** Five major Alpine passes and the long distance

# 40 Alpenbrevet Platinum Tour

The Platinum Tour is enormous. There are lesser distances in the Alpenbrevet event – a Silver Tour of three passes and 132 kilometres (82 miles), and a Gold Tour of four passes and 172 kilometres (106 miles), and both are demanding – but the Platinum Tour is *beyond* demanding. The Grand Tours (the Tour de France and the Tours of Italy and Spain) don't do five passes this big in one stage any more. It's inhumane.

All three Swiss tour routes start and finish in Meiringen, and they share some but not all of the same climbs. None of the challenge routes have much flat riding in them, and the first pass on the Platinum Tour, the Grimselpass, starts just 30 kilometres (18.5 miles) outside Meiringen. It's 26 kilometres (16 miles) long and there are some beautiful high-altitude lakes on the way to the summit.

But even they don't compare with the mountains to the west. They look huge as you climb, and when you reach the top of the pass you see that they are. The Finsteraarhorn is 4,274 metres (14,022 feet) high, behind that the Jungfrau is 4,158 metres (13,642 feet), and the brooding Eiger lies between the two at 3,970 metres (13,020 feet). It's a world of ice and snow, a world you are about to leave on the spectacular descent into Oberwald and the idyllic valley below. The source of the River Rhone lies at the head of this valley, and a little lower down, where the river runs through Ulrichen, you start to climb the giant Nufenenpass, the second highest paved road in Switzerland at 2,478 metres (8,130 feet). It's not as long as the Grimsel and it climbs in two breathtaking sections of hairpin bends, one near the start and one near the top. Between them you ride up a valley alongside the Agen stream, where the head of the valley is at 2,000 metres. The summit of the Nufenen is pockmarked with small lakes and shattered rocks and surrounded by snowy peaks. It's also the border between German-speaking Switzerland and the southernmost canton, where they speak Italian.

That's where you go now, down into the Ticino Valley, through Airolo for a long downhill-trending trek to Biasca, which is only 300 metres above sea level. It could be quite warm here when you do the ride, as the Alpenbrevet is held in July, and doing this ride outside it is only possible from mid-June to mid-October. The passes are closed the rest of the time. Temperature and scenery changes, from snowy roads to palm-lined avenues, are a feature of the Alpenbrevet.

The next leg involves a long route march up the Blenio Valley, where the Passo del Lucomagno starts. This is also listed as the Lukmanier Pass on the event website. It's the lowest of the five passes at 1,915 metres (6,282 feet), but still a tough proposition with a view to die for when you get to the summit and see the Sontga Maria Lake in the rocky valley below. You pass the Upper Grindelwald Glacier on the long descent. Then there's a quite difficult and dispiriting section to Disentis. The road undulates, climbing a little on the side of a mountain and over a low ridge. None of these hills are famous, but their quick succession takes its toll.

Disentis is the start of the Oberalppass, a 20-plus kilometre climb that takes a while to get going. You ride along a steadily rising shelf above a very young River Rhine then make a break for the summit up some much steeper slopes. The descent takes you to Wassen and back to the scenery you started in.

Wassen is the start of the Sustenpass, the final one of the day, but an incredible climb with an even more incredible descent. You pass the end of the Stein Glacier, where in summer the ice melts into a huge lake called the Steinsee. This is really worth seeing because glaciers have definitely receded in the Alps over the last 20 to 30 years. You rarely get

**Racers in the Tour of Switzerland with the High Alps in the background**

to ride this close to one. A long straight section after the first two gives you a chance to look, but keep an eye ahead and watch your speed for the hairpin bend at the bottom.

The rest of the descent is very technical and demands every bit of your attention. Eventually, though, you roll into Innertkirchen for the final sting of the Alpenbrevet. There's

a really tough climb between here and the finish. It's not long but it's a real slap in the face after all you've been through. You will need to keep a bit of strength back for it, so even though you are near the finish, take the chance to eat after descending the Susten to ensure you have some firepower left in your legs.

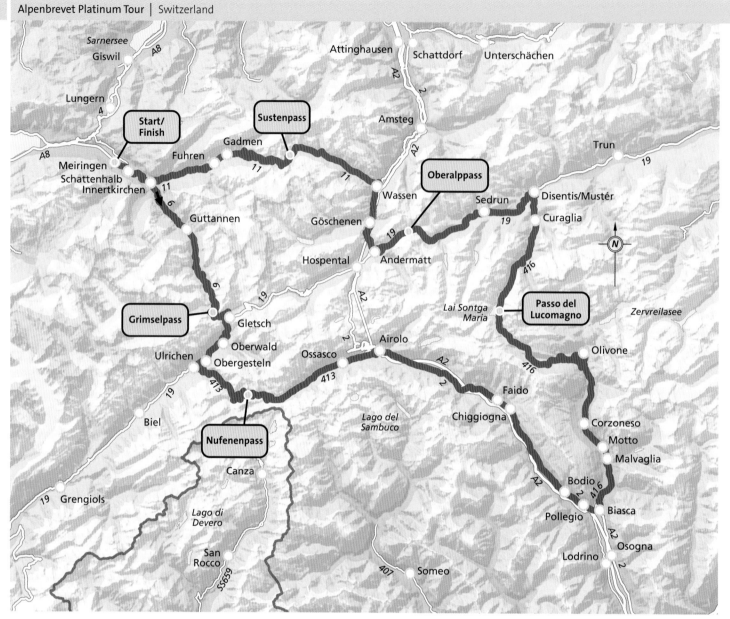

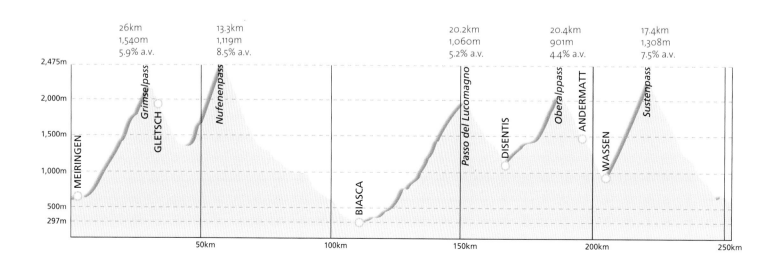

# ▌Directions

▲ From Meiringen go southeast over the Grimselpass and turn right through Gletsch, then left in Ulrichen to climb the Nufenenpass. Descend past the start of the St Gotthard Pass and continue through Airolo to Biasca. Turn left to ride up the Blenio Valley then climb the Passo del Lucomagno. Turn left in Disentis to climb over the Oberalppass. Go right in Andermatt, through Wassen, and turn left to climb the Sustenpass back to Meiringen.

**Website**
www.alpenbrevet.ch

**Date**
End of July.

**Why the name?**
It's in the Alps and *brevet* is a French word that used to be used a lot as a word for a long-distance cycling challenge. It conveys that the event is purely there to be done, and not for competition. Indeed, the Alpenbrevet organisers publish finishers' times, but not the order in which they finish.

**Anything else?**
The Swiss Alps are an adventure playground for cyclists – there are challenges everywhere you look.

**Don't forget**
There may be bad weather. The Alpenbrevet organisers will change the route if that's so, but if you do it independently you must pick a window of good weather. What is already an incredibly hard challenge could become a terrible and frightening experience if you don't. There are some long tunnels on the route. They are lit, but, nevertheless, small front and rear reflectors on your bike will help your safety. Lights are even better. Training should include some regular long rides in hilly terrain. You should also try to simulate long mountain climbs by repeatedly climbing the same hill at a much harder pace than you would ride on the day, or by doing 45-minute rides on a turbo trainer with the front wheel supported six inches higher than normal. Ride those training sessions harder than you would during the challenge, too.

**Early Swiss road-building required great ingenuity to take people over the high passes**

Italy

The Italian Lake District

**Distance** 258 kilometres / 161 miles
**Total climbing** 4,050 metres / 13,284 feet
**Route key** Two medium-sized mountain climbs and several others of differing lengths, including some very steep ones

# **41** Tour of Lombardy

The Tour of Lombardy is cycling's fifth monument, and Italy's second after Milan–San Remo. It's a classic that's run at the end of each racing season and, because of this, it has been called 'The Race of the Falling Leaves'. Like all classics, the Tour of Lombardy is demanding. Its route is long and has a serious amount of climbing in it, but the scenery is stunning.

The Italian Lake District lies north of Milan on the way to the Alps. Long lakes fill the bottom of steep-sided, towering valleys where roads cling to the lake shores, and villages full of muted pastel houses flow like coloured ribbons along their edges. The valleys are Lombardy's race route, and the transition between each one requires a back-breaking climb, where the race is decided. Over the years these climbs have become some of the most famous in cycling.

You'll probably have to try this challenge on your own, as although there has been a Tour of Lombardy all-comers event as well as the pro race, it didn't run in 2012. The DIY option works though, because it's quite easy to find your way around the route and the area is well populated, so you don't get the feeling of isolation you would in bigger mountains.

The start and finish have varied a great deal since the first race in 1905, although the race has travelled over many of the same roads and hills. The 2012 start was in Bergamo, an old city that's part of the north Italian corridor of commerce and industry that stretches from Milan to Venice.

To start with, the route does a flattish loop east then west at first, climbing the Colle dei Pasta before returning to Bergamo. It's a nice warm-up for the first real challenge, the Colle di Valcava. This is the highest point of the ride, a genuine mountain climb that reaches 1,333 metres (4,372 feet) and is incredibly steep in places. The descent is long and twisting and takes you almost to the foot of the next climb, the Colle Brianza. This leads to twin round lakes, the Pusiano

and Annone, then through Sormano to the hardest passage of this race, a short and super-steep climb called the Muro di Sormano, then the Colma di Sormano, the second highest on the route. There's no good advice for the Muro di Sormano; it is steep all the way – so steep that you hardly notice the 25 per cent section because the rest is so bad. It's a battle of survival, and the only mindset to have is that if you are still pedalling and going forwards, then you are winning.

The climb leads over a mountain ridge and down to Lake Como, the most iconic lake on the route, and you get to know it well in the next 10 kilometres (6 miles), riding along the shore. Watch out for the sea plane that takes off and lands on the lake to take people on spectacular sightseeing flights around the mountains. Eventually you arrive in Bellagio at the elbow of land where Lake Como and Lake Lecco meet, and where you turn your back on them to take on the most famous climb of the Tour of Lombardy. It's one of the most famous in cycling: the Madonna del Ghisallo.

The Ghisallo was one of the first climbs included in this race, which when it was first run stuck to the flat valley roads. But they were hard back then; most were just powdery trails, and many of them had railway lines running down the middle. Some of the wiser riders carried their bikes over to ride between the tracks, because the road was smoother there. The first winner, Giovanni Gerbi, went further, as winners often do. He went round the route the day before the race building little earth ramps next to the rails so he was able to cross over them without dismounting.

When road conditions improved, the organisers put in other obstacles, otherwise the whole bunch would have stayed together all the way round. This would have made the Tour of Lombardy ordinary, and classics can't be ordinary. The Madonna del Ghisallo was enough at first; it's a tough climb, especially on its early slopes where there's some 14 per cent climbing, but as racers got fitter and bikes better, more climbs were added.

At the same time the Ghisallo became special in cycling for another reason. The climb is named after the chapel on its summit, which is dedicated to cyclists. The name and picture of every cyclist killed on Italian roads is in there, and so are jerseys and bikes of some of cycling's biggest legends. So much memorabilia was donated to the chapel over the

years that a modern museum has opened next to it. Both are worth visiting and spending some time in after the ride.

Two short, sharp climbs follow the Ghisallo's descent, then you climb up to Villa Vergano. This deceptive hill is not too bad at the start but it has a very steep second half. From the top of that one it's only 9 kilometres (5.75 miles) to the finish in Lecco, right at the southern edge of Lake Lecco, squeezed in between the lake and a lovely green mountain called Monte Barro.

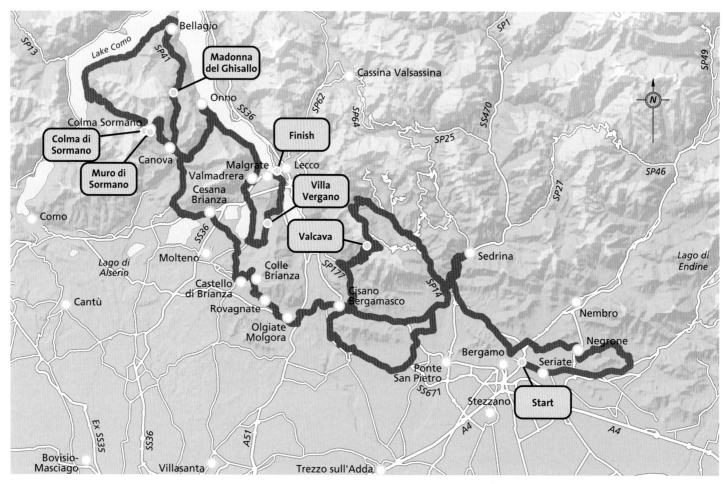

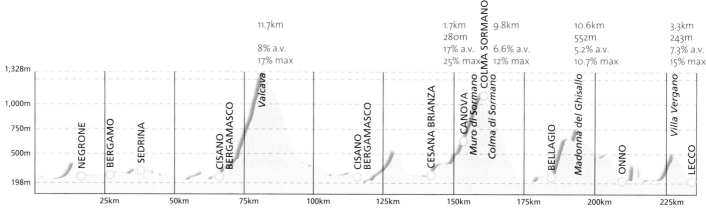

Lombardy's breathtaking countryside is a joy to ride through – a heady mix of lakes and mountains

Magnus Ljungqvist on the Lake Lecco road

## Directions

▲ From Bergamo, follow the SS42 east, then go north towards Valpredina, then southwest towards Albano, where you head north to Negrone. Head west through Bergamo, turning northwest along the edge of the Parco della Rocca to pick up the SS470 and follow this to Sedrina. Turn left after crossing the bridge and follow the road along the other side of the River Brembo to Almenno San Bartolomeo.

▲ Turn left in Brembate di Sopra and go through Presezzo and Terno d'Isola to Villa d'Adda. Continue north then northeast to Cisano Bergamasco. Follow signs over the Colle di Valcava and after the descent follow the SP14 and SP175 back through Cisano Bergamasco to cross the Adda at Brivio. Follow the SS342 to Monticello, turn right and follow the SP58 over the Colle Brianza. Turn right in Dolzago then left on the SP49 and follow this road to Cesana Brianza to turn right on the SS42. Turn right on the SS41 then fork left to Canova and climb the Muro di Sormano then the Colma di Sormano.

▲ Descend to Nesso on the Lake Como shore, where you turn right. Follow the road to Bellagio, where you turn right to climb the Madonna del Ghisallo. Continue until just after Canova, turn left to Onno then go right and follow the Lake Lecco road to Parè, where you turn right and go through Valmadrera and follow the Lake Annone road. Turn left in Imberido to climb to the Villa Vergano and continue through Galbiate to Lecco.

**Website**
www.gazzetta.it/Speciali/GiroLombardia/en/

**Date**
Usually on the second Sunday in October.

**Why the name?**
It's a race around the Lombardy region, which had autonomy before the unification of Italy.

**Anything else?**
There are steep climbs up to villages on the valley sides away from the lakes all over this area. And there are other lakes to visit east and west of the Tour of Lombardy route.

**Don't forget**
The climbs aren't too high, so there won't be big temperature changes to worry about. The route is also quite densely populated, so you are never far from somewhere to buy food and drink. The downside of that, though, is that the valley roads are quite busy, so take care. Bergamo is even busier, so watch out when navigating your way around there. The hills here are steep, so include some training in which you use higher gears than you normally would to climb. There's no better way to build cycling-specific strength.

**Distance** 290 kilometres / 181 miles
**Total climbing** 1,970 metres / 6,462 feet
**Route key** One long climb at halfway and five further significant ones during the last 25 miles of the race

# **42** Milan–San Remo

Milan–San Remo is one of cycling's monuments. An old race that has been running since 1907, it is the first of several big races each year known as the spring classics. Those races include three more of the five monuments: Tour of Flanders, Paris–Roubaix and Liège-Bastogne-Liège, all of which are in northern Europe. Milan–San Remo runs from Italy's largest northern city to the Mediterranean coast then goes along it. There isn't a better race to usher in cycling's spring period, and Milan–San Remo is often called La Primavera, which is the Italian word for spring.

Milan–San Remo is long, and the cyclosportive version of the pro race covers every metre of the pro route. It's a long day in the saddle, but it is made slightly more comfortable by being run in June, rather than the mid-March date on which the pro race is held. The 2013 pro race was hit by snow, rendering the first big obstacle of the race, the Passo del Turchino, impassable and making the rest of it a test of resolve and resistance to hypothermia as much as the festival of speed it usually is.

The pro race is often won by a sprinter nowadays, a fact you'll find surprising if you tackle Milan–San Remo's hills. The Turchino comes first, after a long, flat trek across the Piedmont plain from Milan to Novi Ligure, a city close to the birthplace of Italy's iconic cyclist Fausto Coppi.

Coppi won Milan–San Remo three times, as well as almost every other big race in cycling, many more than once. He was hailed as the greatest cyclist ever until Eddy Merckx. Merckx won Milan–San Remo a staggering seven times between 1966 and 1976. Nobody has eclipsed Merckx yet.

The Turchino is a genuine mountain climb, and when the pro race is run in March it often sees the racers effectively passing from winter into spring. Piedmont has cold winters, and the north side of the Turchino has a Piedmont climate,

but once over the summit the effects of the Mediterranean are felt.

The sea lies at the end of a valley after the Turchino's descent, where you turn right and ride along the coast, heading for San Remo. Sounds simple, doesn't it? Well, it's not. There are headlands between the beaches of the Costa Azzurra, headlands called *capi*, and they make significant hills to cross before the finish.

Capo Mele is the first, but then Capo Cervo and Capo Berta come next. From there it used to be a flat run in the race to the finish, but too many Milan–San Remos were ending in a big group sprint, so the organisers decided to put some diversions into the hills behind the coast. Il Poggio di Sanremo was the first, but when that wasn't enough they added a longer and harder hill called La Cipressa.

They are both tough, not because they are steep, but because you have ridden well over 200 kilometres (124 miles) by now, so they hurt. Watch out on their descents, too, as they are quite technical. Many a Milan–San Remo has been won with a death-defying descent of the Poggio, the end of which is so near the finish. Take care because the sharp bends can catch you out and very often there's a sheer drop on one side of the road and a solid wall on the other.

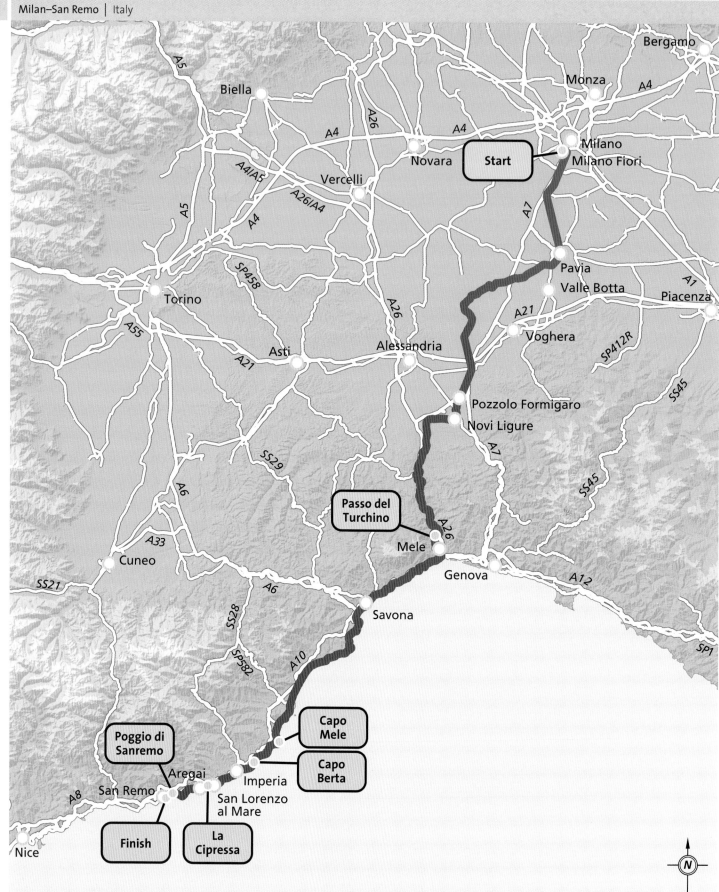

The Milan–San Remo cyclosportive is run in the fine weather of June

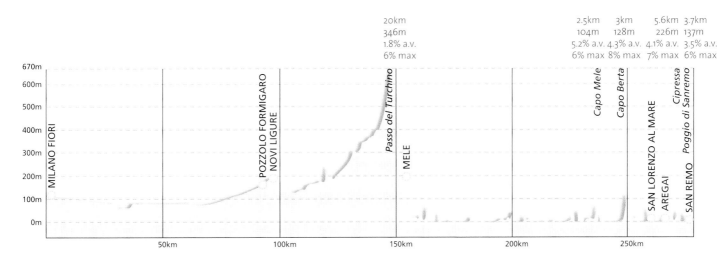

| | | | 20km | | 2.5km | 3km | 5.6km | 3.7km |
| | | | 346m | | 104m | 128m | 226m | 137m |
| | | | 1.8% a.v. | | 5.2% a.v. | 4.3% a.v. | 4.1% a.v. | 3.5% a.v. |
| | | | 6% max | | 6% max | 8% max | 7% max | 6% max |

# Directions

▲ Start in Milano Fiori to the southwest of Milan and head south on the SS35 through Binasco and Pavia. Continue south over the River Po and turn right then left to go through Sannazzaro de' Burgondi to Pieve del Cairo. Turn left on the SP221 then continue south through Pozzolo Formigaro to Novi Ligure. Go round the west side of Novi Ligure and turn right on the SP155. Follow this road to join the SS456 to climb over the Passo del Turchino and descend through Mele to the coast. Turn right and follow the SS1 coast road to San Lorenzo al Mare, where you turn right to climb over La Cipressa on the SP47. Rejoin the SS1 at Aregai and follow this road to the first right after rounding Capo Verde to climb over the Poggio. Rejoin the SS1 into San Remo.

**Norwegian national champion Kurt Asle Arvesen loves training in Italy**

**Website**
www.milano-sanremo.org

**Date**
Early June.

**Why the name?**
It's usual practice in cycling to replace the 'to' in place-to-place races with a dash, hence Milan–San Remo.

**Anything else?**
If you do this outside the event, don't end the ride in San Remo where the new race and the sportive ends (on the street that is straight on when you get to the Via Fume roundabout just after entering San Remo). Instead, go left at the roundabout, down the Via Fume and turn right on the Via Roma (the SS1 road) and ride into town. That's the traditional finish of Milan–San Remo. It's the finest road in town and the backdrop for many great victories, including those of Coppi and Merckx. The new finish came in about five years ago, and doesn't have the emotional attachment for bike fans yet.

**Don't forget**
You'll be looked after on the organised event with feed stations, and it's run in June so the weather shouldn't be a problem, although it could be very hot. Drink plenty and ensure that some of what you drink contains electrolytes to help keep all your body systems functioning properly. Your training should include some long rides with as many hills in them as possible. Really push yourself hard on those rides, but rest well before and after doing them. Work on your nutrition strategy, and if you are riding the event, find out what nutrition products are available on the day and use them in training so you are well prepared. If you ride this outside the event, it's probably best to do so as a group and have a support vehicle, although it is truly rewarding to ride all this way without any help or company at all.

Valtellina

**Distance** 129 kilometres / 80.6 miles
**Total climbing** 4,888 metres / 16,032 feet
**Route key** Three iconic mountain climbs

# 43 A Stage of the Tour of Italy

There is a stage of the Tour of Italy for all to ride – exactly like if you want to try a stage of the Tour de France, there's the Etape du Tour. But the Tour of Italy's all-comers stage hasn't been established for as long as the Etape, and none of the events so far have had the qualities I wanted to reflect.

For me, and this is purely personal, the Passo di Stelvio is the most beautiful climb ever used by Tour of Italy, or the Giro as it's known in cycling, and I wanted the ride to do both sides. I also wanted to start and finish in the Valtellina, which is an amazing playground for the Giro because so many famous Giro climbs are located in and around this valley. And I wanted to reflect another characteristic the Giro has that the Tour de France didn't have until 2012: some super-steep climbs that the Tour of Spain has also copied. So this ride isn't an actual stage, but more a reflection of several stages rolled into one.

The ride starts with the super-steep climb, not as a warm-up, because that doesn't do it justice, but more as a tasty hors-d'oeuvre. The Mortirolo is an icon in cycling, a climb that turns pro racers inside out. It's not very fashionable to quote Lance Armstrong any more, but even he said that the Mortirolo was the hardest climb he'd ever done. And in Lance's world that's a compliment.

There are three ways to the top, and are all steep, but the steepest route starts in Mazzo di Valtellina, and that's the way the Giro climbs it. There's a sign at the foot of the climb saying that it's dangerous, and warning motor vehicles not to go any further. The Mortirolo is that serious, but despite the dire warning it starts relatively easily (if you call 7 and 8 per cent climbing easy). The road is very narrow, but quite well surfaced.

Then the nightmare begins: a stretch of 11.6 per cent from Piazzola Otta to Ca' d'Batista is a prelude to the frightening

mid-section of the Mortirolo. From the third to the ninth kilometre the average gradient is almost 13 per cent, with four sections of back-breaking 18 per cent, making an incredible height gain of just over 800 metres (2,624 feet) in 6 kilometres (3.75 miles). This is the crux of the Mortirolo.

It really is incredible. The road writhes and twists upwards, searching for weaknesses in what is virtually a rock wall. It's oppressive here in high summer. Trees crowd the road and remove any sense of location. For most cyclists this is a dark tunnel of pain: just you, the bike and the mountain. Only the most talented can even think about racing up this slope. For everyone else it is just survival. No wonder the great climbers love the Mortirolo. One of the greatest was Marco Pantani, who had some amazing moments here before his death from a cocaine overdose in 2004. There's a plaque dedicated to Pantani 8 kilometres (5 miles) up the climb on its steepest corner. Continue to the top of the climb then retrace and take the right fork back down into the Valtellina, heading for the main course.

The Stelvio starts in Bormio, and it's 48 kilometres (29 miles) over the top and down the other side to Prato allo Stelvio, 48 kilometres of 70 hairpin bends that soar 2,757 metres (9,043 feet) into the sky, up and down what looks like a rock wall from the bottom. It's the highest paved road in Italy, the fourth highest in Europe, a feat of engineering that sprang from colonial necessity when Austria had to control its interests in Italy. You still see the Stelvio's Austrian name, Stilfser Joch, on the pass and the maps.

The climb begins in a long gorge that contains several dark tunnels that can be more of a problem coming down than they are going up. They are all unlit and therefore you should slow right down and remove your sunglasses before entering each one.

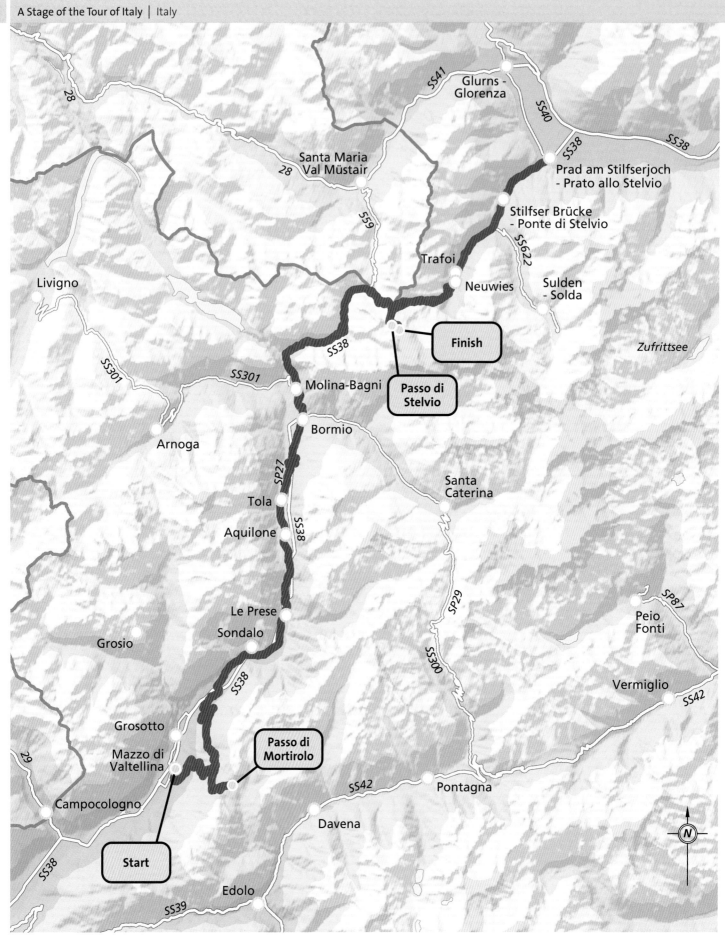

Livigno

SS28

Santa Maria
Val Müstair
28

SS41

Glurns -
Glorenza

SS40

SS38

SS38

SS38

Prad am Stilfserjoch
- Prato allo Stelvio

Stilfser Brücke
- Ponte di Stelvio

SS622

559

Trafoi

Neuwies

Sulden
- Solda

SS301

SS38

**Finish**

*Zufrittsee*

SS301

Molina-Bagni

**Passo di
Stelvio**

Arnoga

Bormio

Santa
Caterina

SP27

Tola

SS38

Aquilone

SP29

Peio
Fonti

SP87

Le Prese

Sondalo

Grosio

SS300

Vermiglio

SS42

SS38

Grosotto

Mazzo di
Valtellina

**Passo di
Mortirolo**

Campocologno

SS42

Pontagna

29

SS38

Davena

**Start**

N

Edolo

SS39

The climb's average gradient looks tough, but an added difficulty is presented by the Stelvio's famous hairpin bends. There are 20 on the southwest ascent, the way this route climbs the first time, and 48 to negotiate over the other side. Most of them are quite flat but they have steep ramps of straight road in between them that make a mockery of average gradient figures.

The first part of the climb follows the natural line carved out by a stream; the first hairpins come when the wall of the valley side has to be overcome. Look upwards at this point and the traffic above you shuttles left and right as it makes its way to a higher valley, where the gradient eases for a short while.

The valley ends where the Umbrail pass comes up from Switzerland to join the Stelvio, and from there the summit is visible for the first time. It's a further 3 kilometres (2 miles) and over 250 metres (820 feet) higher, but it is there, snow-capped and shimmering in the thin air.

The top is spectacular; you can see down the whole of the northeast side from there. Coil after coil of hairpin bends flow down the long valley, disappearing as they straighten into what is the first part of the northeast ascent. This is the side of the mountain that the Giro has used most often; the side that Fausto Coppi climbed when he put the Stelvio in the cycling history books in 1953.

Descend to Prato, turn around, and you can follow Coppi, Charly Gaul, Eddy Merckx, Bernard Hinault and all the other greats who have written their names on the northeast side of the Stelvio. It's one of the best tests in cycling, and one that any cyclist should be proud of completing.

**The Tour of Italy is in many respects even more beautiful than the Tour de France**

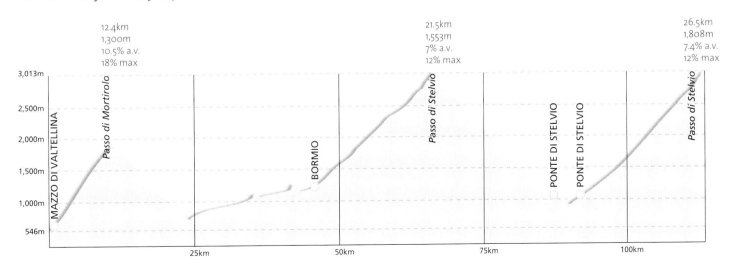

The Stelvio is an exercise in patience as well as lung capacity

# Directions

▲ Start riding south from Mazzo di Valtellina, to where the Mortirolo starts. You will see signs to the Passo della Foppa, as they are on the same climb. Ride to the top, turn around and descend but go right at the fork in the road. Turn right in Grosio and ride through Bormio and over the Stelvio to Prato allo Stelvio. Turn around and retrace your route up the Stelvio's northeast face, then descend to Bormio and continue through Grosio to Grosotto. Or you could just stop at the top of the Stelvio if you have back-up transport. All the hard work is done by then.

**Website**
www.valtellina.it/eng/index.html

**Date**
Any time the passes are clear. June to early September is best.

**Why the name?**
It climbs three of the most famous ascents in the Tour of Italy's history.

**Anything else?**
Another iconic Giro climb, Passo di Gavia, also starts in the Valtellina. It's where Andy Hampsten became the first American to win a Grand Tour, when he survived an awful snow-wrecked stage to take the lead of the 1986 Giro.

**Don't forget**
You have to do this one on your own or in a group, which is why I kept the distance down to just over 80 miles. There are huge changes of altitude, so watch the weather forecast, dress accordingly and take a rain-/waterproof even if it's sunny. You'll be able to get water and food in Bormio or Prato. Your training should include some strength work for the Mortirolo's steepest bits. You need very low bottom gear, at least 34 x 12, but even then you'll end up pedalling quite slowly, so to simulate that in training try climbing hills in a higher gear than you normally would. Do them seated and standing up to build all-round strength.

Trentino

**Distance** 142 kilometres / 88.75 miles
**Total climbing** 3,960 metres / 12,988 feet
**Route key** Two major climbs

# **44** La Leggendaria Charly Gaul

Charly Gaul is a cycling legend – one of the best mountain climbers the sport has ever seen. He is a rare breed, because pure climbers like Gaul don't often win the biggest races, such as the Tour de France and the Tour of Italy, but Gaul did. The reason for this is that pure climbers may excel when the road goes upwards, but they lose time during the rest of a three-week race. The only way they can win is if they get enough lead in the mountains, which is exactly what Gaul did.

But Gaul was a Luxembourger, so why is his memory celebrated by a cyclosportive event in Italy? Because Gaul had one of his best racing days here, on a climb called Monte Bondone. It was a day that helped the fans christen Gaul the Angel of the Mountains, because, small and frail though he looked, he flew uphill at a pace no one could match.

Gaul's celebrated Italian exploit occurred way back in 1956. Gaul was particularly good in conditions that shouldn't have suited him because he was so thin. Cold didn't seem to affect him, or maybe he could just suffer it and push himself more than the rest. The final mountain stage of the 1956 Giro d'Italia was cold and wet, with snow banked up at the sides of the roads on the mountain passes.

Gaul was lying 24th overall, 16 minutes behind the race leader, but with 242 kilometres (150 miles) and several high passes, Gaul still thought he could win. He attacked halfway through the stage and simply danced away from the rest. They could do nothing about his attack, and Gaul took back all his deficit and enough time to win the race overall. He couldn't walk by the end of the stage, which took him nine hours to complete, and only 49 of the morning's 89 starters even made it to the top of Monte Bondone. That's why they celebrate Charly Gaul here.

The event starts in Trento and in 2013 it had a very racy feel. The international cycling body, the UCI, made it one of the rounds of what they call their World Cycling Tour. This is meant as a world championship for age-group riders, and those wanting to ride have to qualify in one of the 13 events around the world that lead up to the final's September date. La Leggendaria Charly Gaul is one of the rounds, but the final was also on a similar route in September. Details of the World Cycling Tour can be found on the UCI's website, www.uci.ch, but basically their aim is to promote racing for all-comers on the sort of routes that professionals race on.

Of course, you don't have to participate in the race to experience La Leggendaria Charly Gaul route and follow him up Monte Bondone. Like all the challenges in the book, the ride can be attempted at any time when the mountain passes are open. The start is in Trento, and Monte Bondone's summit is not far from the city, so the logistics of a solo or group ride aren't a problem.

The first 7 kilometres (4.5 miles) are flat, but then the climbing starts. The first hill leads to Palù di Giovo, home of Italian racing legends Francesco Moser and Gilberto Simoni. The route then descends to go through Trento again, where it crosses the River Adige.

There are 30 kilometres (19 miles) of flat riding now before the second climb, called Viota, which takes the route to 1,563 metres (5,127 feet), where there is an amazing view over the Lago di Cei. Ten kilometres of downhill cycling leads to another flat section, then Monte Bondone starts.

The climbing begins by the lake with 3 kilometres (2 miles) of uphill riding, then almost a mile of descent, but it's an appetite whetter. Monte Bondone starts after that in Ciago, and it's incredible. The road meanders through some villages, taking a natural but long line towards the top, then after the tiny hamlet of Candriai it heads straight for the summit up a series of dizzying hairpin bends.

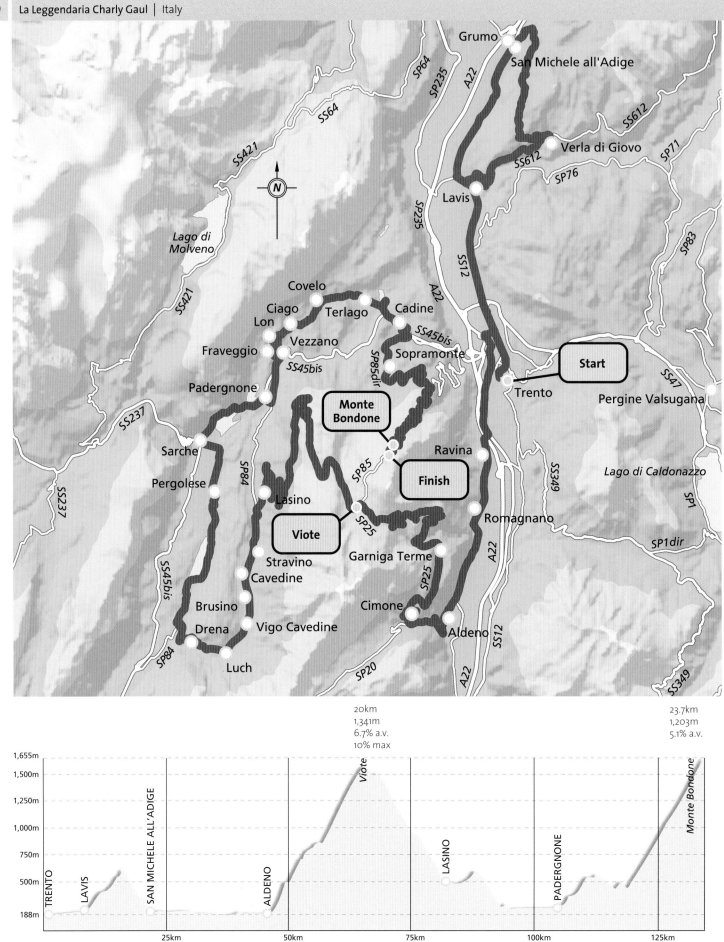

20km
1,341m
6.7% a.v.
10% max

23.7km
1,203m
5.1% a.v.

# Directions

▲ Start in Trento and head north on the SP76, then the SS12. Turn right in San Michele all' Adige and go uphill to Palù di Giovo. Descend through Lavis then retrace the earlier route on the SS12 but turn right, staying on the SS12, over the Adige to Ravina, and turn right in Aldeno to climb the Viote. Descend through Madruzzo then turn left in Lasino and follow the SP84 through Drena. Go north to Sarche, Padergnone then Vezzano, then turn left to begin the Monte Bondone climb.

**Website**
www.laleggendariacharlygaul.it

**Date**
July.

**Why the name?**
Many organised events in Europe take the names of famous racers.

**Anything else?**
Trento is right on the edge of the Brenta Alps, and Lake Garda is just to the southwest. Both are great places to ride.

**Don't forget**
You will be pretty well looked after in this event, and just need to match your race clothing to the weather conditions. Outside the event the same applies to how you dress, but take an extra top layer and gloves in case the descents are cold. Training-wise, there are no particular demands on this route requiring special preparation.

**The Giro d'Italia in Trentino with the race leader's pink jersey prominent in the centre of the peloton**

The Dolomites

**Distance** 138 kilometres / 86 miles
**Total climbing** 4,190 metres / 13,743 feet
**Route key** Five mountain passes above 2,000 metres

# **45** Maratona dles Dolomites

The Dolomites are a unique, sawtooth collection of sheer rock walls and pinnacles deep in the heart of the Alps. They get their name from the rock they are made from, a kind of limestone discovered by the French mineralogist Déodat Dolomieu, where some of the calcium has been replaced by magnesium. This has a weird effect on its colour. Mostly, in flat light or on dull days, dolomite is grey, just like normal limestone, but at other times it can look dusky yellow or even a delicate pale pink.

The Giro d'Italia loves the Dolomites today, but it didn't come here until 1937, maybe because this region was a mystery to most Italians. For centuries there was no clear delineation as to what was in Austria and what was in Italy, and the border has moved north and south over time. Now the Dolomites are part of three Italian provinces, Trentino, Belluno and South Tyrol, but many people still speak German as well as Italian, especially in South Tyrol.

The Maratona is one of Europe's blue ribbon cyclosportives, and with good reason. It's not as long as some others, but it packs in five mountain climbs that go beyond the 2,000-metre contour, plus two more that break 1,800. That's a hard day in the saddle by anybody's standards.

The route is really clever. There are three different-length rides in the organised Maratona, one of 55 kilometres (34 miles), one of 106 kilometres (65 miles) and this route, the full Maratona, which follows parts of the 55- and the 106-kilometre loops, plus an additional section of its own. It means you are never too far from the start in Pedraces and the finish a little further down the road at Corvara on the longest ride.

As you might expect with a lot of uphill riding to fit in 86 miles, the climbing starts shortly after you get going, with the Passo Campolongo. Where that climb's descent ends, the

Passo Pordoi begins. This is big and has featured a lot in the Giro d'Italia. There's a statue of Fausto Coppi at the summit of the Pordoi, from where you can see the crown of the Dolomites, their highest point, La Marmolada.

Dolomite peaks tend to have a special shape. The mountainsides slope like any others, but the peaks stick out at the top like teeth – not sharp canine teeth, blocky ones like molars, or, in La Marmolada's case, like a crowned head sitting on the mountain's shoulders. It's in the sheer walls of these peaks that you see the subtly changing colours of dolomite.

The Passo Sella is also a Giro favourite, another of Coppi's stomping grounds. He is still talked about a lot in cycling, even more so in Italian cycling, but just imagine what it took to pedal up here way back in 1953, when bikes weighed 12 or more kilograms and the lowest of their 10 gears was 46 x 24. If you want to see Coppi in action, search the internet using 'Coppi Passo Sella 1953 on video'.

At 2,244 metres (7,362 feet), the Passo Sella is the high point of the ride, part of a heady passage of climbs that ends with a long descent from the Passo Gardena to pass a second time through Corvara. Four climbs are down, but you've only done 55 kilometres (34 miles). A second time up the Campolongo is the prelude to some respite, where the route undulates for 20 kilometres (12 miles), although undulate is a relative term in this mountainous setting. Don't get carried away on the early climbs, because testing times are still to come in the form of two more giant climbs.

Whereas you were already high up when you started some of the climbs already accomplished, the Passo Giau climb starts at the lowest point on the route, so it's a long way vertically to the top. Passo Giau is huge, and a regular climb in the Giro d'Italia. It's the steepest of the Maratona climbs, but the most rewarding because its summit is

spectacular. Instead of looking like a tooth or a crown, the rocky summit that towers over the top of the pass resembles a sinister castle, like something from *The Lord of the Rings*.

There's a long descent off the Pordoi with some very sharp hairpin bends, although not as tight as those you meet going up. Then there's the last climb. Well, two climbs really, as you go up the Passo Falzarego, which is like a ladder on the side of the Passo Valparola. So, once you've climbed the Falzarego, you have the last bit of the Valparola to do.

Neither is as steep as some of the others, but you will be tired now. However, after pacing yourself over all the other climbs, you can push it a bit on the Passo Falzarego, because from the top it's 20 kilometres (12 miles) to the finish: 15 kilometres (9 miles) downhill and 5 kilometres (3 miles) up a steady rise to the end. That bit is cruel, but adrenalin and joy from being so close to achieving something memorable helps you cope.

**The Dolomite foothills**

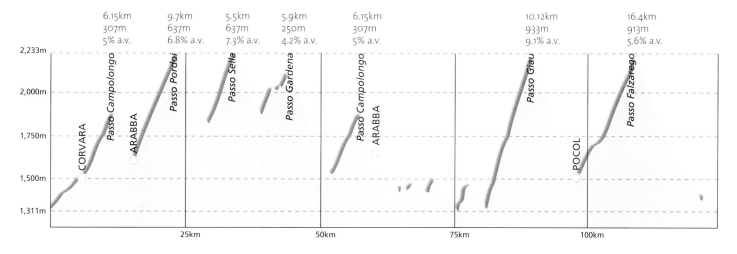

# Directions

▲ Start in Pedraces and go south then southwest to Corvara, turn left and climb the Passo Campolongo. Descend to Arabba and turn right to climb the Passo Pordoi and Passo Sella then the Passo Gardena, and descend to Corvara. Turn right and climb the Passo Campolongo again, descend to Arabba but turn left and follow the road to Cernadoi, where you turn right and go through Colle Santa Lucia and left before Selva di Cadore to climb the Passo Giau and descend to Pocol. Turn left to climb the Passo Falzarego and the Passo Valparola and descend through San Ciascian, then turn right to go through La Ila to the finish.

## Website
www.maratona.it

## Date
End of June.

## Why the name?
Very often sportive names are not self-explanatory; this one is.

## Anything else?
Two famous Giro d'Italia climbs are near this route: La Marmolada and Tre Cime di Lavaredo. The Marmolada is the mountain, not the pass that tends to be called by the same name in cycling. The pass is actually the Passo di Fedaia, and it runs to the north of the Marmolada's peak, from Canazei in the west to Caprile. Tre Cime di Lavaredo is accessed from Cortina d'Ampezzo.

## Don't forget
Go through your usual high-altitude procedure. Check the weather forecast and dress accordingly, and take a wind-/waterproof and thin gloves in case there are big temperature differences between the valleys and mountain tops. You need to simulate long climbs in training by riding the longest in your area several times in a session. Alternatively, do 45-minute to one-hour rides on your turbo trainer with the front raised 6 inches to simulate riding uphill.

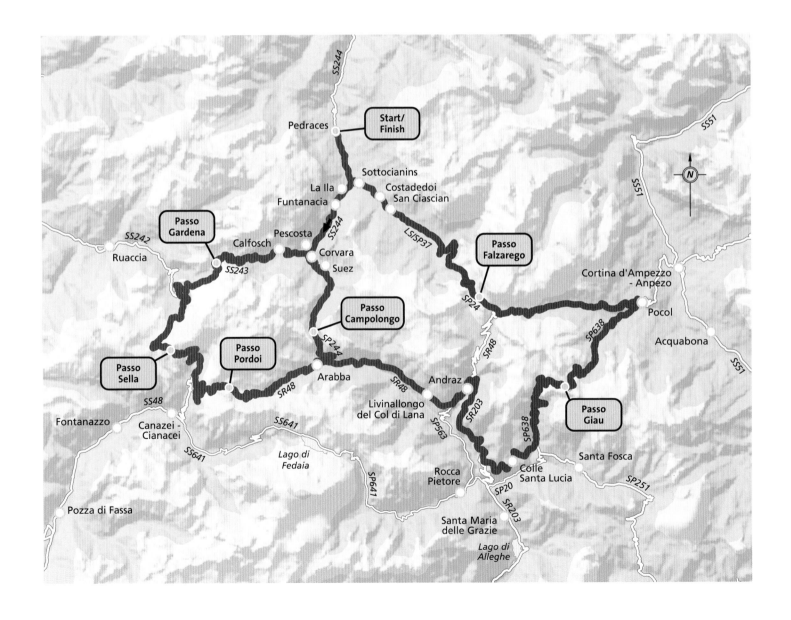

Veneto

**Distance** 198 kilometres / 123 miles
**Total climbing** 3,750 metres / 12,300 feet
**Route key** One fairly big mountain climb and several small hills

# 46 La Pinarello Cycling Marathon

This is the ride for you if you fancy rubbing shoulders with some cycling greats. Pinarello bikes have supplied some of the biggest names in cycling through their team sponsorship over the years; Sir Bradley Wiggins and Team Sky are the latest in a long line. Wiggins is still racing of course, and some Sky riders did the 2012 event, which the Pinarello family call 'La Pina'. And 'family' is the key word of the Pinarello Cycling Marathon; it and their bike company are a real family business, and they like to invite former Pinarello racers to take part, regarding them as part of their extended family. The five-time Tour de France winner Miguel Indurain is a 'La Pina' regular.

The ride starts and finishes in Treviso, starting in the Piazza dei Signori, which is the beating heart of Treviso in the way only Italian town squares can be. This lies north of the River Paive and the route does a little tour of a couple more piazzas before heading northwest to Volpago del Montello.

You climb up a bean-shaped hill called Il Montello then ride the road that runs its length, from where there are fantastic views north to the Alps. In 1950 the most violent tornado ever recorded in Europe hit here, flattening everything in its path and killing 23 people. The second small climb comes 20 kilometres (12.5 miles) later, as a final warm-up for this ride's big one.

The road undulates all the way to Possagno, where a restored temple stands on a hill. The climb of Monte Grappa starts here. The incline is easy at first, just a valley road, but then it clambers up the valley sides in a dizzying series of hairpin bends. This section is steep: the hairpins follow a mountain cornice to a false summit, where just before, the gradient is 22 per cent. The short descent is a real relief.

The road is less engineered now, using natural lines to work its way to the summit of Monte Grappa. The road over the mountain passes below the summit, but in the Pinarello event riders are expected to follow the road that spears off to the very top, the Cima Grappa. Ride up, take in the view and ride back, passing the Sacrario Militare as you do so.

Monte Grappa played a key role during World War I, when the writer Ernest Hemingway was a volunteer ambulance driver here, and has been used three times in the Tour of Italy route. There is also an annual race, Bassano to the summit of Monte Grappa, which used to be a professional race but is now only for riders aged under 23. Despite how difficult it is to climb, the mountain is loved by local cyclists, particularly by one. Ginesio Ballan has ridden up the mountain well over 1,000 times, and once did it 273 times in a single year.

The route descends Monte Grappa along a long spine of rock leading down from the summit to Feltre in the upper Piave Valley, which the route follows as it turns south towards Treviso. Feltre is at the foot of an historic Tour of Italy climb, the Croce d'Aune, after which the Italian bike component manufacturer Campagnolo named an equipment range during the 1990s.

You ride around the base of the Grappa range following a tributary of the Piave then follow the wide river as it flows between two blocks of mountains. The route passes through an archway of the Castello di Quero, built to guard this river entrance to the Feltrina district, then wanders up another tributary valley, over a small climb called Combai, to Follina, from where it follows the Soligo River southwest to join the Piave once more. You then climb the road up Il Montello, but not quite to its summit, before descending to Treviso.

Of the challenges in this book, this is one that's best done as part of the official event. The effort and warmth that the Pinarellos put into ensuring that everyone has the best experience they can is huge. La Pinarello is a template that other cyclosportive organisers should try to copy.

Riders in the Tour of Italy leaving a stage start from Treviso

# Directions

▲ From the Piazza dei Signori head northwest on the Via Calmaggiore then right on the Via Canova to turn left onto the SS13. Go right on the Viale Luzzatti then continue northwest on what is effectively the same road to Volpago del Montello. Go through the town centre on the SP248 but go straight where it bends sharp left to climb Il Montello. Turn left at the summit crossroads, follow the road then turn right on Via Generale Vaccari. Turn left on Via Medaglie d'Oro, then left at the bottom onto the SP77.

▲ Turn right at Nogarè then left in Cornuda and right in Maser to Monfumo, Pederobba and Cavaso del Tomba to Possagno. Turn left then go right in Fusere-Tuna to climb Monte Grappa, following the summit road. Then, after visiting the summit, turn right and continue on the same road you followed up over the other side down to Seren del Grappa. Head east on the Via Feltre then turn right to Tomo and Villaga then go left on the Via Dueca to Anzù, where you follow signs south to Sanzan.

▲ Turn left over the River Piave at the first bridge then follow the river road south to San Vito, turn left to Valdobbiadene and continue east on the Via Piva through Case Marche and Guietta. Go left on the Strada Fontanelle and climb through Combai. Descend to Follina where you turn right and go through Sottoriva and take the right fork in Solighetto. Then go left in Falzè di Piave to Ponte della Priula, where you turn right to cross the River Piave. Follow the SS248, carrying straight on where it bends left to follow the spine road up Il Montello. Turn left on the Via degli Alpini, follow this road to the SP90, then turn right on the SP56 and left on the SP55 back into Treviso.

## Website
www.lapinarello.com

## Date
Mid-July.

## Why the name?
Pinarello is a bike brand started by Giovanni Pinarello in 1952, although his family were involved in manufacturing bikes under other names long before that. Giovanni was a cyclist before he was a manufacturer, and his passion for the sport has always been evident in his products and in his support and sponsorship of so many teams and individuals over the years.

## Anything else?
Some of the hills you ride are foothills of the Dolomites, a cyclist's adventure playground.

## Don't forget
Dress for the weather and take the usual wind-/waterproof in case it changes. The food and drink support on La Pinarello is excellent; energy drinks and bars are supplied by an Italian brand, Enervit, so try to get some before the event to see if their products suit you. Training should include some high-gear hills to condition you to the steep climbs, and make sure you do some core condition training.

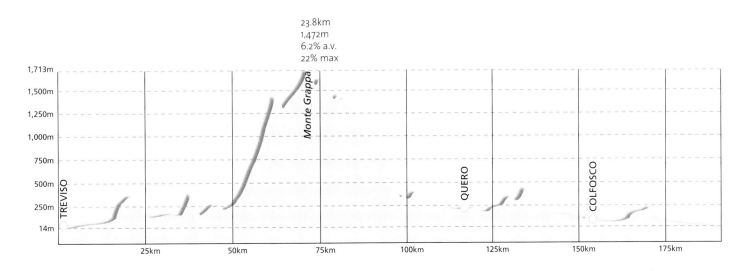

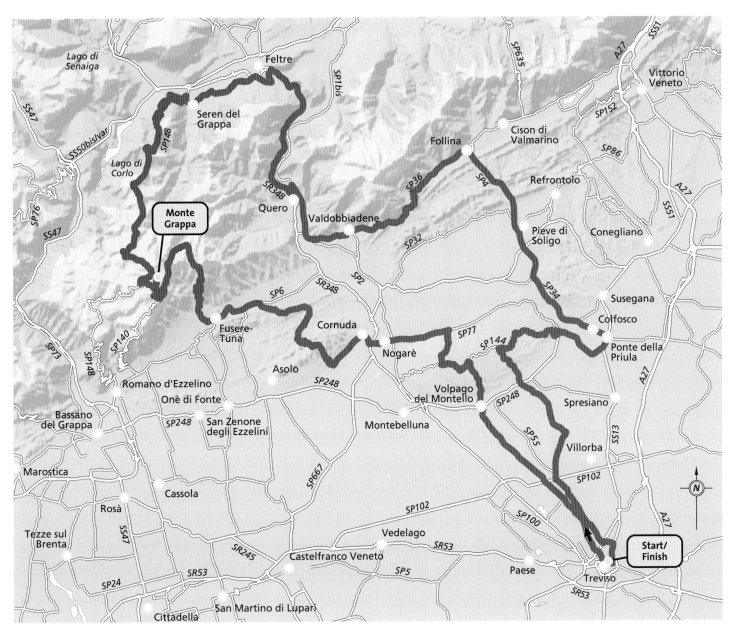

Tuscany

**Distance** 205 kilometres / 128 miles
**Total climbing** 2,383 metres / 7,818 feet
**Route key** The off-road sections of the Strade Bianchi, three blocks of hills rising to 610 metres (2,000 feet) and a long, generally undulating route

# 47 L'Eroica

Flanders is one of Europe's cycling hotspots, Tuscany is another. More champions come from this region than from any other part of Italy. Gino Bartali was one of them, the man who occupies the number two slot in Italian cycling history after Fausto Coppi. Bartali was Coppi's biggest rival. Called the Tuscan Lion by fans, he was an attacking cyclist who was also a war hero. Bartali worked against the Italian fascist regime and the Nazis during World War II, a war that deprived him of the best part of his career. He won the Tour de France in 1938 and in 1948, bookending the war almost, but the Tour was held only once between those years. How many could Bartali have won but for the conflict?

L'Eroica is an event that harks back to the days when country roads were made of hard-packed stone. Most have been overlaid by tarmac or other solid surfaces, but in Tuscany an old network of hard-packed chalk roads still exists. They are called the Strade Bianche, the White Roads, and they are located around Siena, where they are still used by the locals.

One of those locals is a cyclist called Dario Cioni. He was a good pro racer whose last team was Team Sky and he now works for them in PR. He explained how the White Roads work when I did a ride with him there a few years ago. 'In Tuscany there are lots of ridges and valleys, and the White Roads were built in a loose grid pattern over them. One road runs along the top of each ridge, one parallel to it along each valley bottom, then the third type of White Road links the two at intervals by going up from the valleys across the ridges and then down into the next valley.'

L'Eroica is a retro event, like the Retro Ronde in Belgium, but instead of being tagged onto a pro race, like the Retro Ronde is to the Tour of Flanders, L'Eroica has spawned one.

The Strade Bianche race is fast becoming a classic, even though it only dates from 2007, when it was called Monte Pasche Eroica, and it's a classic because of the White Roads. So if you don't have a retro bike suitable for the L'Eroica event, this route on the White Roads is worth doing because it's an incredibly scenic bike ride with a growing race heritage.

There's a marked L'Eroica trail that follows the event route. It starts and finishes in Gaiole in Chianti and uses a half-and-half mix of surfaced roads and White Roads to provide a fascinating route through a timeless landscape.

The event has four distances: 38, 75, 135 and 205 kilometres (24, 47, 84 and 128 miles), all with the 50/50 off-road mix. The marked 205-kilometre route, the one described here, has 15 sections of White Road. The first comes after just over 10 kilometres (6 miles) at the top of the first big hill.

The route is hilly; the first big climb goes up to the Castello di Brolio and it starts shortly after the village of La Madonna. Then, after a long downhill section, the route undulates, still switching from road to off-road, through the outskirts of Siena then south to a long, twisting main-road climb called the Poggio di Montalcino, where you cross the highest point on the ride.

The Montalcino descent is steep and twisting, so be careful. A longish White Road section, the seventh of the ride, comes after Torrenieri, which is around halfway. A few miles of provincial road come next, then you are back onto another long White Road section, some of which last for 7 kilometres (4.5 miles). Some of them, like this one that goes through Buonconvento, even pass through villages, which adds to the feel of riding through a much older landscape.

The White Roads require some technique, and there are things you need to be aware of, but they don't present too

Many Tuscan vineyards were planted by the Romans, and the landscape has hardly changed in two millennia

much of a problem in dry conditions, although they can be hard going. It's best to ride on the smoothest bits of each section and avoid anything that looks loose, so the sides and middle of the road are best avoided unless the smooth line goes over them.

This has consequences on corners, because sometimes the ideal line through a corner would mean crossing loose gravel. If you do that you can end up slipping and falling. Follow the smoothest line instead.

In contrast, the White Roads are a very bad experience in heavy rain. They can get quite soft in places and difficult to ride on. The Tour of Italy did a White Roads stage a few years ago, and a deluge turned the stage into agony.

The final block of more hilly terrain starts near Asciano at 90 miles. There are two climbs to point out in this section. The first goes up to Radda in Chianti and is the steepest and longest, and the second is shorter and peaks at the end of a long forested section, just three miles from the finish.

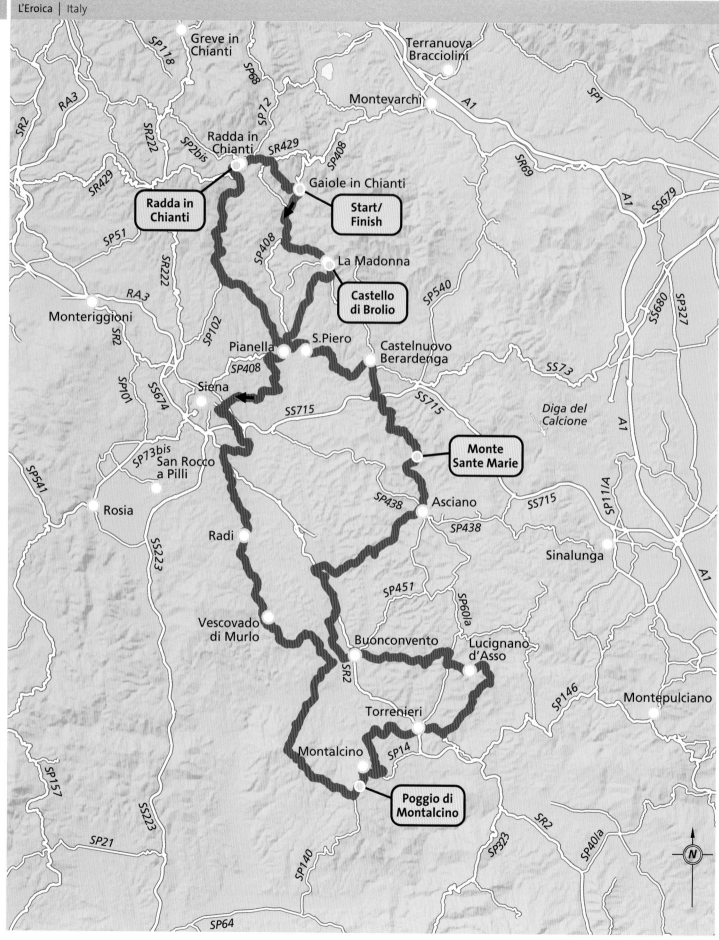

Greve in Chianti

Terranuova
Bracciolini

Montevarchi

Radda in
Chianti

Gaiole in Chianti

**Radda in
Chianti**

**Start/
Finish**

La Madonna

**Castello
di Brolio**

Monteriggioni

Pianella          S.Piero

Castelnuovo
Berardenga

Siena

**Monte
Sante Marie**

San Rocco
a Pilli

Asciano

Rosia

Diga del
Calcione

Sinalunga

Radi

Vescovado
di Murlo

Buonconvento

Lucignano
d'Asso

Montepulciano

Torrenieri

Montalcino

**Poggio di
Montalcino**

N

# Directions

▲ Start in Gaiole in Chianti and follow the permanent L'Eroica route markers to La Madonna, climbing the Castello di Brolio. The route crosses its return leg en route to Siena then heads south through Radi to start the Poggio di Montalcino shortly after descending a smaller climb, the Castiglione del Bosco.

▲ From Montalcino go north then east, through Torrenieri, left on the Strade Provincale 71, then right then left past Lucignano d'Asso to Buenoconenvto. Continue west over the river and turn right to go through Ponte d'Arbbia then right to Asciano, where the Monte Sante Marie climb starts, then head for Castelnuovo Berardenga to begin the final loop after the earlier crossover point, northwest. The Radda in Chianti climb starts at 196 kilometres, and there is another short one after that. Then it's downhill, mostly, into Gaiole in Chianti.

**Dario Cioni riding towards Siena**

## Website
www.eroicafan.it

## Date
October.

## Why the name?
*Eroica* is Italian for heroic, and it refers to an earlier time in cycling when bike racers seemed like heroes. They were certainly revered as such by race fans. The heroic spirit of cycling has many references in Italian literature, and it was these that inspired the organisers to celebrate the way this older generation raced and the conditions they faced with a retro bike event. The first event was held in 1997 and interest has grown so much that L'Eroica has also become a foundation set up to protect the White Roads of Tuscany.

## Anything else?
Tuscany is a great place in which to have little cycling adventures of your own making. The terrain undulates in the area where L'Eroica is held, but is more mountainous in the north and east. The Tuscan coast is worth exploring, too.

## Don't forget
The full Eroica is a long day in the saddle. If you ride the event on a retro bike, the organisers reckon that 12 hours is a good effort. The White Roads definitely drag at your tyres, even if they are bone dry, which can make dust a problem. It's hard work even on a modern bike, and it's worth considering splitting the distance over two days. You need to be as strong as possible and have several long rides under your belt. Some long mountain bike rides might help your preparation. There are lots of villages in which to buy food and drink along the route.

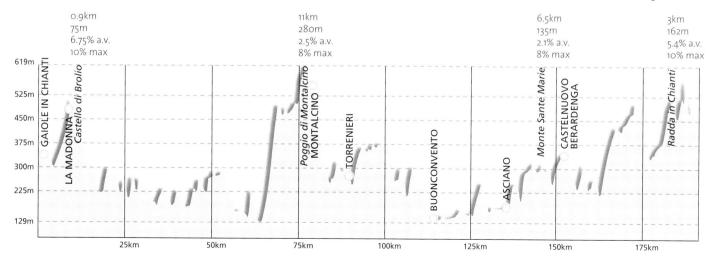

Spain

Basque Country

**Distance** 198 kilometres / 123 miles
**Total climbing** 2,733 metres / 8,965 feet
**Route key** Three climbs including one up a spectacular mountain above the sea

# 48 San Sebastian Classic

The San Sebastian Classic is Spain's only classic race. Spanish cycling has a leaning towards stage races, and Spanish riders tend to be better at that sphere of racing than they are at single-day races. But there's such enthusiasm for any kind of cycling in the Basque country that it was the best place for Spain to try to grow a race that could stand comparison with the other great European single-day races. They've certainly done it with the San Sebastian Classic.

The race is called Clásica San Sebastián–San Sebastián in Spanish, Donostia–Donostia Klasikoa in the local Basque. This is another part of Europe that's fiercely proud of its native language and its regional identity, and it has used cycling to express both. As well as providing many of Spain's best riders, including five-time Tour de France winner Miguel Indurain, the Basque country has a bike-racing team called Euskaltel-Euskadi competing in the world's biggest races. (Euskaltel is the name of a Basque telephone company.)

The Clásica San Sebastián has been going since 1981, and its first winner has gone on to score the most victories so far. His name is Marino Lejarreta and he has won three times. He's a Basque, and in a way his career represents the stoicism and endurance that people from this part of the world pride themselves on. Not many cyclists have ever completed all three Grand Tours in the same year, but Lejarreta has done it four times and holds the record. His best was 1989, when he was fifth in the Tour de France, 10th in the Giro d'Italia and 20th in the Vuelta a España. That's a lot of hard yards.

Tough racers are often forged in tough terrain, and the Basque country has plenty of that. San Sebastián is a delightful seaside resort, with a perfect crescent beach and some handsome rocky headlands, but inland it's wild and hilly. The race starts and finishes in San Sebastián and does a large loop into the hills around the back of the resort, then heads east to climb a mountain called Alto de Jaizkibel, which towers out of the Atlantic Ocean. It's a dramatic place, and it's where most of the dramatic moments of the race have occurred over the years.

There is no Clásica San Sebastián all-comers event yet, so this route is a slightly shorter version of the pro race, but it contains the most important parts, including Jaizkibel. One benefit of this route is that it misses the final few kilometres through San Sebastián's busy port area. These roads are closed to other traffic when the pros race to the finish.

The first section of the route goes around San Sebastián's bay, past Lasarte-Oria, where Tom Simpson won Britain's first ever world professional road race title in 1965 (only Mark Cavendish has won that since), and down to another seaside resort called Zarautz. You continue along the coast then turn inland to climb a steep hill called the Alto de Garate, then head further inland for the long climb up the Urola Valley.

Next there's a long descent on a main road, then some smaller roads leading to an undulating section that ends at the foot of Alto de Jaizkibel. Get ready because this is good. Jaizkibel is a long, thin mountain, running east to west, with the sea on one side and a lush valley on the other. The route leads to the middle of the valley, then west along the mountain's south side before turning east to climb its ridge.

For the first couple of kilometres you climb above an inlet, its fishing villages getting smaller behind you, then you crest the ridge and see the Atlantic. It's amazing, and the sea keeps you company almost all the way to the top.

The descent twists and turns down to Hondarribia, where you head west then south to climb a smaller hill on the race route. The route is complicated here, so this version aims to simplify it yet still contain the crux of what race riders face, before finishing in Lezo, on the eastern edge of San Sebastián.

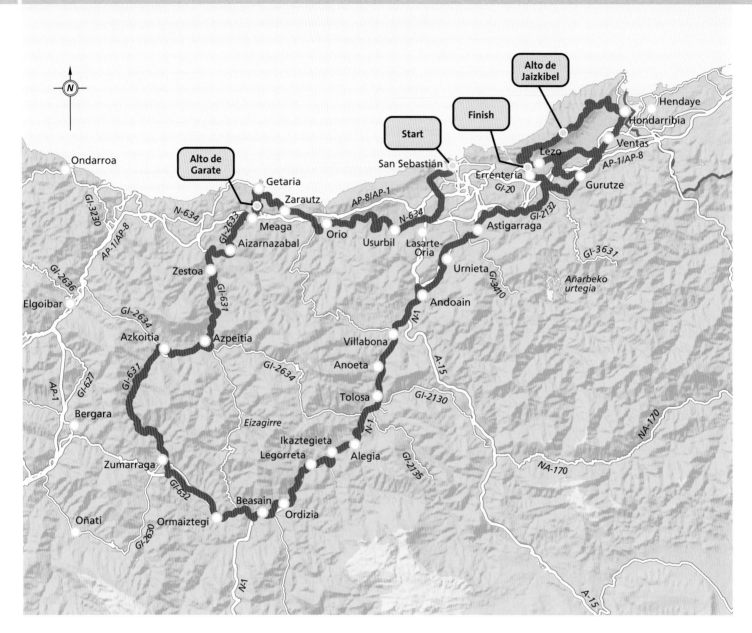

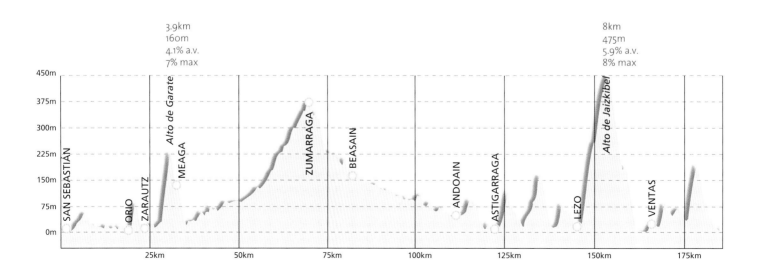

3.9km
160m
4.1% a.v.
7% max

8km
475m
5.9% a.v.
8% max

San Sebastián's bay is the perfect backdrop for the start of this ride

# Directions

▲ Start in the centre of San Sebastián, near the seafront, and head west around the bay through Antiguo and Ibaeta to go south to Errekalde. Cross the motorway and go through Usurbil to follow the River Oria then cross it at Orio and head for Zarautz. Ride northwest along the coast road to Getaria, where you turn left to climb the Alto de Garate. Continue over the summit and turn right in Meaga and follow this road into the Urola Valley.

▲ Follow the river upstream all the way to Zumárraga. Continue south through the town then turn left at the big roundabout and follow the main road to Beasain. Turn left and follow a smaller road that follows the River Oria, joining the main road again at Alegia, to Andoain. Turn right and head to Hernani, but go around the east side of town to Astigarraga. Turn right and keep to the road just south of the main AP-1\AP8 and follow this to Arragua, where you turn right and head for Ventas.

▲ Turn left at the first roundabout, turn left (third exit) at the next roundabout, go over the main road junction and take the second exit at the next roundabout. Follow this road through Lezo to begin the climb of Jaizkibel. Descend to Hondarribia then turn right at the airport and retrace the way you went before over the Ventas roundabouts, but take the third exit at the last one. Turn left at the next junction and follow this road to Gurutze, where you turn right. Continue uphill then descend to Lezo.

The Basque Country is unlike the rest of Spain, with its own weather and its own culture

### Website
http://clasica-san-sebastian.diariovasco.com

### Date
The race is held on the first weekend following the end of the Tour de France, so it's usually very early August.

### Why the name?
It's a classic race on a classic route that starts and finishes in San Sebastián.

### Anything else?
The Raid Pyrenees starts here, a west to east long-distance route right across the Pyrenees that takes several days to complete. You can follow a specified route over a number of stages or design your own raid.
www.raidpyrenees.com

### Don't forget
You are going to need transport back to the start, although it's not far and you could ride, provided you take care in San Sebastián's streets. A support vehicle is always useful on a ride like this, where there is no official event that anyone can ride. Make the usual weather forecast checks and take a wind- or waterproof top. There's no real high altitude on this route though. Summers are hot and humid in the Basque country, autumn can be very pleasant, and winters fairly mild apart from in the highest mountains. Spring tends to be wet and sometimes cold.

**Distance** 205 kilometres / 128 miles
**Total climbing** 3,500 metres / 11,480 feet
**Route key** Three Tour de France mountain climbs

# 49 Quebrantahuesos

Quebrantahuesos is said by many to be the best cyclosportive event in Spain. It has a glorious mountain route, it's a real challenge and it has a truly evocative name. Quebrantahuesos is a giant bird of prey, also known as the bearded vulture, lammergeyer or, more ominously, bone-crusher, and this ride goes through its habitat. The bird feeds like a vulture on the carcasses of dead animals, which it expertly butchers, but the Quebrantahuesos is not just after meat; it loves the juicy marrow inside animal bones. That's how the bird gets its bone-crusher nickname, because it carries off long bones and drops them from a great height onto a hard rock, then swoops down to pick the marrow out of the shattered remains.

Your journey on the path of the bone-crushers starts in Sabiñánigo, an often-used stage town on the Tour of Spain, because it's at the foot of the Spanish side of the Pyrenees. The route heads west at first, to Jaca, then turns north to climb into the mountains up the Aragon Valley.

This leads to the Col du Somport. This used to be a busy main route between Spain and France, but now the Somport tunnel takes most of the traffic away from it and the summit is a lonely, wild place today. The 9 kilometres (5 miles) of the old road on the Spanish side and slightly less on the French are almost traffic-free. The descent into France twists and turns, so treat it with respect and ride within your skill level.

It's nearly 40 kilometres (24 miles) downhill from the top of the Somport, where there's an aid station in the event, to Escot and the start of the shorter but very much sharper, especially near the top, Col de Marie-Blanque. It's a nice name with a grim heritage, because Marie Blanque was a famous professional mourner in the Bearn region. Her services were required at any respectable funeral, so much so that they named a mountain after her.

The Marie-Blanque's eastern descent is also quite technical, and it ends in the Ossau Valley, where you head south towards Spain again. The Pyrenees look magnificent here, especially as you approach one of their most distinctive peaks. The Pic du Midi d'Ossau juts up out of the range like a dark triangle with two top points that reach nearly 3,000 metres (9,842 feet). It's so distinctive that it can be seen from Pau, nearly 50 miles to the north.

You're heading for the final climb now, the highest of Quebrantahuesos, the Col du Pourtalet. It's known locally as the stairway climb because it goes up in three definite steps, which each average around 7 per cent. Counting down the steps will help at this stage of the ride, and you can recover on the flatter sections in between.

With the Pic du Midi d'Ossau behind you and peaks on either side, this is the territory of the bone-crusher, and if you are fortunate enough to get a sighting of this shy bird of prey, most likely it will be here. The high peaks are its home, where the jagged rocks act as its butcher's slabs. The Pourtalet's descent is spectacular at the point where you pass a series of long lakes, the largest of which, the Búbal, has a short climb at the end of it.

It's called the Puerto de Hoz de Jaca, where *puerto* is Spanish for mountain pass. Although it has a meagre height gain of about 75 metres (246 feet), it's quite steep. It can catch you out if you hit it in too high a gear, which is a temptation after the long descent off the Pourtalet, but once at the top it's almost all downhill to Sabiñánigo.

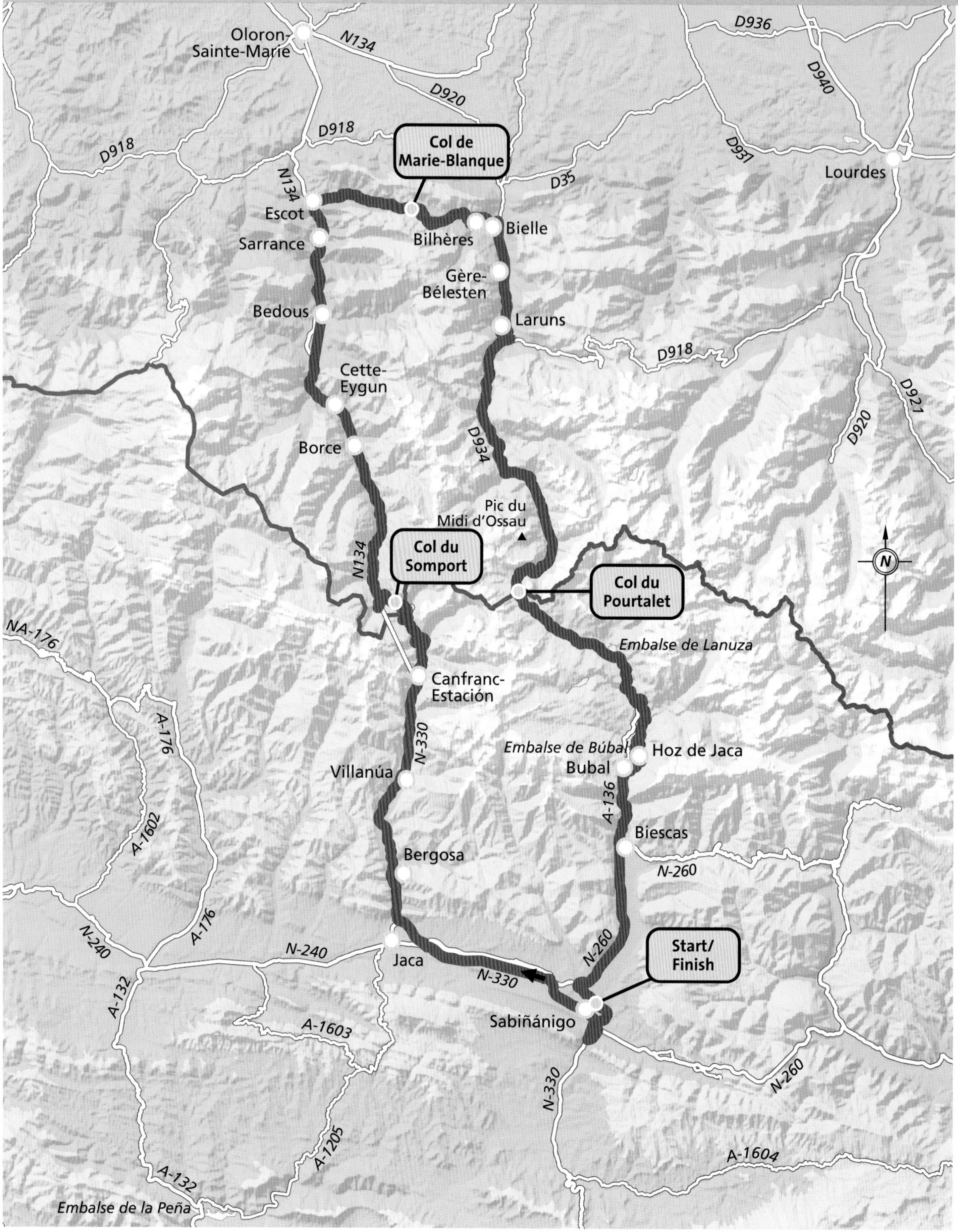

Oloron-Sainte-Marie

N134

D936

D920

D918

D918

D935

D940

Lourdes

**Col de Marie-Blanque**

D35

N134

Escot

Bielle

Sarrance

Bilhères

Gère-Bélesten

Bedous

Laruns

D918

Cette-Eygun

D934

Borce

N134

Pic du Midi d'Ossau ▲

**Col du Somport**

**Col du Pourtalet**

D920

D921

N

NA-176

Embalse de Lanuza

Canfranc-Estación

A-176

N-330

Embalse de Búbal

Hoz de Jaca

Villanúa

Bubal

A-1602

Biescas

A-136

Bergosa

N-260

A-176

N-240

N-240

N-330

**Start/Finish**

N-260

A-132

Jaca

N-330

Sabiñánigo

N-260

A-1603

A-1205

N-330

A-1604

Embalse de la Peña

A-132

# Directions

▲ Start in Sabiñánigo and go northwest on the A23 to Jaca. Turn right and head north on the N330, going around the Somport Tunnel to cross the Col du Somport and descend into France on the N134. Continue to Escot, where you turn right on the D294 to climb the Col de Marie-Blanque. Descend to Bielle, where you turn right on the D934 to climb over the Col du Pourtalet, then descend on the A136, turning left after Escarrilla. Stay right to go over the Hoz de Jaca climb, then join the N260 back to Sabiñánigo.

**Website**
www.quebrantahuesos.com

**Date**
Late June.

**Why the name?**
The route is named after a bird of prey that lives in this part of the Pyrenees.

**Anything else?**
The organisers of Quebrantahuesos, which is known in Spain as La Quebranta, also organise a mountain bike challenge and a triathlon of the same name.

**Don't forget**
The event is always oversubscribed so entries are selected by lottery; details are on the website. If you want to do this event, enter it as soon as you possibly can. This ride involves some high-altitude stuff, so pay close attention to the weather forecast and take an extra layer because it will be colder on the tops of the climbs. The Pyrenean climate can be capricious, and the weather can change quickly, with sudden thunderstorms a possibility. If you do this ride outside the event, you will need to take plenty of food and drink with you, because the villages are quite spread out.

The distinctive Pic du Midi

Tour de France riders racing in the Pyrenees

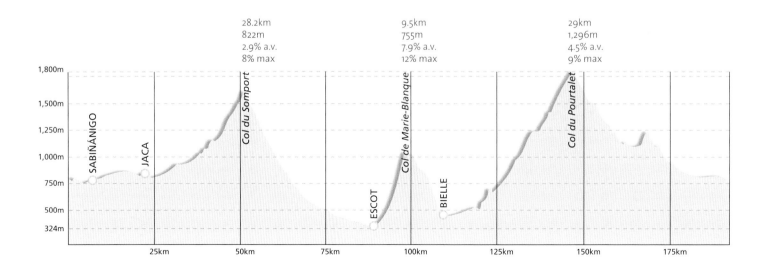

28.2km
822m
2.9% a.v.
8% max

9.5km
755m
7.9% a.v.
12% max

29km
1,296m
4.5% a.v.
9% max

Eastern Pyrenees

**Distance** 142 kilometres / 88.6 miles
**Total climbing** 4,124 metres / 13,527 feet
**Route key** Two Tour de France climbs, one of which you ascend twice,
so three Tour de France climbs really, then a much less well known but very tough climb in Spain

# **50** Val d'Aran Cycling Tour

Val d'Aran is a deep, wide valley in the far north of Spain. The Río Garona, which starts high on the Spanish side of the Pyrenees and is fed by waters from the glaciers in the Maldetta Massif, flows through it into France, where it becomes the Garonne.

The Val d'Aran Cycling Tour starts in a town called Vielha, on a bend of the Garona. The route crosses into France via a Tour de France climb, takes on another, then returns to Spain up the first climb, but in the opposite direction. It ends with a hellish slog up a tiny road to some remote villages, followed by a hectic descent then a short climb back to Vielha.

The Val d'Aran looks amazing. The river weaves along the bottom like carelessly laid silver thread. A rich, green strip of meadow lies on either side, then a wide belt of dark forests climbs towards a band of rock that's topped in places by snowy peaks. Colour is full strength here and contrast is sharp, whatever the season. In summer the valley is a stark, primary blue and green set against dark grey rock and flecks of white snow. It's an incredible place, like a lost world valley.

The first section runs down the valley to Bossòst and the start of the Col du Portillon. It's been on the route of 18 Tours de France since 1957, the most recent being in 2006. Climbing from Spain, it's just over 8 kilometres (5 miles) of regular 7 per cent gradient. The road is smooth, the trees are full of birdsong; it almost goads you into pushing hard, but don't: there's a long way and harder climbs to come.

You cross into France at the summit of the Portillon, then the descent is narrow in places with lots of irregular turns. It takes you to Bagnères-de-Luchon, from where you head north along the Pique Valley to begin the hardest climb of this ride.

The Port de Balès would be a toughie in any ride. It's quite new to the Tour, having been included for the first time in 2007 after a new road, the first one with a tarmac surface, was laid across the top. This is an old-style climb, up a back way made for locals. Very often these were established to avoid busier routes patrolled by customs officials. The Port de Balès connects Mauléon-Barousse with Luchon, where there's a far more obvious way of getting there, along the road you've just ridden.

The Port de Balès is very Pyrenean. The road follows natural lines – there's nothing artificial or engineered about its twists and turns. It's narrow and steep in places, and it's very difficult to climb with a good rhythm. The summit is high and wild and the descent is sketchy in places, with some rough sections leading down to the start of a far more famous Tour de France climb, the Col de Peyresourde. You descend the final part of the Peyresourde's east side and ride back into Bagnères-de-Luchon.

Now the route climbs the side of the Col du Portillon you descended earlier. It's a longer climb, a little harder too, with one very steep section in the middle and another nearer the top, but your reward is a wonderful view at the summit. Look west and you can see the ski station of Superbagnères, where the 100-bedroom Grand Hôtel, an exact copy of the one in the centre of Paris, draws your eye. And in the opposite direction lies the luxuriant Val d'Aran.

The Portillon descent is great; a smooth road and regular turns take you down to Bossòst in a flash, ready for the last big effort of the day. The Guardader d'Arres climb is almost unknown in the wider cycling world, but it has a fierce reputation locally. It climbs to well over 1,220 metres (4,000 feet), where there's a straggle of villages on the side of the Planet des Barrancs mountains, and it is certainly the second-hardest climb of this ride after the Port de Balès. It's short but unrelentingly steep. The descent demands respect too, but once you are down, the finish isn't far, although cruelly it's all uphill to get there.

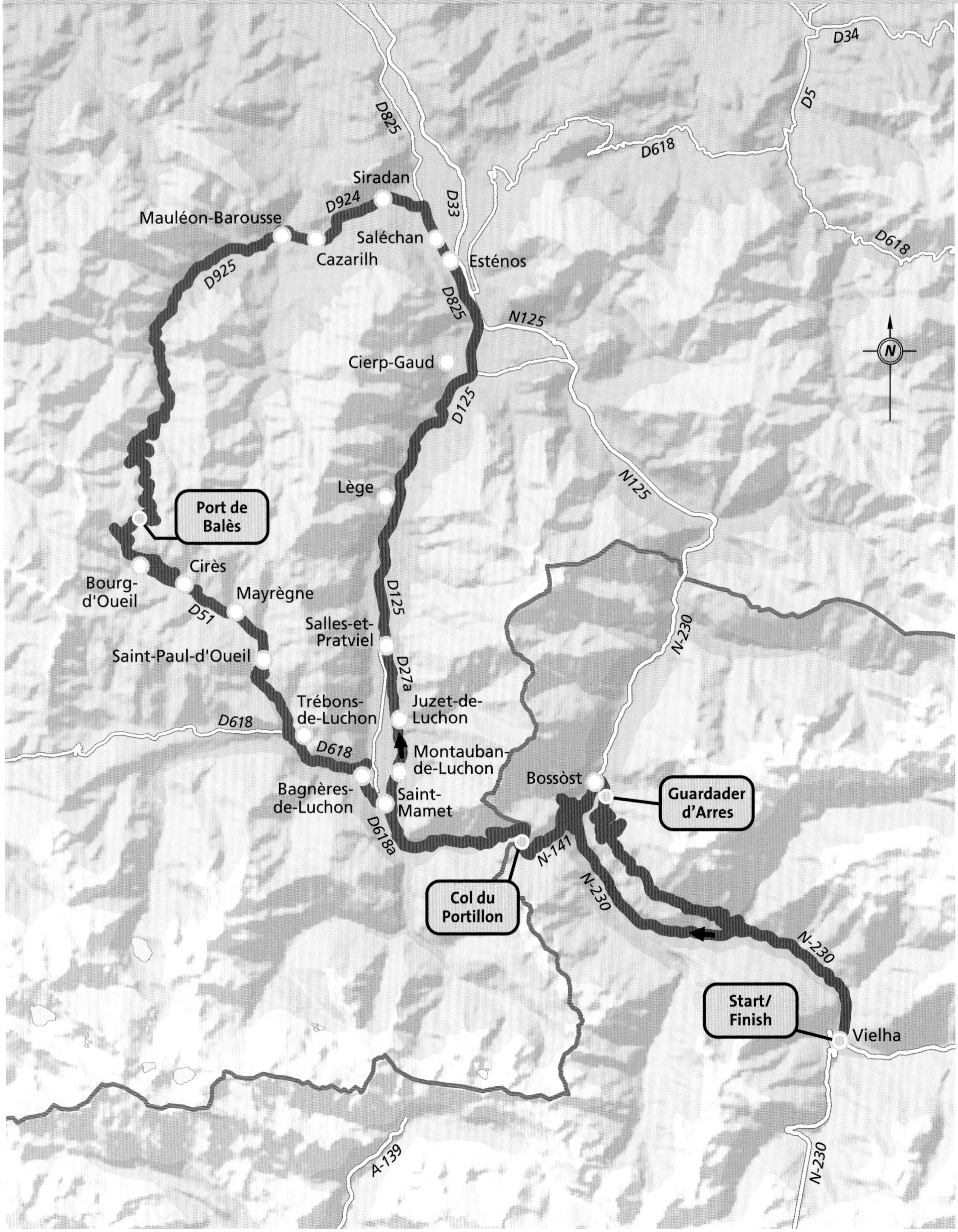
D34
D5
D825
D618
Siradan
D33
D924
Mauléon-Barousse
Saléchan
Cazarilh
D618
Esténos
D925
D825
N125
Cierp-Gaud
N
D125
N125
Lège
Port de Balès
Cirès
Bourg-d'Oueil
Mayrègne
D125
D51
N-230
Salles-et-Pratviel
Saint-Paul-d'Oueil
D27a
Trébons-de-Luchon
Juzet-de-Luchon
D618
D618
Montauban-de-Luchon
Bossòst
Guardader d'Arres
Bagnères-de-Luchon
Saint-Mamet
D618a
N-141
N-230
Col du Portillon
N-230
Start/Finish
Vielha
A-139
N-230

**Bossòst in the Val d'Aran**

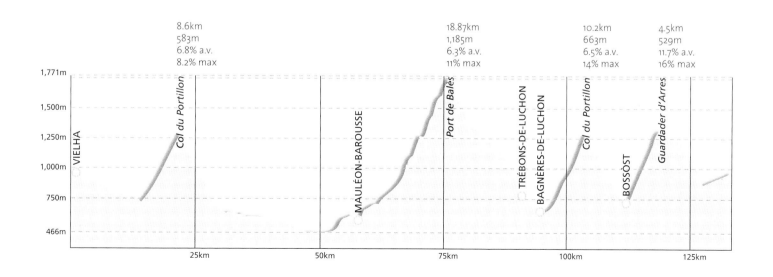

|  | 8.6km | 18.87km | 10.2km | 4.5km |
|---|---|---|---|---|
|  | 583m | 1,185m | 663m | 529m |
|  | 6.8% a.v. | 6.3% a.v. | 6.5% a.v. | 11.7% a.v. |
|  | 8.2% max | 11% max | 14% max | 16% max |

1,771m

1,500m

1,250m

1,000m

750m

466m

VIELHA · Col du Portillon · MAULÉON-BAROUSSE · Port de Balès · TRÉBONS-DE-LUCHON · BAGNÈRES-DE-LUCHON · Col du Portillon · BOSSÒST · Guardader d'Arres

25km    50km    75km    100km    125km

# Directions

▲ Start in Vielha and go north then northwest on the N230. Turn left on the outskirts of Bossòst on the N141 to climb the Col du Portillon. Descend to Bagnères-de-Luchon and follow the D27A, D125 and D825 north to turn left on the D924 to Mauléon-Barousse, then climb the Port de Balès and descend to the D618, where you turn left to Bagnères-de-Luchon. Turn right and return to Spain over the Portillon and turn left after the descent. Take the first right in Bossòst and climb the Guardader d'Arres, then descend to the main road where you turn left to Vielha.

**Website**
http://sport.be.msn.com/uciworldcyclingtour and click on 'Show Calendar'

**Date**
September.

**Why the name?**
It's called the Val d'Aran Cycling Tour to fit in with the marketing of the UCI's World Cycling Tour, which it is part of.

**Anything else?**
Continuing up the Val d'Aran provides access to some remote side valleys that penetrate some of the wildest parts of the Spanish side of the Pyrenees. Mountain bikers love this area and there are 400 kilometres of marked trails for them to follow. In 2013 the Val d'Aran Cycling Tour was a qualifying event in the UCI World Cycling Tour.

**Don't forget**
Any ride in the Pyrenees requires careful study of the weather forecast so you can correctly judge what to wear. The more local the forecast the better. There is support in the Val d'Aran Cycling Tour, so your food and drink needs will be taken care of. Just take the normal water-/windproof layer you should always carry on mountain challenges like this.

The Tour de France winds through the lush, green mountain scenery of the Pyrenees

**Distance** 139.2 kilometres / 87 miles
**Total climbing** 4,160 metres / 13,648 feet
**Route key** Mastering the hardest climb in cycling

# 51 A Stage of the Vuelta

The Tour of Spain is the third and youngest of cycling's three Grand Tours, the three-week stage races that are the ultimate test of cycling speed, all-round ability and endurance. The first Tour of Spain took place in 1935, but it had a shaky start due to the Spanish Civil War and World War II. Now, the Vuelta a España, which is what they call the race in Spain, has been run continuously since 1955. The organisers recently followed the lead of the other Grand Tours, the Tour de France and Giro d'Italia, by giving everyone the chance to enter a cyclosportive event run on one of the stages used by the race. It's called the Etapa de la Vuelta, but it hasn't yet visited the most dramatic feature of recent Tours of Spain, a climb in the Asturias called Alto de l'Angliru, but referred to simply as El Angliru.

El Angliru is a climb that strikes fear into the hearts of many pro racers, but also delight in the few who are steep mountain specialists. It's so steep that racing up it has only been possible since the development of compact chainsets. To climb it on ordinary racing gears would mean a slow-motion slog to the top, because El Angliru is far from ordinary. It is a challenge that every cyclist should attempt.

To give an idea of what a stage of the Tour of Spain is like, I've chosen stage 15 of the 2011 Vuelta that ran from Avilès to the top of El Angliru. The Etapa might visit this iconic climb one day, although it might not because it's a stage planner's nightmare. The organisers might never run a mass participation event that ends on El Angliru, so riding the 2011 stage 15 route is the best way to combine the experience of a Vuelta stage with the achievement of mastering the hardest climb in cycling.

That's no idle boast. It's hard to pick a single quote to sum up how tough El Angliru is, because there are so many. 'You go at 9 kilometres per hour. It's hell, there is nothing like it,' says the 2002 winner, Roberto Heras. 'Nothing like this

has ever been seen before. Riders will be getting off their bikes and walking. If you are not fit, don't come,' said Pedro Delgado after a reconnaissance of El Angliru before its first use in 1999. 'If you stay sitting, your front wheel goes up in the air. If you stand up your back wheel slips,' reckons top climber Fernando Escartín.

Nothing like it had ever been seen in cycling when El Angliru was first introduced. In terms of steepness, it's the king. A wicked road to nowhere that was placed in the Vuelta to raise its profile as a spectacle. And it worked.

The route starts in Avilés near the northern Spanish coast. This is Basque country, which is Spain's cycling stronghold. The sport is big here and the geography breeds tough racers.

There are three other climbs on the route, and they get progressively harder, but this ride is all about El Angliru, and you should try to conserve as much energy for it as you can.

Asturias is a rugged place of jagged peaks and lush valleys. As it closes on El Angliru, the route follows a humid tree-lined valley, past old mine workings, while the gradient slowly racks up towards the start of the climb. You climb the Alto del Cordal, which is tough, then you descend, and then it's El Angliru.

The first slopes are an anticlimax. El Angliru doesn't live up to its billing. The road wanders up a lush shoulder of meadowland until it reaches a village called Las Ablanosas, where things start to get grippy. The hairpin bends tighten; their inside line becomes very steep. But still the gradient on the straights is around 8 per cent, scraping 9 per cent in places. This still isn't the real Angliru.

That begins at El Caborno, after which every kilometre section's average hovers at around 13 per cent, but if average gradient was El Angliru's only problem then it wouldn't be the climb it is. The gradient is rarely at its average. It jumps

Another feature of racing in the Tour of Spain is the crosswinds on the high central plateau

around up a series of curves and ramps, each with its own name, connected by stretches of lesser gradient. Lagos at 8 kilometres (5 miles) into the climb is 14.5 per cent, Les Picones at 9 kilometres is 20 per cent, Cobayos at 10 kilometres is 21.5 per cent. Then it gets silly. La Cueña les Cabres is the steepest part of the climb at 23.5 per cent and 10.5 kilometres (6.5 miles) into the climb. The road used to be dangerously narrow until the local authorities spent thousands of euros widening it. You can have problems here if pedal force overcomes tyre friction, making your rear wheel spin and causing a loss of traction. Even gifted climbers can stumble here and the not so gifted simply keel over.

Once this stretch is beaten, El Angliru is nearly over, but it's still not an easy passage to the top. The El Aviru ramp is

21.5 per cent, Les Piedrusines at 12 kilometres (7.5 miles) is 20 per cent. Then suddenly it's over. Just 500 metres (1,640 feet) of relatively easy climbing leads to the summit and almost to the peak of a mountain called La Gamonal. The height gain of the second half of El Angliru is phenomenal, getting on for 800 metres (2,624 feet) in 6 kilometres (3.75 miles).

Take your time and spread your effort up the steepest sections. If you feel your rear wheel slip then move your weight backwards; if your front wheel lifts, move it forwards, but do both smoothly. Above all, keep your pedalling as smooth as possible and try to apply power through as much of each pedal stroke as you can. Oh, and you need a head for heights because in places the exposure of this mountain road is chilling. Take extreme care coming down.

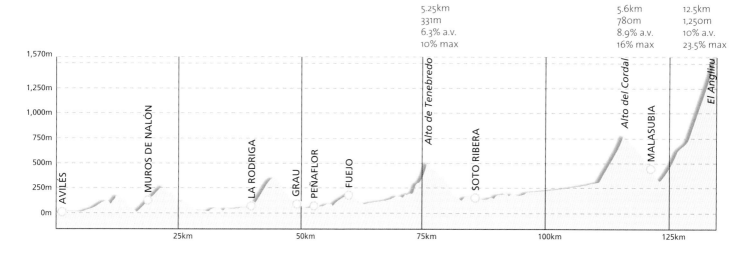

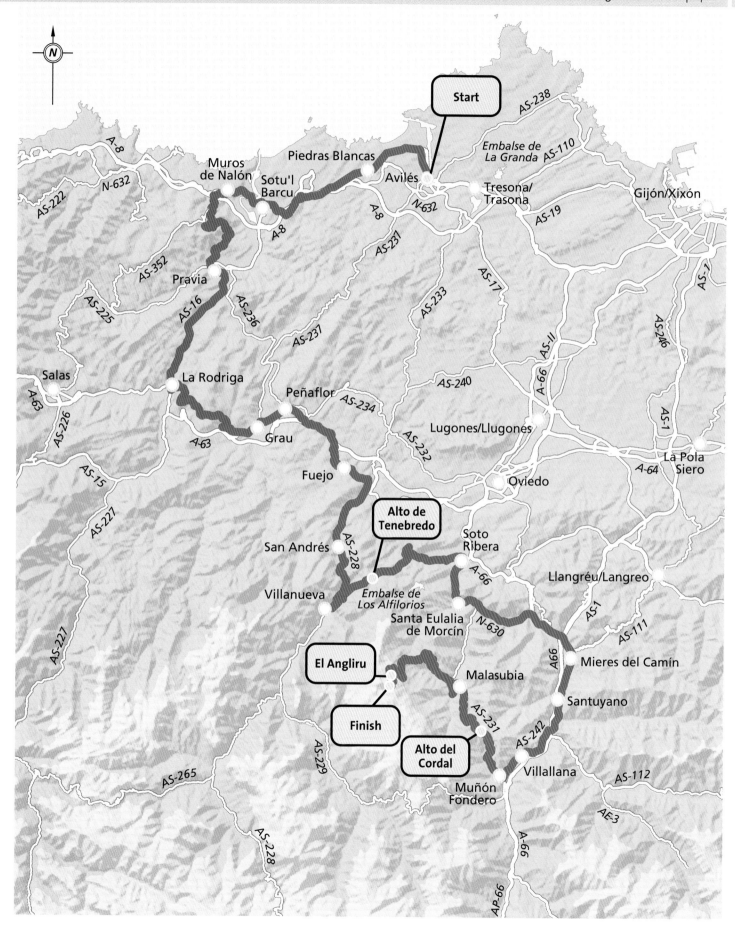

**Riders on a Tour of Spain stage in Asturias**

# ▌Directions

▲ Start in Avilés and head north towards the coast then southwest through Piedras Blancas to Muros de Nalón. Take the third exit at the roundabout then keep left and follow this road south through Pravia, keeping left up the valley of the Río Narcea. Turn left to La Rodriga, where you turn left to climb Alto de la Cabruñana. Descend to Grau and head northeast to Peñaflor, then follow the road that runs between the Río Nalon and the motorway.

▲ Go under the motorway and take the first exit at the roundabout, then go left in Fuejo and follow the Río Trubia to Villanueva, where the Alto de Tenebredo starts. Descend to Soto Ribera, where you go right and follow the Río Caudal Valley through Mieres del Camín and Uxo to Muñón Fondero, where you cross the motorway and start the Alto del Cordal climb. Descend to Malasubia to start El Angliru.

**Website**
www.etapadelavuelta.com

**Date**
Best done between April and October.

**Anything else?**
There are at least three ways to the final steep ramps of El Angliru, opening up the possibility of a Cinglés du Ventoux-type challenge. You can't go over the climb and down the other side; El Angliru's final part just leads to the top.

**Don't forget**
This ride is best done with some support, so a vehicle that could carry spares and assist with direction-finding would be a great help. Without that, you need to carry plenty of food and drink, but make the last food you eat well before El Angliru. The weather in Asturias is likely to be hot and humid in summer but possibly cool and wet in spring and autumn, so plan for that and check the local forecast.

A compact chainset is a must for climbing El Angliru. Even talented climbers like Alberto Contador have used gears as low as 34 x 28 to race up its slopes. Training should include lots of hills, lots of climbing out of the saddle and core strength work, too. Try doing some sessions where you climb a steep hill in a higher gear than you would normally use. Do it a number of times in each session, alternating riding out with riding in the saddle each time up. When you are out of the saddle, focus on riding smoothly and not moving your bike around too much or weaving across the road. Make your transitions to and from riding out of the saddle as smooth as possible.

Andalucía

**Distance** 147 kilometres / 92 miles
**Total climbing** 3,420 metres / 11,217 feet
**Route key** The highest paved road in Europe

# 52 La Pico del Veleta

There's a sign at the foot of the Col de la Bonette in the French Alps that claims it is the highest paved road in Europe. It's not. Despite locals building an extra loop above the old pass on top of the Bonette so it would be higher than the Col d'Iseran and enter the Tour de France record books as the highest the race ever climbs, its 2,802 metres (9,192 feet) are dwarfed by a road in the Sierra Nevada, which runs just below one of the two highest peaks there. The Pico del Veleta stands at 3,394 metres (11,135 feet) and the road passes just under 200 metres below it, so at 3,200 metres (10,498 feet) it is the highest paved road in Europe. It's also possible to ride an off-road trail almost to the Pico del Veleta summit, but more of that later.

The effects of high altitude will definitely kick in if you ride up here. The percentage of oxygen in the air remains the same as it is at sea level the higher you go: 21 per cent. However, atmospheric pressure drops as altitude increases, so the pressure on individual gas molecules is reduced and they spread out. That means there are fewer oxygen molecules for each breath taken at altitude than there are at sea level. Less oxygen per breath means you must breathe deeper and more often, and your heart must work harder to pump blood around your body to keep your muscles going. But both these things are finite, so there comes a point when altitude will slow you down. Don't fight it; just relax and ride within yourself and your comfort zone.

A number of challenges, organised and other, include the Pico del Veleta, but the simplest is a circuit that climbs the mountain, descends the other side, then runs along its edge so that you can see the whole mountain, absorb its scale and fully realise what you have achieved.

Pico del Veleta can be seen clearly from the city of Granada. It's one of the two highest peaks on the Sierra Nevada mountain range. The classic way to climb it by bike begins in Cenes de la Vega, quite close to the centre of the beautiful Moorish city, which is already over 700 metres high.

A series of four ramps separated by easier stretches make up the classic Pico del Veleta route. After a tough first four kilometres, including two sections of 8 per cent climbing, the first ramp ends in Pinos Genil. One kilometre of 4 per cent leads to the start of the second ramp, which leaves the Genil Valley by a series of hairpin bends that wriggle upwards between sparse but tall pine trees.

Even though there is enough precipitation in the Sierra Nevada to give good snow cover, the lower slopes are still quite arid as the snow falls mostly above 2,000 metres. However, there is still some water around, but since it comes in big seasonal gushes it has carved out deep canyons and gorges that cut through all of the lower slopes of the Sierra Nevada range. There are a few deep canyons close to the route, plus a number of caves where people used to live – this is one of the oldest inhabited areas of Spain.

The road surface is good and quite wide, to help the transport that goes to and from the Sierra Nevada ski resort most days. Even so, as the road climbs over the lip of the Genil Valley, the everyday world is left far behind. Replacing it is a true wilderness of rock, scree and parched bushes. It doesn't look or feel at all like Europe any more, a feeling reinforced by the huge birds of prey – Egyptian vultures with their massive wingspan – that patrol the air.

The section from Pinos Genil averages 7 per cent in a constant fight against gravity. Then, at a place called El Purche, with spectacular views, the slope relents, becoming almost flat for just over a kilometre. The third ramp, a stretch of 5 and 6 per cent climbing, where the route traces a natural run of higher ground that leads steadily upwards, goes on for 11 kilometres (7 miles). Relief comes at the intersection with the summit of another climb, the Collado de las Sabinas, where there is another welcome flat section.

On any normal big climb you should be at the top by now, but Pico del Veleta isn't a normal climb. There's another section of just under 7 per cent climbing to go. This is where you feel the extra scale of this challenge. The Spanish sports altitude centre is at 2,300 metres (7,546 feet); this last section takes you 900 metres higher.

Just before the summit, a gravel track goes off to your left. This is the limit road. It's rideable if you have thick tyres, and every year a cycling challenge called El Limite starts in Granada and comes up here, 46 kilometres (28 miles) uphill to 3,300 metres (10,827 feet). The paved road tops out only 100 metres lower and is a kilometre less of climbing.

The rewards for getting up this high are many: the view, the achievement, being in an environment far removed from everyday life. More immediate, though, is the descent. You've ridden over 28 miles uphill, now it's time to get your revenge on gravity. Going down is exhilarating, a rush of experiences, but one of the most notable is the glowing sensation when your shivering muscles gradually warm up as you begin to feel the full effects of the Andalucían sun. It's like lowering yourself slowly into a warm bath.

The descent ends in Órgiva, followed by around 50 kilometres of at first undulating then mostly flat road. The distinct peak of the Pico del Veleta mountain is visible to the left of its sister, Mulhacen. Then comes the unforgettable sight of Granada's proud profile, as its towers and castellated walls come into view at the end of the final drag.

**Andalucía is a sun-kissed joy for cyclists**

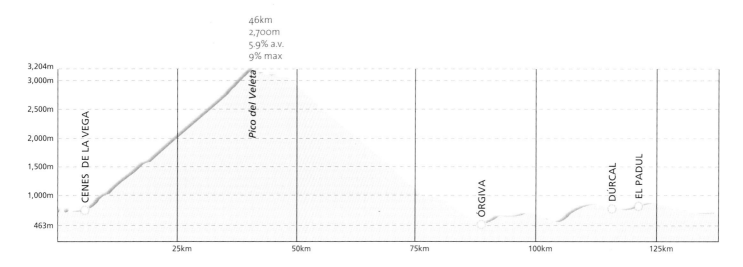

46km
2,700m
5.9% a.v.
9% max

3,204m
3,000m
2,500m
2,000m
1,500m
1,000m
463m

CENES DE LA VEGA

Pico del Veleta

ÓRGIVA

DÚRCAL

EL PADUL

25km    50km    75km    100km    125km

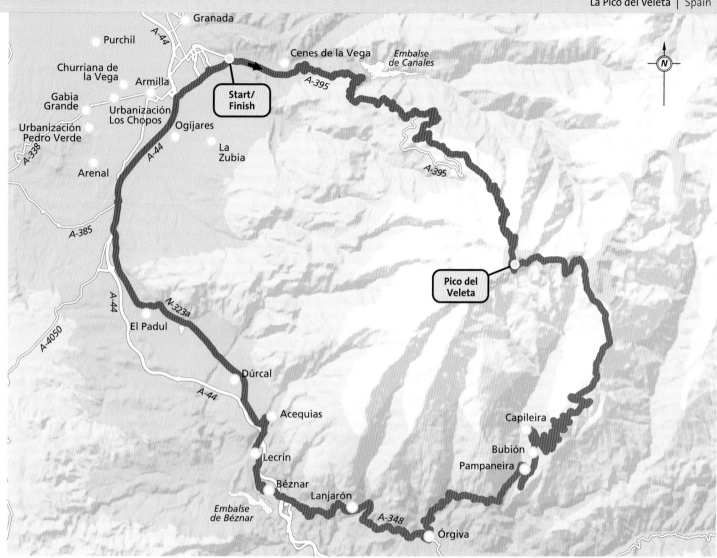

# ▮ Directions

▲ Start in Granada and follow the A395 east past Cenes de la Vega. Continue on this road for the first part of the climb, then turn left on a bend about 1.8 kilometres after Hotel El Guerra before taking the right fork 200 metres down that road. Continue uphill, keeping left to the summit of the Pico del Veleta road, then descend to Órgiva, where you turn right and follow the A348 over the A44 onto the N323a. Continue north, shadowing the motorway around the northeast side of Dúrcal and El Padul, then continue along the road parallel to the A44 motorway back to Granada.

## Website
www.sierranevadalimite.com

## Date
The cyclosportive El Limite takes place in early July, but you can do the ride described here any time the Pico del Veleta road is open.

## Why the name?
Pico del Veleta is named after one of the two summits of the Sierra Nevada mountains.

## Anything else?
There's lots of great cycling in the Sierra and in Andalucía, which is a fantastic winter cycling destination, though you probably won't be able to do the Pico del Veleta during the winter. For information contact www.vamoscycling.com; they are British experts on cycling in Andalucía.

## Don't forget
Cycling at altitude requires you to be as fit as you can through training. Some people are extra-sensitive to the effects of altitude, so if you feel increasingly light-headed as you go higher, or get a headache, feel dizzy or experience chest pains, it's best to stop and go back down. Andalucían weather is generally fine during the summer, but it will be cool on top, so take an extra layer. Also, the sun's ultraviolet rays get stronger the higher you go, so sunscreen is a must. The descent is the other potential danger. It's a long way to ride downhill so you mustn't let your mind wander. There are several quite technical sections, particularly at 50 kilometres and from 60 to 80 kilometres, which is a long way to suffer the repeated braking into sharp hairpin bends.

# INDEX

# ACKNOWLEDGEMENTS

The AA wishes to thank the following photographers and organisations for their assistance in the preparation of this book. Every effort has been made to trace the copyright holders, and we apologise in advance for any unintentional omissions or errors. Abbreviations for the picture credits are as follows – (t) top; (m) middle; (b) bottom; (l) left; (c) centre; (r) right.

Front cover by *Rupert Fowler*
*Alamy* – Image Source 19; Liv Friis-Larsen 21; Aflo Foto Agency 48t; Les Ladbury 61; BlueMoon Stock 85; Jordan Weeks 91b; imagebroker 112, 133tl, 175, 188; Steve Thomas 168, 181; LOOK Die Bildagentur der Fotografen GmbH 176; Mere Sport 179; Tips Images/Tips Italia Srl a socio unico 183; Danita Delimont 199
*Luc Claessen* – 5, 115, 117, 121, 123, 124-125bl, 125br, 128, 130t, 130bl, 130br, 135, 140-141, 143, 145, 152, 153, 159, 163, 166, 173, 187, 191, 193, 196, 205, 206, 210, 213
*Corbis* – Tim De Waele 119, 138, 146t, 160, 164, 214, 216, 218; David-Hevia/Demotix 202
*Stephen Flemming* – 22, 34
*Garmin* – 8, 9tl, 9tr
*Getty Images* – Bryn Lennon 156, 158
*Andy Jones* – 25, 26, 33, 37, 51, 53, 87, 89, 99
*Rick Robson* – 39, 42-43, 44ml, 44mc, 44mr, 48ml
*Chris Sidwells* – 7bl, 7bc, 7br, 11, 12, 13, 15, 17, 29, 30t, 30bl, 30bc, 30br, 44t, 46, 48mr, 54, 57t, 57b, 63tl, 63r, 63bl, 67, 69t, 69ml, 69mr, 71, 73, 75, 77, 78, 81, 82, 91tl, 91tr, 92, 95, 96, 101l, 101tr, 101br, 103, 105, 106, 108, 109, 111, 133tr, 137l, 137tr, 137br, 140l, 146b, 149tc, 149tr, 149c, 171, 180, 184, 201, 209, 220
*Kath Sidwells* – 4

**Download the race routes in this book at theaa.com/cycling-race-routes**